Paweł Stachura / Piotr Śniedziewski /
Krzysztof Trybuś (eds.)

# Approaches to Walter Benjamin's *The Arcades Project*

**Bibliographic Information published by the Deutsche Nationalbibliothek**
The Deutsche Nationalbibliothek lists this publication in the Deutsche Nationalbibliografie; detailed bibliographic data is available in the internet at http://dnb.d-nb.de.

**Library of Congress Cataloging-in-Publication Data**
A CIP catalog record for this book has been applied for at the Library of Congress.

This publication was financially supported
by the Adam Mickiewicz University in Poznań.

Printed by CPI books GmbH, Leck.

ISSN 1434-0313
ISBN 978-3-631-73637-1 (Print)
E-ISBN 978-3-631-73638-8 (E-PDF)
E-ISBN 978-3-631-73639-5 (EPUB)
E-ISBN 978-3-631-73640-1 (MOBI)
DOI 10.3726/b12006

© Peter Lang GmbH
Internationaler Verlag der Wissenschaften
Frankfurt am Main 2017
All rights reserved.
Peter Lang Edition is an Imprint of Peter Lang GmbH.

Peter Lang – Frankfurt am Main · Bern · Bruxelles · New York ·
Oxford · Warszawa · Wien

All parts of this publication are protected by copyright. Any utilisation outside the strict limits of the copyright law, without the permission of the publisher, is forbidden and liable to prosecution. This applies in particular to reproductions, translations, microfilming, and storage and processing in electronic retrieval systems.

This publication has been peer reviewed.

www.peterlang.com

Approaches to Walter Benjamin's *The Arcades Project*

# LITERARY AND CULTURAL THEORY

General Editor: Wojciech H. Kalaga

VOLUME 52

# Introduction

The present volume about Benjamin's *Arcades Project* derives from research conducted by the European Tradition Research Team at the Faculty of Polish Philology of Adam Mickiewicz University in Poznań. The team has been working since 2005 on several ambitious projects studying links between Polish literature, culture and European cultural heritage. The aim of the research is a synthesis of transformations of European cultural heritage in Poland.

According to the authors whose texts are included in this book, Walter Benjamin is one of the most important figures of modern culture. That is why he is presented both as a philosopher, or rather as a critic of modernism entangled in tradition (mainly Jewish), but also as a writer *tout court*. Philosophical and philological readings are accompanied by essays presenting the complex biography of Walter Benjamin and numerous, often unexpected, parallels which indicate traces of his reflections in works of other artists. In consequence, *The Arcades Project*, which can be described as Benjamin's *opus vitae*, is not only a picturesque history of Parisian arcades of mid-19th century. It is also a polyphonic text, composed of quotations, commentaries and footnotes, a discussion of the sense of history and the literary work of art which surprises with its meandering quality.

Authors of the essays are sensitive to the complexity of the philosopher's thought and the surprising structure of his most important work. That is why their reflection is directed by the typically Benjaminesque principle of "indirect approach" i.e. a precise, but indolent observation. This approach is characteristic of the *flâneur*, Benjamin's favorite figure.

# Table of contents

Frequently Cited Editions .................................................................................9

Philosophical Approach

*Adam Lipszyc*
Return of the gaze. The name as idea and dialectical image ........................13

*Agata Bielik-Robson*
Man as Name Giver: Some Non-Elective Affinities between
Benjamin and Heidegger .................................................................................27

Biographical Approach

*Katarzyna Kuczyńska-Koschany*
Benjamin, a Jew ................................................................................................43

*Roman Kubicki*
A Discourse of the Master Benjamin with Death and Life .........................55

Textual Approach

*Jerzy Kałążny*
In the Labyrinth of Benjamin's *Arcades Project*: The Flâneur, the Collector,
and the Gambler as Readers of the Nineteenth Century ............................65

*Lidia Banowska*
Paris in Walter Benjamin's *Arcades Project* – on the Threshold of
Modernity..........................................................................................................79

*Jerzy Borowczyk*
The Poet of Awakening ................................................................................. 105

*Wiesław Ratajczak*
Photography and *The Arcades Project*....................................................... 117

*Piotr Śniedziewski*
*The Arcades Project*, or the Melancholy of "Editing" ............................... 127

Context-Based Approach

*Krzysztof Trybuś*
Benjamin as a Commentator on Norwid ............................................................. 151

*Michał Mrugalski*
Myths in the Polish People's Republic. Iwaszkiewicz *avec* Benjamin ............... 161

# Frequently Cited Editions

References to the following books will be made parenthetically in the text:

- Walter Benjamin, *Selected Writings*, ed. Michael W. Jennings and Marcus Bullock, Howard Eiland, Gary Smith, vol. I–IV (Cambridge, MA: Belknap Press of Harvard University Press, 1996–2003). Cited as *Selected Writings*.
- Walter Benjamin, *The Arcades Project*, trans. Howard Eiland and Kevin McLaughlin, prepared on the basis of the German volume edited by Rolf Tiedman (Cambridge Mass.: The Belknap Press of Harvard University Press, 1999). Cited as *The Arcades*.
- Walter Benjamin, *The Origin of German Tragic Drama*, trans. John Osborne (London – New York: Verso, 1998). Cited as *The Origin of German Tragic Drama*.
- *The Correspondence of Walter Benjamin 1910–1940*, ed. Gershom Scholem and Theodor W. Adorno, trans. Manfred R. Jacobson and Evelyn M. Jacobson (Chicago and London: The University of Chicago Press, 1994). Cited as *The Correspondence of Walter Benjamin 1910–1940*.

# Philosophical Approach

Adam Lipszyc

# Return of the gaze. The name as idea and dialectical image

**Abstract:** The paper offers a detailed analysis of the development of Walter Benjamin's epistemological project from his *Ursprung des deutschen Trauerspiels* to the *Arcades Project*. The author sets the development against the background of the linguistic turn, the essential feature of the 20th century philosophy, understood here as an attempt to focus on the singular. Benjamin is seen as moving from the epistemology conforming rather clearly to the general move of the linguistic turn to the one which sets the paradoxical 'image in language' at the very center of the epistemological endeavors. By referring to Lévinas, Gadamer and Foucault by means of contrast and comparison, the author argues Benjamin's focus on the image, far from undoing the linguistic turn, in fact rescues its very essence.

**Keywords:** Walter Benjamin; linguistic turn; image; name; Hans-Georg Gadamer

The most characteristic mark of the 20th century philosophy was the linguistic turn. This gesture, undertaken in different ways by thinkers representing different philosophical schools, essentially boiled down to the establishing of an unbreakable bond between human thought and the realm of language. If we set aside early Wittggenstein and a few similar philosophical enterprises, we may say that the linguistic turn was to break with absolutist claims of modern philosophy, or perhaps of the philosophical tradition as such. The linguistic notion of cognition was to account for human finiteness, individuality and corporeality, as well as for our involvement in the historical element and for the variety of human experience. Now, the acceptance of such a notion often puts such categories as image, vision and gaze into the enemy's camp, into the camp of those who defend the realm of absolute concepts purified of the contigent word. Thus, on the one side of the barricade we would have the concept and the image, the Platonic belief in the possibility of conceptual vision of the absolute truth outside of the cave, and on the other side – the word, understood as the basic element of the relative and the plural.

The essential point of reference of my rather modest inquiry is a certain general point about the 20th century linguistic turn and about its hostility towards the visual. It states, roughly, that when philosophy gives up vision as such and embraces the idea of the linguistic mediation of experience, it risks a dialectic return to the oculo- and logocentrism it tried to escape; on the other hand, the liguistic notion of human experience can defend its intellectual assets, if, paradoxically enough, at its very center it will accept a certain notion of the image.

It seems that one of the prominent figures in the 20th century philosophy that has understood this (or whose intellectual development at least agrees with the above postulate) was Walter Benjamin. In the following I will simply try to show how and why at a certain stage of development a theory of image becomes a central part of Benjamin's philosophy of language.

Having expressed these two high-flown declarations (the one concerning the linguistic turn as such, and the other concerning the general structure of Benjamin's thought), I may now submerge into the element of the schoolish in which I shall move in this essay. The plan is simple: first, I shall sketch Benjamin's theory of the idea and of the origin presented in the foreword to his book on Baroque and then I shall take a look at certain aspects of the thoery of dialectical image as presented in the file N of the arcades project. Similarities and contrasts between these two theories should give some substance to the general declarations I have formulated. Yet, in order not to bore the reader with Benjamin only, from time to time I shall be referring also to Emmanuel Lévinas, as well as to Michel Foucault and Hans-Georg Gadamer.

It is well known that the methodological foreword to the *Ursprung des deutschen Trauerspiels* is one of the most eccentric of all Benjamin's texts (see *The Origin of German Tragic Drama*, pp. 27–56). Certainly, to a large extent it can be blamed for the fact that nowadays we refer to Benjamin's book on Baroque as "would-be *Habilitationsschrift*". The foreword is composed of short pieces with separate titles, but the whole text can be easily divided into three bigger parts. The third part deals mostly with the failed reception of the German Baroque drama and, although highly interesting, will not be my concern here. The first two part, on the other hand, are of strictly philosophical nature and present a deeply insane methodology of the work. The first of the two – from the beginning of the text till the fragment entitled "Das Wort als Idee" – presents Benjamin's theory of ideas, while the second one develops it further by introducing the category of the origin. Let as have a look at this idiosyncratic conceptual edifice.

In its critical dimension the first part of the foreword is an attack on the notion that truth may become the object of cognition. Cognition is an intentional relationship; it is a form of possession. Yet, truth does not enter any relationships and in particular – any intentional ones. "Truth – according to the famous formula – is the death of intention" (*The Origin of German Tragic Drama*, p. 36). Benjamin identifies the intentional, possessive act of cognition with vision which is characteristic of Neoplatonic paganism. Hence, he claims quite consistently that truth cannot become the object of the mystical, intellectual or of any other kind of vision.

It is perhaps worth noting that if we take into account the identification of the philosophy of vision with paganism as well as the Biblical sources on which Benjamin draws, the criticism is reminiscent of Emmanuel Lévinas's attack against the ontological approach in theology. The author of *Totality and Infinity* insisted that the relation with transcendence cannot be of intentional nature, for the intentional cognitive act would violate the strict otherworldliness of the divine. He also liked to link such an immanentist approach to paganism. The solution which Lévinas offers is to recognize the ethical nature of the true relation with transcendence. God is present in the world only as a trace which we come into contact with only by doing good to the other.

Although in its critical aspect Benjamin's approach may be largely similar to Lévinas's attack, his positive proposal goes into a completely different direction. All reservation aside, Benjamin does not want to reject epistemology as such and shift to ethics, although the proper term here would be perhaps rather "gnoseology" or "gnosis." For if Lévinas represents the ethical trend in Jewish thought, Benjamin belongs to a deeply Gnostic tradition which looks for a relation with transcendence in sparks of the divine dispersed in the created, but also fallen world. Yet, one might object that such a gnoseological-gnostic notion of the sparks also objectifies truth and turns it into the object of vision. How can we defend this notion without resorting to the gesture of Lévinas who urges as to leave epistemology and turn to ethics?

In the book on Baroque Benjamin's positive proposal is based on a complex edifice which involves the categories of idea, concept and phenomenon. Benjamin develops here the notion of the philosophical treatise which aims at what he calls the representation of idea. The representation of idea (which is identical with the non-intentional representation of truth) occurs simultaneously with salvation of the phenomena, for the uncertain being of the phenomena finds the foundation and the refuge in the ideas. The Platonic terminology is used here in a partly ironic way. For, as we shall see, Benjamin aims at a misprision of the Platonic categories, which will endow them with a peculiarly Jewish-Gnostic character. This, by the way, offers another possiblity of comparison with Lévinas who has also executed a misprision of the Plotinian notion of trace and built it into his strictly ethical interpretation of Jewish tradition.

Ideas are not the average or common essence of the phenomena belonging to a ceratin class. More importantly, though, Benjamin rejects not only such a notion of ideas as "summaries" of the phenomena, but also the Christian-Neoplatonic notion that the idea shines through the phenomenon as the symbolized shines through the symbolizing. Such a notion of symbol would obviously be corralated with the conception that the cognition of truth has the nature of a vision. As we sall see, Benjamin does use the concept of symbol and does link it to the ideas, but he understands it in a more subtle and subversive way.

What *are* the ideas, then, and how can they be represented? This question cannot be answered without a reference to the Benjamin's notion of the concept. The representation of the ideas and salvation of the phenomena would not have been possible without the mediating work of the concepts. This implies that concepts are not identical with ideas and they are not the true aim of the cognitive process, but at the same time they are indispensable for it. In the empirical reality the phenomena are submerged in a false, immanent unity of the appearance. If they are to partake in the ideal unity of truth, they need to be broken, fragmented and reshuffled. This job is done by the concepts. Salvation of the phenomena is possible only by virtue of their conceptual fragmentation which at the same time enables the representation of the ideas. It must be also noted that because the ideas do not appear behind the phenomena thanks to the process of symbolic shining-through, the concepts that aim at the representation of the ideas should try to single out what is extreme rather than what is average in the phenomenal world. The concepts are able to bring about the representation of the ideas by creating, so to speak, a field of forces between the extremes. Benjamin himself prefers another metaphor, i.e. the metaphor of constellation. This key category is introduced by the famous proportion: "Ideas are to objects as constellations are to stars" (*The Origin of German Tragic Drama*, p. 34).

At this stage it is perhaps worthwhile to note two things. First, the notion of salvation through fragmentation not only points to one of the constant elements of Benjamin's thinking, but it also shows his links with the Gnostic tradition and offers a partial answer to the question about the possibility of epistemology free of the immanentist possessiveness. To put it in theological terms: between the divine world and the immanent world there is such an unbridgeable gap that we may even say that the divine world does not exist at all, for it was destroyed by a catastrophe which gave birth to the immanent world. The reconstruction of the divine (or, in less mythological terms: a passage from the immanent to the transcendent) must involve destruction and a reshuffling of the false totality of the phenomenal. It is this approach that is to guarantee us that we break here with the Neoplatonic belief in vision and the notion that the transcendence shines through the immanent in a symbolic way. If Benjamin is right, then between the pagan Neoplatonism and the ethical perspective of Lévinas there is still a place for the Gnostic position which is "gnoseological," but not immanentist.

But is this true? After all, Benjamin's stellar metaphors – and this is the second issue I want to refer to at this stage – are definitely of visual nature. If in discussion of Benjamin's theory of ideas we stress not the destructive, but the evocative moment, it may turn out that the theory is not so much the effect of a Gnostic misprision of Platonism, but rather a certain mutation of the philosophy of vision which is not so easily distinguishable from Neoplatonic conceptions, especially those which would more eagerly penetrate the realms of negative theology. For example Charles Taylor, a rather naive chap deeply embedded in the tradition of Christian Neoplatonism and resistant to any Gnostic nuances, convinces his readers in the *Sources of the Self* that the idea of constellation is just a more complicated version of the Neoplatonic symbol which offers the miracle of epiphany.[1] This is obviously a massive simplification, but there is something to it. Who is Benjamin? A Jewish Gnostic looking for his language in the Neoplatonic realm of light? A Neoplatonic thinker who tries to make his own tradition more complex by means of certain Gnostic conceits? An answer to these questions should emerge from what follows.

Be that as it may, in the most important, final fragment of the first part of the foreword, entitled "Das Wort als Idee," Benjamin's offers a decisively antivisual move. He asks about the way the ideas are given and immediately answers this question by claiming that they are of linguistic nature. More precisely, they represent the aspect of the word which makes it a symbol. Yet, as I have already mentioned, what is meant here is not the symbol in Neoplatonic sense. Rather, the symbol is here the dimension of the word, which is a remnant of the paradise speech of pure naming. Benjamin relies here on his own meditations from the essay "On Language as Such and on the Language of Man" which develops such a conception of the pure language (see "On Language as Such and on the Language of Man," in: *Selected Writings*, vol. I, pp. 62–74). This pure language was destroyed (an event identical with the fall of the Tower of Babel and of the Fall of Man) and since that time apart from the aspect of names the language of humans has also had the fallen communicative aspect. Yet, the sparks of names are still present in the fallen language. Now, in the foreword to the book on Baroque the ideas are identified precisely with such names. This is also why Benjamin may claim that the task of philosophy, i.e. representation of the ideas, is of anamnetic nature, for the task boils down to a rememberance, recovery of the fragments of the pure language. Yet, this anamnesis is not a recovery of *the primal image*, but rather a

---

1   See Charles Taylor, *Sources of the Self. The Making oft he Modern Indentity* (Cambride: Cambridge University Press, 1996), pp. 478–479.

recovery of a *primal hearing*. This is also why – and here the idea of the Jewish-Gnostic misprision of Platonism becomes quite explicit – according to Benjamin it is not Plato, but Adam, the father of all people, who is the father of philosophy.

The identification of idea with name has at least threefold consequences. First, the Neoplatonic world of vision is unambiguously rejected in favor of the Jewish world of hearing. Second, this approach underlines the nature of the treasure which the philosopher tries to regain. The pursuit is not aimed at the generality of the concepts that would swallow the phenomena. The general concepts play only a mediating role in the fragmentation and reshuffling of the phenomena, but the ideas, the true object of the philosophical quest, are characterized by the stubborn individuality of names. It is true that Benjamin defines the ideas as that what is truly general, but since they appear above the order of the concepts from the *unaufgehoben* tensions between elements of the phenomena, this true generality is in fact a higher form of individuality. Third, then, we can see clearly that Benjamin dreams of a model of relation between philosophy and the phenomena, on which philosophy does scorn the phenomena from its high throne, but it also does not limit itself to gathering facts.

The latter intention comes to the fore especially in the second part of the foreword, which discusses perhaps the most obscure category that Benjamin ever introduced, namely the category of the origin. Here the static, slightly scholastic model based on the categories of the phenomenon, concept and idea is confronted with reality in the form in which its phenomenal nature is most painful for the philosophical Eleatism – with the realm of the historical. Although Benjamin attacks the Hegelian contempt for the facts and conditionally supports the nominalist approach to history, he also believes that the thought penetrating the variety of facts does not have to end up as a slave of the phenomena. In this part of the foreword it is clear that Benjamin belongs to the rather large camp of thinkers who try to sneak between the Skylla of Platonism and the Charibda of historicism.

A rather childish historicism is surely the result of the neo-Nietzschean critique of all Platonism in relation to history, as presented by Michel Foucault in his essay entitled "Nietzsche, genealogy, history."[2] The essay is worth looking at before we focus on Benjamin's category of the origin. Genealogy which disperses all the ideal, stable entities is presented here as a perfect cure against metaphysics. Genealogy calmly analyses *Entstehung* and *Herkunft*, the becoming and the

---

2   See Michel Foucault, "Nietzsche, Genealogy, History," in: *Language, Counter-Memory, Practice: Selected Essays and Interviews*, ed. Donald F. Bouchard, trans. Donald F. Bouchard, Sherry Simon (Ithaca: Cornell University Press, 1977), pp. 139–164.

descent of different phenomena and forms, showing their contigency and lack of internal unity. It avoids searching for *Ursprung*, the origin, for to search for it would mean to surrender to Platonism. In fact, Foucault links the pursuit of the origin with the philosophy of image: "This search is directed to «that which was already there,» the image of a primordial truth fully adequate to its nature, and it necessitates the removal of every mask to ultimately disclose an original identity".[3]

Does this criticism affect Benjamin's concept of the origin? No, at least if we stick to Benjamin's intentions: in his conceptual edifice this category is precisely designed to point to the third way between Platonism and historicism. Now, the origin is closely linked to the idea, for the former is the way in which the latter presents itself in the historical reality. Benjamin writes: "in every original phenomenon a determination of the form in which an idea will constantly confront the historical world, until it is revealed fulfilled, in the totality of its history" (*The Origin of German Tragic Drama*, pp. 45–46). Yet, as we already know, the ideas are not general concepts which subsume the phenomena and/or which symbolically shine through the phenomena. From a certain perspective the nominalist historicism is right: "This consideration would seem to do away with the distinction between the *questio juris* and the *questio facti* as far as the highest objects of philosophy are concerned" (*The Origin of German Tragic Drama*, p. 46). And yet, as Benjamin says, "philosophical history, the science of the origin, is the form which, in the remotest extremes and the apparent excesses of the process of development, reveals the configuration of idea" (*The Origin of German Tragic Drama*, p. 47). The key to this process is to be found in what Benjamin calls "the double insight" which combines discovery with re-cognition and is able to find an incomplete repetition of an idea in the constellation of fragmented phenomena. Instead of a self-identical, unchanging image which ignores the stream of becoming, Benjamin offers us a notion of truth revealing itself only in repetition in this very stream.

The category of the origin certainly demands a closer analysis. Here I would only like to point out that it is not at all clear if (similarily as in the case of constellation), all the precautions notwithstanding, Benjamin has not come dangerously close to the Neoplatonic understanding of symbol, and hence not far from conceptions that can be affected by Foucault's criticism. For could not such a Christian Neoplatonist as Hans-Georg Gadamer accept the notion according to which idea appears time and again in the phenomenal world in the incomplete form, only to appear fully in the totality of its history? And although the locus of epiphany is not a single phenomenon, but a constellation of fragmented phenomena, the

---

3   Foucault, "Nietzsche, Genealogy, History," p. 142.

suggestion remains valid. Is the notion that the anamnesis of the "philosophical historian" should be a restoration of a primal hearing, rather than of a primal vision, truly helpful? Also here Gadamer would not need to object and certainly no objection would be heard from Paul Ricoeur, a postheideggerian supporter of "the hermeneutics of hearing"[4] who at the same time offers a purely Neoplatonic conception of symbol. And from the other, anti-Platonic, Jewish camp, Emmanuel Lévinas would have a right to ask if the true disintegration of the intentional consciousness does not demand the complete break with the idea of anamnesis – also the acustic one – in favor of the notion of a certain past that cannot be retrieved in the act of remembering and re-presentation, in favor of a diachrony which guarantees a truly anti-Platonic gap between transcendence and immanence.[5]

Certainly, Benjamin's and Gadamer's intentions are essentially different. In Benjamin's conviction that every idea is a monad, and hence that the representation of one idea is in fact the representation of the whole world, (see *The Origin of German Tragic Drama*, pp. 47–48) we may trace the Gnostic, impatient desire to grasp the whole knowledge here and now, the desire which is absent from Gadamer's patient project which treats history as the chain of subsequent forms of traditions through which the eternal truth shines forth. Whereas, then, in Gadamer the origin or revelation would be homogeneously present in the medium of tradition as such, for the ecstatic Benjamin the philosopher who discovers the origin organizes the whole reality around it and does not want to hear about other manifestations of the idea, for – paradoxically enough – he uncovers the absolute center in the repetition. It also does not need to be explained how far from Gadamer's universe is the Gnostic idea of the fragmentation of the phenomena and of the destruction of the immanent appearance, which in Benjamin is linked to the cognitive impatience by means of the theological vision of the world as fallen. Still, it seems that the conceptual apparatus which Benjamin uses at this stage – in particular the otherwise exciting, iconoclastic idea of anamnesis of the primal hearing – does not guarantee the full articulation of his position and its clear differentiation from the Neoplatonic hermeneutics.

It should be noted that an important development of these meditations on the concept of origin can be found near the end of the great essay Benjamin devoted to Karl Kraus, where the category is located immediately in the linguistic sphere (see "Karl Kraus," in: *Selected Writings*, vol. II, part 2, pp. 453–454). Benjamin

---

4   Paul Ricoeur, *Interpretation Theory: Discourse and the Surplus of Meaning* (Fort Worth: Texas Christian University, 1976), p. 31.
5   See Emmanuel Lévinas, *Otherwise Than Being or Beyond Essence*, trans. Alphonso Lingis (Dordrecht: Kluwer Academic Publisher, 1991).

sketches here a philosophy of the destructive, punishing quotation which calls the word by its name, tears it out of its context and at the same time summons it to its origin. His bold reasoning involves additionally the category of rhyme which seems to play the role of a linguistic paraphrase of the moment of re-cognition that is indispensable for the discovery of the origin. As far as the problem of differentiating Benjamin's project from Neoplatonism, this direction of inquiry might be promising, for the subversive, even cruel aspect of the turn towards the origin is underscored here much stronger than in the book on Baroque. But the reflections are presented in such a telegraphic form that a serious assessment of this new approach is hardly possible. Thus, I propose to follow a different path.

Now, in the very middle of the file N of the arcades project, between other notes that are to sketch the methodology of the work, one stumbles upon the following fragment: "In studying Simmel's presentation of Goethe's concept of truth, I came to see very clearly that my concept of origin [...] is a rigorous and decisive transposition of this basic Goethean concept from the domain of nature to that of history. Origin – it is, in effect, the concept of *Ur*-phenomenon ectracted from the pagan context of nature and brought into the Jewish context of history. Now, in my work on the arcades I am equally concerned with fathoming an origin" (*The Arcades*, 462). This important fragment forms a link between the two fundamental works. What happens with the methodology of the book on Baroque in the work on Paris?

There are three fragments in the N file where we can find the category of concept. It seems that they ascribe to it a role which is rather similar to the one it played in the book on Baroque. One of them reads: "What matters for the dialectician is to have the wind of world history in his sails. Thinking means for him: setting the sails. What is important is *how* they are set. Words are his sails. They way they are set makes them into concepts" (*The Arcades*, p. 473). Or similarly, although with slight modifications: "Being a dialectician means having the wind of history in one's sails. The sails are the concepts. It is not enough, however, to have sails at one's disposal. What is decisive is knowing the art of setting them" (*The Arcades*, p. 473). These remarks explain the third fragment which links the category of the concept to the category of salvation we already know: "On the concept of «rescue»: the wind of the absolute in the sails of the concept" (*The Arcades*, p. 473). Thus, also here the concepts do not constitute the realm of the historian's aims, but rather the set of his tools. And just like in the book on Baroque, they are the instruments of salvation.

Yet, already here we may note an important change. In the would-be *Habilitationsschrift* the historian himself was not so much involved in the historical process. Just like the café-writer from the "One-Way Street" he bent over the historical phenomena like a surgeon and cut them with his concepts (see "One-Way Street," in: *Selected Writings*, vol. I, pp. 475–476). It is true that at the very end of the foreword Benjamin points to certain analogies between Baroque and Expressionism that establish a special relation between his own present and the past he studies. In the very work on the arcades he claims also that in the book on Baroque he tried to "expose the seventeenth century to the light of the present day" (*The Arcades*, p. 459). Yet, in the earlier work the historian was certainly not a sailor traveling the oceans of the historical events. Now he himself is subject to the historical powers, but thanks to a skillful setting of the conceptual sails he can make good use of the wind of history. Hence the positioning of the historian in history, his own present, becomes an essential element of the cognitive mechanism.

The second change pertains to the category of salvation which is now invested with a more dramatic sense. In the book on Baroque Benjamin referred to the category of salvation taking as his point of departure the Platonic intuition that what is fleeting needs grounding in what is stable – although certainly he proposed a strongly Gnostic interpretation of this intuition, on which the grounding involved a moment of destruction. Now salvation seems to turn against a double sociohistorical enslavement. First, it turns against the false immanence of the apparent happiness, that enclosed the past generations, and second, it turns against the delusive appearance and barbarity of the historical transmission itself. The latter idea finds its fullest articulation in the theses "Über den Begriff der Geschichte" and in the postulate that history must be brushed against the grain.

Both modifications set in motion the methodological construction of the book on Baroque. This transformation is also linked to a change that is crucial in our context. In the methodology of the arcades project we shall not find the third crucial methodological category of the book on Baroque, i.e. the category of the idea. Apart from the passage I have quoted above we shall not find the category of the origin, either, the very concept that was to link the idea with history. Is there an equvalent of these categories here? Yes, there is. I suspect that you will not be very surprised if I say that the equivalent of the idea (or rather of the origin as the historical mode of its presence) in the book on Paris is the category of the dialectical image.

Two observations should provide sufficient evidence. First, when talking about the category of the dialectical image, Benjamin uses the concept of constellation which previously he linked with the ideas. Let us look at a well-known passage: "To thinking belongs the movement as well as the arrest of thoughts. Where thinking comes to a standstill in a constellation saturated with tensions – there the dialectical image appears" (*The Arcades*, p. 475). Second, if in the passage quoted above the origin was identified as the transposition of *Urphänomen* into the realm of history, the same term refers to the dialectical image: "The dialectical image is that form of the historical object which satisfies Goethe's requirements for the object of analysis: to exhibit a genuine synthesis. It is the primal phenomenon of history" (*The Arcades*, p. 474).

Thus, just like in the book on Baroque the work of concepts was to bring about the simultaneous salvation of the phenomena and representation of the ideas, here the same work is to bring about a similar salvation and the flash of the dialcetical image. And here, too, the work of the concepts is a violent form of liberation. In the book on Baroque Benjamin spoke of the fragmentation of the phenomena. Here the historian must bring about a double destruction which corresponds to the double nature of enslavement. First, he breaks the narrative continuity of history and tears phenomena out of it, opposing the catastrophe of the barbarious cultural transmission. Second, such a destruction uncovers the phenomenon in its truth, i.e. in its broken nature that was hidden in the mythical dream of culture. In other words, it uncovers it as the locus of unfulfilled expectations, as a gate through which the Messiah has not entered. For the fact that the historian himself is involved here in the historical process means first and foremost that the dialectical image is a constellation which forms itself between what has been and the moment of awakening in the "now of knowability," when an especially ambiguous element of the past world becomes readable and the collective dream of the past generations reveals itself as the bleak landscape of allegory, the sign of the fallen creature.

Setting aside other properties of the dialectical image, as well as certain inconsistencies in Benjamin's description of this category, we have to ask now about the relation between the dialectical image and the realm of language. It would seem that the use of this category means a withdrawal from the panglotticism characteristic of early Benjamin. Yet, in one of the crucial fragments of the file N, we read: "[…] image is that wherein what has been comes together in a flash with the now to form a constellation. […] Only dialectical images are genuine images (that is, not archaic [like the images of Jung who wants to keep as in the mythical dream rather than head towards the emancipatory awakening]); and the place where one encounters them is language" (*The Arcades*, p. 462). In what sense are the dialectical images present in language?

I think that we shall not be very far from Benjamin's intentions if we assume that the dialectical image is a form of name's presence. This can be discerned in the way Benjamin writes about both categories. Thus, we saw that the dialectical image appears like a lightning, *blitzartig*. But in the important theoretical text entitled "Doctrine of the Similar" the same word refers to the manifestation of the mimetic aspect of language. Yet, the mimetic or magical aspect of language is precisely the remnant of the paradise language of names in the human, fallen speech (see "Doctrine of the Similar," in: *Selected Writings*, vol. II, part 2, p. 697). In the same context Benjamin writes also that the momentary perception of similarity – identical with the contact with the sphere of names – flashes by, *huscht vorbei* ("Doctrine of the Similar," in: *Selected Writings*, vol. II, part 2, p. 695), and in the fifth thesis "On the Concept of History" the same verb refers to the "true image of the past" ("On the Concept of History," in: *Selected Writings*, vol. IV, p. 390). And the identification of the dialectical image with a form of presence of the name is also suggested by the most general structure of Benjamin's thought: if we treat the early text "Über Sprache überhaupt und über die Sprache des Menschen" as paradigmatic for his whole philosophy, it will be clear that every action of redeeming or saving character (the work of the philosopher, as well that of the historian, critic and translator, if we were to list the most important Messianic figures in Benjamin's work) is about recovery of names. In the case of the dialectical image this recovery becomes also a moral gesture of justice done to the past individual suffering.

I suggest, then, that if we bracket for a moment all the essential moments of dramatization that I pointed to above, there is a strict analogy between the model based on the triad of phenomenon/concept/idea (origin) and between the one based on the triad of phenomenon/concept/dialectical image. All the more visible is the fundamental difference between them: whereas in the former model the name understood as idea cannot have anything to do with an image and should be recovered by means of the anamnesis of the primal hearing, in the latter model the name assumes precisely the form of an image. What has happened here? How seriously are we to treat this visual metaphor? Is this "return of the gaze" a concession to the optical Platonism and Neoplatonic understanding of symbol?

It seems to me – and actually this is the only thing I want to say here – that this is not the case and that, moreover, the use of the optical trope of image paradoxically enables Benjamin to give a better expression to his earlier intuitions. In order to understand it, it may be helpful to look at the constrast between Benjamin's theory and Gadamer's hermeneutics I have already referred to above. As we have already seen, if we rely upon the categories from the book on Baroque, the articulation of the indubitable differences between Gadamer and Benjamin may encounter certain difficulties. If I am not mistaken the situation is much better when we are dealing with the model based on the category of the dialectical image.

Gadamer is a philosopher of continuity, of the calm flow of the linguistic stream of tradition in which truth manifests itself. In his universe language does not stumble upon any limits, but – paradoxically enough – it is this seemingly fully panglottic vision of human experience that is also explicitly rooted in the Neoplatonic tradition of emanation and of the symbolic presence of truth in the contingent world.[6] It is as if the unbroken, purely linguistic order, spreading over all human reality, was perfectly equivalent to the perspective of the Neoplatonic philosophy of vision. The consequences of this situation are, by the way, lethal for Gadamer's thought: pace his declarations according to which his philosophy accounts for historicity, finiteness and individuality, in fact it leads us back to the quite traditional logocentrism. In Gadamer's philosophy the linguistic turn ends with capitulation and Wilhelm von Humboldt humbles himself before Hegel.

Benjamin does not let the linguistic order to pass fully into the optical order, but rather he inserts a heterogeneous motif of image into the very center of the linguistic realm. The image is not something primal, prior to language, but rather somether posterior to it – it is a lump of individuality that precipitates from and in language. The name as the dialectical image breaks the smooth flow of the historical narrative which, although of linguistic nature, all to easily turns into the element of the general. Without surrendering to the philosophy of vision criticised in the book on Baroque, this hybrid of the linguistic and optical categories enables a better articulation of the moment of discontinuity, of the Gnostic rending of the phenomenal order which aims at the salvation of the phenomena and in the socio-historical dimension – at doing justice to the individual suffering of those whose history is the object of the study. Moreover, the introduction of this moment of rending establishes also the individuality of the very subject of cognition who achieves the redemptive knowledge not through participation in the extra-individual stream of the historical transmission, but rather through the act of subversive trasnscendence of the narrative continuity and a stellar clash of his own present with the isolated object of knowledge. As a result, the reference to the category of image enables to retain the gains of the linguistic turn and stops the panglottic vision of the world from slipping into Neoplatonism and the philosophy of pure vision ignoring all finiteness. It seems then – and let us conclude with this – that it is precisely thanks to this move that Benjamin is able to protect individuality against the omnivorous machine of the general and save the honor of the name.

---

6   See especially Hans-Georg Gadamer, *Truth and Method*, trans. Joel Weinsheimer, Donald G. Marshall (London – New York: Continuum, 2006), pp. 469–484.

## Bibliography

1. Walter Benjamin, "Doctrine of the Similar," in: *Selected Writings*, ed. Michael W. Jennings and Marcus Bullock, Howard Eiland, Gary Smith, vol. II, part 2, (Cambridge, MA: Belknap Press of Harvard University Press, 1999).
2. Walter Benjamin, "Karl Kraus," in: *Selected Writings*, ed. Michael W. Jennings and Marcus Bullock, Howard Eiland, Gary Smith, vol. II, part 2, (Cambridge, MA: Belknap Press of Harvard University Press, 1999).
3. Walter Benjamin, "On Language as Such and on the Language of Man," in: *Selected Writings*, ed. Michael W. Jennings and Marcus Bullock, Howard Eiland, Gary Smith, vol. I (Cambridge, MA: Belknap Press of Harvard University Press, 1996).
4. Walter Benjamin, "On the Concept of History," in: *Selected Writings*, ed. Michael W. Jennings and Marcus Bullock, Howard Eiland, Gary Smith, vol. IV (Cambridge, MA: Belknap Press of Harvard University Press, 2003).
5. Walter Benjamin, "One-Way Street," in: *Selected Writings*, ed. Michael W. Jennings and Marcus Bullock, Howard Eiland, Gary Smith, vol. I (Cambridge, MA: Belknap Press of Harvard University Press, 1996).
6. Walter Benjamin, *The Arcades Project*, trans. Howard Eiland and Kevin McLaughlin, prepared on the basis of the German volume edited by Rolf Tiedman (Cambridge Mass.: The Belknap Press of Harvard University Press, 1999).
7. Walter Benjamin, *The Origin of German Tragic Drama*, trans. John Osborne (London – New York: Verso, 1998).
8. Michel Foucault, "Nietzsche, Genealogy, History," in: *Language, Counter-Memory, Practice: Selected Essays and Interviews*, ed. Donald F. Bouchard, trans. Donald F. Bouchard, Sherry Simon (Ithaca: Cornell University Press, 1977).
9. Hans-Georg Gadamer, *Truth and Method*, trans. Joel Weinsheimer, Donald G. Marshall (London – New York: Continuum, 2006).
10. Emmanuel Lévinas, *Otherwise Than Being or Beyond Essence*, trans. Alphonso Lingis (Dordrecht: Kluwer Academic Publisher, 1991).
11. Paul Ricoeur, *Interpretation Theory: Discourse and the Surplus of Meaning* (Fort Worth: Texas Christian University, 1976).
12. Charles Taylor, *Sources of the Self. The Making oft he Modern Indentity* (Cambride: Cambridge University Press, 1996).

Agata Bielik-Robson
# Man as Name Giver: Some Non-Elective Affinities between Benjamin and Heidegger

**Abstract:** The aim of this presentation is to point to certain convergences between Benjamin's and Heidegger's essays on language which the author will call "non-elective affinities." Although there is no direct influence between them, the source of the affinities is nonetheless obvious. Both Benjamin and Heidegger draw on the same precursorial texts: Hamann's essay from 1762, *Aesthetica in nuce*, as well as his polemic with Herder written ten years later, *Des Ritters von Rosencreutz letzte Willensmeynung über den göttlichen und menschlichen Ursprung der Sprache*. Both refer to the same quotations and make similar allusions to Hamann's leading thesis according to which everything ultimately is language and language manifests itself in everything.

**Keywords:** Hamann; Heidegger; "Unterwegs zur Sprache"; "On Language as Such and on the Language of Man"; philosophy of language

*Heil dem Erzengel über die Reliquien der Sprache Kanaans! [...]*
*Ich rede mit euch, Griechen! weil ihr euch weiser dünkt,*
*denn die Kammerherren mit dem gnostischen Schlüssel.*[1]
Johann Georg Hamann

The aim of my presentation is to point to certain convergences between Benjamin's and Heidegger's essays on language which I will call here "non-elective affinities". Although there is no direct influence between them, the source of the affinities is nonetheless obvious. Both Benjamin and Heidegger draw on the same precursorial texts: Johann Georg Hamann's famous essay from 1762, *Aesthetica in nuce*, as well as his polemic with Herder written ten years later, *Des Ritters von Rosencreutz letzte Willensmeynung über den göttlichen und menschlichen Ursprung der Sprache*. Both refer to the same quotations and make similar allusions to Hamann's leading thesis according to which everything ultimately is language and language manifests itself in everything. However, these affinities between Benjamin and Heidegger are not exactly the kind Goethe would call *Wahlverwandtschaften*: despite certain similarities – most of all their analogous insistence on *die Nennkraft*, the power of naming as the essence of human language, most perferctly revealing itself

---

1 Johann Georg Hamann, *Sokratische Denkwürdigkeiten/Aesthetica in nuce*, ed. Sven-Aage Jorgensen (Stuttgart: Philip Reclam Verlag, 1968), p. 81, 117.

in poetry – the overall contexts, in which they formulate these sometimes striking analogies, differ rather fundamentally. They both revise the same precursorial texts of Hamann, but the more they revise it, the more they invest in their ow *clinamen* from the source, and the less they appear to have in common with each other. We could say, therefore, that the exercise in finding out the non-elective affinities aims in fact at the demonstration of *the greatest possible difference* which gains its *Gestalt* precisely by the contrast with the common starting point. A careful reading of Benjamin's essay "On Language as Such and on the Language of Man," written in 1917, will be able to show us an alternative "way to language" that is only to a certain point *unterwegs* with Heidegger, and then, precisely in the moment of their closest affinity, departs from him radically.

## A Kabbalistic Rhapsody

*Aesthetica in nuce* has a subtitle, *eine kabbalistische Rhapsodie*, which also perfectly fits Benjamin's late variation on Hamann: just like kabbalah and after its techaning, the famous Magus of the North, Benjamin develops the theme of the ultimate linguistic nature of reality by following closely the greatest "relic of the Kaananites", the Hebrew Bible: "In what follows, says Benjamin, the nature of language is considered on the basis of the first chapter of Genesis […] on the discovery of what emerges of itself from the biblical text with regard to the nature of language."[2] He thus conceives language in the broadest possible way, as a universal communication of mental meanings, encompassing and enjoining into the stream of constant interaction everything that exists.[3] "There is no event or thing in either animate or inanimate nature that does not in some way partake of language, for it is in the nature of all to communicate their mental meanings," he says (OL, p. 315). And then, by alluding to Hamann's letter to Herder, where he calls this "kabbalistic" theory of language both self-evident and dangerously "abyssmal", he formulates his task as a philosopher of language: "The view that the mental essence of a thing consists precisely in its language – this view, taken

---

[2] Walter Benjamin, "On Language as Such and on the Language of Man," trans. Edmund Jephcott, in: *Reflections. Essays, Aphorisms, Autobiographical Writings* (New York: Schocken Books, 1978), pp. 321–322. From now on in the text as OL.
[3] See for analogy Hamann: "Rede, daß ich Dich sehe! Dieser Wunsch wurde durch die Schöpfung erfüllt, die eine Rede an die Kreatur durch die Kreatur ist; denn ein Tag sagts dem andern, und eine Nacht thuts kund der andern." In *Sokratische Denkwürdigkeiten*, p. 36.

as a hypothesis, is the great abyss into all linguistic theory threatens to fall, and to survive suspended precisely over this abyss is its task" (OL, p. 316).[4]

What does the language communicate? It communicates "mental being corresponding to it" (OL, p. 316), which is at the same time mental meaning and mental essence. This is communicated not *through* language but *in* language which clearly suggests that for Benjamin language is coextensive with everything. There can be no perspective external to language, as it is assumed by the "bourgeois" conception of language which treats it merely as a medium between three extralinguistic entities, as in Charles Pierce, more or less – the thing denoted, the speaker and the recipient of the information. This bourgeois, pragmatic conception of language, implies Benjamin, is but the further development of the first false step taken in Paradise – first lapse, when Adam and Eve went for what Blake used to call a "false tongue," the language of questioning stolen from the Tree of Knowledge of Good and Evil. The false tongue of opinionation, ruling its verdicts as if from the non-situated outside – the wretched favourite idiom of the Blakeyan "Idiot Questioner," as well as Socrates in Hamann's rendering, called by him derisively *der weise Idiot Griechenlands* – is to be blamed for tearing the immanence of language, its "uninterrupted flow" (OL, p. 331), as coextensive with the whole of Creation. It introduces *false transcendence*, located in the isolated, separate, questioning human subject, which at the same time is the most ominous characteristics of the Fall. The subject, who uses language as a tool for mediating his opinions, deepens the Fall by further degenerating language into what Kierkegaard – and after him both Benjamin and Heidegger – call "platter" (*das Geschwätz, das Gerede*). Poetry locates itself on the opposite pole to this "bourgeois," pragmatic misuse of language: away from abstract and non-situated questioning, and close as possible to the activity of naming, *nennen*, which restores to things their original honour of proper names.[5] "It is the linguistic being of man to name things" (OL, p. 317), and "the language of poetry is partly, if not solely, founded on the name language of man" (OL, p. 330).[6]

---

4   Heidegger formulates his task in a surprisingly similar manner: "The saying 'language is language' allows us to balance over the abyss as long as we stick to what it says," in *Unterwegs zur Sprache* (Stuttgart: Verlag Günther Neske, 1959), p. 12 (in my translation). From now on the text as US.

5   See again Hamann, *Sokratische Denkwürdigkeiten*, p. 38: "Poesie ist die Muttersprache des menschlichen Geschlechts; wie der Gartenbau, älter als der Acker: Malerey, – als Schrift: Gesang, – als Deklamation: Gleichnisse, – als Schlüsse: Tausch, – als Handel".

6   "The theory of proper names is the theory of the frontier between finite and infinite language [...] the proper name is the word of God in human sounds [...]. The proper name is the communion of man with the creative word of God" (OL, p. 324).

This is why the primary problem of language is not the correlation of an artificial system of signs with the order of things: quite to the contrary, "the primary poblem of language is its magic" (OL, p. 317). It may sound a little surprising on the part of Benjamin who will later on show himself as an intransigent critic of everything mythical[7], but here magic is simply understood as a principle of universal interaction: "To whom does the lamp communicate itself? The mountain? The fox? But here the answer is: to man." And to an imagined bourgeois Idiot Questioner, who would doubt the existence of such magical correspondence, Benjamin answers by paraphrasing Goethe's famous line from the *Xenien*, concerning the common substance of eye and sun: "This is not anthropomorphism [...]. If the lamp and the mountain and the fox did not communicate themselves to man, how should he be able to name them?" (OL, p. 317) Precisely: why would he ever want to name them? Or rather, why would he ever feel an urge to reveal their essence that goes beyond the pragmatic use of a thing? Things demand from a man to be named, and this silent demand, issued in a lower form of language, "imperfect and dumb,"[8] cannnot be ignored: it must be translated into a higher language and carried forward to God himself. "The bourgeois conception of language [...] – says Benjamin – holds that the means of communication is the word, its object factual, its addressee a human being. The other conception of language, in contrast, knows no means, no object, and no addressee of communication. It means: in naming the mental being of man communicates itself to God" (OL, p. 318). And further: "Man is the namer, by this we recognize that through him pure language speaks. All nature, insofar as it communicates itself, communicates itself in language, and so finally in man. Hence he is the lord of nature and can give names to things [...] God's creation is completed when things receive their names from man [...] Name is not only the last utterance of language but also the true call of it" (OL, p. 319).

Benjamin bases his speculation, in which man figures primarily as a name giver, on two stories of creation offered by *Genesis*. The first story tells about the creation of the world that runs according to the triad "Let there be – He made (created) – He named" (OL, p. 322). God creates (*barah*) by uttering words in the form of a performative (*devharim*) and then, contemplating the things he had made, reveals their names (*shemot*). The second story, however, is qualitatively different; it tells about the creation of man not through word but through making

---

7  See especially his "Goethe's *Elective Affinities*," in: *Selected Writings*, vol. I.
8  "Language itself is not perfectly expressed in things themselves [...] the languages of things are imperfect, and they are dumb" (OL, p. 321).

a copy (*zelem*) of God himself out of a combination of clay (*adamah*) and breath (*ruah*) which simultaneously is also a gift of language.[9] "God did not create man from the word – writes Benjamin – and he did not name him. He did not wish to subject him to language, but in man God set language, which had served Him as a medium of creation, free. God rested when he had left his creative power to itself in man. This creativity, relieved of its divine actuality, became knowledge. Man is the knower in the same language in which God is creator... All human language is only reflection of the word in name" (OL, p. 323).

In the triad, which forms the creation of the world, Benjamin substitutes "He named" for "He saw that it was good," thus implying that in God the act of final judgment is passed via the knowledge of the name, and, moreover, that judging, included into the triad, belongs strictly to the continuous and integral process of creation: "He had cognized it through name" (OL, p. 323). Making the judgment the part of this "uninterrupted flow" is absolutely crucial for Benjamin for it serves him to elucidate the role of the primordial sin which underlies the Fall. Fall is here nothing but *interruption* – or, as kaballah has it, "the blockage of the channels" in the flow of infinite language.[10] Man's sin consists precisely in the way he attempts to pass judgment over creation, taking a stance as if from nowhere; his way of questioning becomes Mephistophelian in its un-creative, destructive rivalry with God's making powers.[11] It is only in this sense that we can speak here of a false tongue and false transcendence: a subject abstracted from the immanence of the ongoing creation, a questioning view from nowhere made up by the impotent Satan precisely as *nothingness*, *Nichtigkeit*, created through the abstraction of pure, isolated inquiry. "The knowledge to which the snake seduces, that of good and evil – says Benjamin – is *nameless*. It is vain (*nichtig*) in the deepest sense, and this very knowledge is itself the only evil known to the paradisiac state. Knowledge

---

9 "In this second story of the Creation the making of man did not take place through the word: God spoke – and there was – but this man, who is not created from the word, is now invested with the gift of language and is elevated above nature" (OL, p. 322).
10 "The life of man in pure language-mind was blissful" (OL, 329), i.e. wholesome and participatory in being itself. On "the blockage of the channels" and their function within the process of creation see most of all Gershom Scholem, *Zur Kabbala und ihrer Symbolik* (Frankfurt am Main: Suhrkamp, 2001).
11 This motif of destructive rivalry between God and man, whose spirit is embodied in Goethe's Mephisto, appears in one of Georg Simmel's essay Benjamin obviously read: "Zu einer Theorie des Pessmismus," in: *Gesamtausgabe*, vol. 5 (Frankfurt am Main: Suhrkamp Verlag, 1992).

of good and evil abandons name, it is a knowledge from outside, the uncreated imitation of the creative word. Name steps outside itself in this knowledge: the Fall marks the birth of the human word" (OL, p. 327).

Benjamin's rendering of the Fall is thus the story of a wrong repetition, an abuse of the logic of *zelem*, or inappropriate *mimesis* of God: seduced by the Mephistophelian snake's *eritis sicut Dii*, first parents, instead of completing God's creation by naming things, wished to imitate what can only belong to the Creator himself: the final touch of judgment. Not only is this spurious but also empty repetition, the one that engenders the unnecessary, *das Nichtige*, the truly nameless that sticks out from the infinite flow of language, the evil itself: "The question as to good and evil in the world after creation – writes Benjamin – was empty prattle (*Geschwätz*). The tree of knowledge did not stand in the garden of God in order to dispense information on good and evil, but as an emblem of judgment over the questioner. This immense irony marks the mythical origin of law" (OL, p. 328).

## The Incongruity

Yet, it may also be argued against this Hamannian-Kierkegaardian variation on the theme of the Fall – and Benjamin will do it himself later on – that there is a certain disquieting incongruity in the double story of creation which has to end in crisis. For, if God had already sealed his creation with the cognizant naming of "that was good", why does he need Adam to complete the process of naming? What is there for Adam to do, but to repeat in "blissful" monotony what had already been done? If he lives in the "uninterrupted flow" of this infinite language, his role dwindles down to an insignificant, transparent transmitter whose existence is not at all metaphysically necessary. But, if there is a *flaw* in creation itself – i.e. if the Fall occurs not due to the accidental misbehaviour of the first people, but due to a necessary catastrophe which prevents creative act from completion and leaves world in the state of imperfection: a truly kabbalistic conjecture – then the second story of creation, which concerns forming of man and his destiny as namer of things, makes more sense. It would mean that God failed to reach the essence of things at the conclusion of his creative act; that, in the end, he did not know or recognized the world he had created. Simply speaking, the whole creatory business got completely out of hand – and that the world, as existent, achieved due to this failure the status of both separation and imperfection. On this reading, the interruption would thus be on God's part and not man's – or rather (and this is, in fact, quite Heideggerian remark) on the part of Being itself: this is at least, as

Lurianic Kabbalah represents the blunder of creation, i.e. as ontologically necessary, for which nothing and nobody can be blamed.[12]

Benjamin seems to be aware of this problem. This awareness manifests itself in few crucial equivocations that plague his early text, not yet very well versed in all those "kabbalistic rhapsodies" which later on will become Benjamin's trademark. First of all, we wonder what could be the state of nature and its language before the Fall; in what sense would it be dumb, imperfect, mute and lower (all Benjamin's formulations) and why would it need human helping translation? "After the Fall, when God's curses the ground, the appearance of nature deeply changed – says Benjamin. Now begins its *other* muteness, which we mean by deep sadness of nature. It is a metaphysical truth that all nature would begin to lament if it were endowed with language..." (OL, p. 329).[13] It is only later, that is in "The Task of the Translator," that Benjamin will develop the notion of translation as – precisely – the interruption which, as de Man, commenting on it, put tersely, "disarticulates and undoes the original", thus testifying to the "blockage of the chanels" which stops *die lebendige Sprache* from continuous flowing.[14] Here, however "translation is (still) removal from one language into another through a *continuum* of transformations... The translation of the language of things into that of man is not only a translation of the mute into the sonic; it is also the translation of the nameless into name... In receiving the unspoken nameless language of things and converting it by name into sounds, man performs his task" (OL, p. 326).[15] But, are

---

12   On the idea of creation as an unavoidable catastrophe see Gershom Scholem, *Über einige Grundbegriffe des Judentums* (Frankfurt am Main: Suhrkamp, 1996).
13   "Because she is mute, nature mourns. Yet the inversion of this proposition leads even further into the essence of nature; the sadness of nature makes her mute" (OL, p. 329). And then: "Over-naming as the deepest linguistic reason for all melancholy" (OL, p. 330).
14   See Paul de Man, "Walter Benjamin's 'The Task of the Translator,'" in: *The Resistance to Theory* (Minneapolis: University of Minnesotta Press, 1986), p. 84. In her most interesting essay, which makes connection between Benjamin's and de Man's version of gnosis, Cathy Caruth claims that especially for the latter reality was nothing but *the fall from meaning*. Only where the seemingly meaningful text falls, i.e. stumbles in its flow – it touches the ground of what just *is* and thus refers to reality. Being is here the darkest, least transparent of all energies, which is resistant to all light and language; it can only be reached by the failure of signification. See Cathy Caruth, "The Falling Body and the Impact of Reference," in *Unclaimed Experience. Trauma, Narrative, and History* (Baltimore & London: The Johns Hopkins University Press, 1996).
15   A view of continuity obviously inherited from Hamann who says: "Reden ist übersetzen – aus einer Engelsprache in eine Menschensprache, das heist, Gedanken in

things simply nameless? Are they endowed with hidden divine names that have to be recovered? Or, are they damaged in their inner name-essences that need to be repaired? These are three separate options and Benjamin's essay does not choose between them definitively; only later on he will go unequivocally for the third solution, which assignes to man a crucial role in the process of redemption, i.e. in a saving completion of the work of creation that became internally and necessarily thwarted. Interruption will still appear as the main characteristics of the Fall, this time however it will also be interpreted *positively* within the antinomian logic of redemption as an indispensable caesura, which grants distinct and separate status to three entities: God, nature, and man.[16]

At this stage, however, a subtle undercurrent of theological contradiction dents into Benjamin's essay. Towards the end he says – First: "The uninterrupted flow of this communication runs through the whole of nature from the lowest forms of existence to man and from man to God…" And then right on: "The language of nature is comparable to a secret password that each sentry passes to the next in his own language, but the meaning of the password is the sentry's language itself. All higher language is a translation of those lower, until in the ultimate clarity the word of God unfolds, which is the unity of this movement made up of language" (OL, pp. 331–332). The first image belongs to the Neoplatonic static vision of a never-ending, self-repeating, continuous cycle of emanation where the kabbalistic word substitutes for Plotinian light. The second image, however, tells a more complex story – precisely, a *story* – in which the flow becomes interrupted, blocked and fragmented into discreet units whose mutual communication is not at all that obvious. Now, it is a task, *ein Auftrag*, performed on the demand which has nothing playful or blissful about itself – quite to the contrary, it is full of tragic lament: an effort which has to be made to bring all this blocked, differentiated, separated, secretive muteness into "the ultimate clarity of the divine word" that was before the creation and must be restored in the messianic future.

---

Worte, – Sachen in Namen, – Bilder in Zeichen…" Hamann's idea seems also to underlie Heidegger's "Setzen ist Übersetzen," pointing to a quasi-linguistic relationship between the matrix of *Sein* and its always, by necessity, half-failed copies in the form of *die Seiende*.

16 This doctrine of separation as a positive condition of further redemptive work appears in Benjamin's thought thanks to the influence of Franz Rosenzweig and his *Star of Redemption*, where God, Man, and Nature are set apart from one another as three isolated points of a triangle that constitutes *die Vor-Welt* of creation. In Rosenzweig's system it is only after their initial separation that the proper relationship of speech can begin.

## Uninterrupted Flow

But this is precisely this mythical phantasy of the "uninterrupted flow" which makes Benjamin, at least in this early essay, strangely close to Heidegger who projects a similar *Sprachkreise* in the closed circulation of *Sagen*, occurring between Being, man, and then Being again. The danger of the ontological obliteration of the middle term – man – is here as distinct as in Benjamin, although unlike in Benjamin, who, having discovered it, gave up on the organic metaphor of the infinite life of language, it is fully welcomed by Heidegger as its self-evident consequence. "How far does man speak the language?", asks Heidegger in the essay called "Die Sprache," opening his *Unterwegs zur Sprache*: not very far, indeed, for it is in fact "die Sprache, die spricht", the language itself that speaks primarily and only lends itself to man (US, p. 17). Man has nothing else to do in this mythic, circular picture than to participate, listen-obey (*Ge-hören*) and witness the glory of the cycle of reciprocity between things and World and between *Sein* and *die Seiende* that passes between his mystified eyes on "the treshold" of *die Unter-Schied*, the inter-cut both constituting and sublating all the difference. This is a truly "uninterrupted flow", belonging to the mythical world from before the Fall, where man is assigned not an active and creative role of a redeemer, but merely a passive, essentially *ja-sagend* role of a witness.

The apparent affinities, therefore, should not mislead us. True, we find in Benjamin a very similar critique of the Cartesian subjectivity as an incipiently nihilistic, mute instance, grounding itself in nothingness, i.e. on the original act of exclusion from the whole of Being. Heidegger also tries to make a move from the nihilizing questioning, which passes original silent No to Being and sets up the mutely functional world of manipulable technological beings, to the act of poetic *Sagen* whose aim is to return man into the cycle of speech and make him again, after Humboldt's definition, a "speaking being". And we find the same concern with poetry as the language of proper names, exercising the right linguistic power, the one of naming, *die Nennkraft*. Yet in Heidegger this naming quickly transforms itself into something else; the sequence from "Die Sprache", which changes *nennen* into *heissen*, *rufen*, *zu-rufen*, and finally into *ein-laden*, turns naming into a vague invitation which is addressed not to separate things but to Being itself, encompassed in its totality, whose subtle, self-withdrawing gift can be properly appreciated only in the language of poetry. "Das Sprechen – writes Heidegger on Georg Trakl's poem, *Der Winterabend* – nennt die Witnerabendzeit. Was ist dieses Nennen? Behängt es nur die vorstellbaren, bekannten Gegenstände und Vorgänge: Schnee, Glocke, Fenster, fallen, läuten – mit den Wörtern einer Sprache? *Nein*. Das Nennen verteilt nich Titel, verwendet nich Wörter, sondern ruft ins Wort. Das Nennen ruft. Das Rufen bringt sein Gerufenes näher" (US, p. 18). The link between naming and word is thus broken, and reveals a deeper ground from which all words originate: the "resonating silence." "Die Sprache spricht als eine ringende Stille" (US, p. 26). This muteness however, has nothing sad or tragic about it; it is not a melancholy sign of imperfection or blockage. Quite to the contary, it is an ultimate reality of Being, its, so to say, natural murmur which never reaches, or rather never intended to reach, the clarity of the divine word.[17] For Heidegger, therefore, poetry names only insofar it names-calls this silence which both appropriates (*eignet*) and disappropriates (*er-eignet*) and thus disrupts the language of words – the best instance here are long, disruptive ellipses in Hölderlin's poems – that is, insofar it is a language "given to death," *gelassen* (calmly-resignedly) witnessing coming and passing of things out of and back to the undifferentiated matrix of Being (US, p. 26). If the flow is so uninterrupted here, it is only because nothing ever gets properly constituted, no being granted a status of separation: here "every *Setzen* is a disruptive *Setzen*", a failed translation that never emancipates itself from the original.[18] In this mythic world, Being, unlike the Hebrew God, plays safe: it disrupts the difference and separation of things before they can interrupt its wholeness. Nothing can ever happen in this perfectly henotheistic, tautological flow of One into One. No crisis – and no reparation.

---

17 The difference between the dark light of Heidegger's *Seyn*, which remains in the *Ab-Grund* as ambivalent and half-concealed (and which, later on, Benjamin will ascribe generally to mythical world) and the clarity of the world of revelation is absolutely crucial in understanding the fundamental non-affinity between the two thinkers: "The highest mental region of religion – says the latter – is at the same time the only one that does not know the inexpressible. For it is addressed in name and expresses itself as revelation" (OL, p. 321).

18 I take the phrase of "disruptive *Setzen*" from Rodolphe Gasché, who, in his book on de Man, *The Wild Card of Reading*, describes by it the Heideggerian operation of Being. In *On the Origin of the Work of Art* Heidegger introduces the metaphor of *die Erde*, the chtonic aspect of Being which shelters everything which emerged in order to return to its matrix. *Die Erde* shelters the constant motion of emergence and disappearance; provides a kind of an umbilical cord, the link of *Nichtigkeit* which ties all beings to their origins and pulls them back to them in their due time. All *Setzen*, therefore, is like *Übersetzen*, a translation which inevitably looses something essential in the process and cannot stand as autonomous towards its original. In the process of *a-letheia*, of coming forth from unconcealedness, Being translates itself into beings, and, as if discontended with the product of such lame translation, withdraws them, thus re-translating them back into the original. See Rodolphe Gasché, *The Wild Card of Reading. On Paul de Man* (Cambridge, Mass.& London: Harvard University Press, 1998), p. 43.

Thus the analogy with Benjamin eventually has to break on the level of nothing else but theology. If we look at Benjamin's essay on language as a yet ambivalent promise of the later development, we shall see clearly that the regulative idea of an uniterrupted flow must be discarded as belonging to the *sphere of the mythic* – strictly opposed to the *sphere of the messianic*.[19] The principle of non-interruption can engender no story, all the more *die Heilsgeschichte*, i.e. an ongoing and open process in which man is assigned a significant redemptive role. In Benjamin, eventually – very much as in Rosenzweig – all elements of the dialogic triangle will become strictly separate, precisely thanks to the interruption that breaks the cycle of speech. Muteness, the zero-point of language, means fallenness into dumb matter – but it also means a liberating severance, a condition we could call, in contrast to Heidegger, a "complete *Setzen*." Dead allegory, which in Benjamin's *The Origin of German Tragic Drama* marks the very opposite of the living flowing speech from his early essay, is an empty sign which signifies only one thing: *separation*. And names, with their secret redemptive *Nennkraft*, which is to rescue the world of things from the deadness of allegory, are given to name each and every thing precisely as severed from the whole, fallen from grace, obstructive, singular and differentiated.

It would seem, therefore, that the Neoplatonic fantasy of an uninterrupted flow (fully embraced by Heidegger, and partially by early Benjamin) versus the traditional Jewish teaching of separation (towards which Benjamin gravitates in his later works) offers the best model to juxtapose two alternative answers to the notorious question *What is being*? Not only it is unfair but also untrue when Heidegger says that "there is no Christian (implicitly also Judaic) philosophy," for it allegedly never asks the question of Being. Well, it clearly *does* and it answers it in a radically different way, employing an alternative "mythical narrative". For, what else is Heidegger doing if not simply translating mythical contents of pre-Socratic narratives into his "four-folds" and "tresholds"? And what else is Benjamin doing if not trying to find an analogous translation for the "narrative" concept of the

---

19 In fact, the ideal of an interrupted flow of the infinite language is still very much Hamannian. See, for instance, the passage from *Des Ritters von Rosencreutz letzte Willensmeynung...*: "Jede Erscheinung der Natur war ein Wort, – das Zeichen, Sinnbild und Unterpfand einer neuen, geheimen, unaussprechlichen, aber desto innigern Vereinigung, Mittheilung und Gemeinschaft göttlicher Energien und Ideen. Alles, was der Mensch am Anfange hörte, mit Augen sah, beschaute und seine Hände betasteten, war ein lebendiges Wort; denn Gott war das Wort. Mit diesem Wort im Mund und im Herzen war der Ursprung der Sprache so natürlich, so nahe und leicht, wie ein Kinderspiel..." – Hamann, *Sokratische Denkwürdigkeiten*, p. 78.

Fall? In this early essay, Benjamin still hovers dangerously close over the waters of myth, but even there he already attempts to de-psychologize the Fall-motif and move it towards ontological necessity. For the being to be, the Fall must have occurred; for the Being to be, a separation-interruption must have taken place.

Fall is thus implied in creation; creation, in fact, is synonymous with the Fall – falling away from intention, from judgement, from meaning. *Die Abgeschiedenheit*, "apartness" – the motif Heidegger deals with in his reflections on Trakl's poem *Der Abgeschiedene* and surrounds with a tragic aura of madness and *Verfallenheit* – appears here as a necessary condition of "coming into being". This is how things begin to be: as abandoned and separate, as "those that have parted" (US, p. 52).[20] This is why in maturing Benjamin, it will be the allegory that will constitute is the most naked and poignant sign of such bare existence. Yet, still and only then – an *existence*. A full *Setzen*, therefore, i.e. the one that truly makes beings come into being, is a self-alienated *Setzen*, which implies its own failure – interruption, blockage, disturbance. Whereas a continuous *Setzen*, like in Heidegger, does not really allows beings to be; their existence reduces itself to belonging to the uninterrupted flow from which they never single themselves out properly (their *Abgeschiedenheit* merely spells a moment of "madness" that needs to be corrected by the *Ruf des Seins*). Experiencing no *break* – only a *treshold* of mutual passage – they never make into the "apartness" of existence.[21]

The answer of the Hebrew tradition to the question of Being, lurking behind Benjamin's essay, is, first of all – separation, a fully endorsed "apartness" that speaks only in allegories, the signs of a broken whole. And, unlike in Heidegger's circular world of "incomplete *Setzen*", there is no turning back on this road of differentiating interruption. The messianic breaks the tautological circle of the mythic. In the beginning is *not* my end; in the beginning is only the beginning.

---

20 The detailed analysis of Trakl's *Der Abgeschiedene* in Heidegger's interpretation can be found in Karsten Harries, "Language and Silence: Heidegger's Dialogue with Georg Trakl," *boundary 2*, No. 2 (1991).
21 We can find an analogous, yet this time fully conscious, move away from Heidegger in Emmanuel Lévinas, who abhorred the circular, uninterrupted motion of what he called "the amphibology of Being and beings." His notion of hypostasis, which he fashions according to the Jewish logic of separation, sets itself against the amphibolic motion of Being (*il y a*) as its "error" and interruption. Hypostasis is thus erroneous – it blocks the logic of the Heideggerian flow – but it is a "felicitous error" which only subsequently establishes a new principle of "separate, singular beings". See most of all his *De l'éxistence a l'éxistant* (Paris: J. Vrin, 1998).

## Bibliography

1. Cathy Caruth, "The Falling Body and the Impact of Reference," in *Unclaimed Experience. Trauma, Narrative, and History* (Baltimore & London: The Johns Hopkins University Press, 1996).
2. Walter Benjamin, "On Language as Such and on the Language of Man," trans. Edmund Jephcott, in: *Reflections. Essays, Aphorisms, Autobiographical Writings* (New York: Schocken Books, 1978).
3. Walter Benjamin, "Goethe's *Elective Affinities*," in: *Selected Writings*, ed. Michael W. Jennings and Marcus Bullock, Howard Eiland, Gary Smith, vol. I (Cambridge, MA: Belknap Press of Harvard University Press, 1996).
4. Paul de Man, "Walter Benjamin's 'The Task of the Translator,'" in: *The Resistance to Theory* (Minneapolis: University of Minnesotta Press, 1986).
5. Rodolphe Gasché, *The Wild Card of Reading. On Paul de Man* (Cambridge, Mass.& London: Harvard University Press, 1998).
6. Johann Georg Hamann, *Sokratische Denkwürdigkeiten/Aesthetica in nuce*, ed. Sven-Aage Jorgenson (Stuttgart: Philip Reclam Verlag, 1968).
7. Karsten Harries, "Language and Silence: Heidegger's Dialogue with Georg Trakl," *boundary 2*, No. 2 (1991).
8. Martin Heidegger, *Unterwegs zur Sprache* (Stuttgart: Verlag Günther Neske, 1959).
9. Emmanuel Lévinas, *De l'éxistence a l'éxistant* (Paris: J. Vrin, 1998).
10. Gershom Scholem, *Über einige Grundbegriffe des Judentums* (Frankfurt am Main: Suhrkamp, 1996).
11. Gershom Scholem, *Zur Kabbala und ihrer Symbolik* (Frankfurt am Main: Suhrkamp, 2001).
12. Georg Simmel, "Zu einer Theorie des Pessmismus," in: *Gesamtausgabe*, vol. 5 (Frankfurt am Main: Suhrkamp Verlag, 1992).

# Biographical Approach

Katarzyna Kuczyńska-Koschany

# Benjamin, a Jew

**Abstract:** The essay is a preliminary study of the Jewish condition of Walter Benjamin, the eminent German-language essayist, historian of culture, and philosopher. The study of Jewish condition encourages a general biographical discussion, and an inquiry into Benjamin's suicide in Port-Bou in Spain, when he was unsuccessfully attempting to escape from war-torn Europe in 1940. The lethal quality of Jewishness during the war led by Nazi Germany is a peculiar complement to Benjamin's great, unfinished work. His marginalia will be of primary importance for the discussion.

**Keywords:** Walter Benjamin; the Jewish condition; Hebrew language; *The Arcades Project*; biography

> In a situation presenting no way out, I have no other choice by to make an end of it. It is in a small village in the Pyrenees, where no one knows me, that my life will come to a close [*va s'achever*].
> Walter Benjamin, in a letter dated September the 25th, 1940, the day before he committed suicide[1]

(In Port-Bou, in a place where he took his life, Benjamin is already commonly known and people are proud that he has been buried there; "at the initiative of the Socialist Party – as Gershom Scholem reports – a plaque commemorating him was placed at the cemetery"[2]).

I have drawn the idea for the title from a sketch *Jesus der Jude* by Lou Salomé, published 1896 in *Neue Deutsche Rundschau* (1896, VII, p. 342), a precursor sketch for presenting Christ as an orthodox Jew. Walter Benjamin, a future freelance intellectual was four years old at that time. Thus it was intended to be only an idea for a title and rather only for it. Reading the correspondence which followed arise of *The Arcades Project* caused things to go another way. Both Jesus and Benjamin constitute tragic characters in Jewish history (this refers especially to Benjamin's formula of fate as being "participation in guilt of everything that is alive"[3]).

---

1 Quoted after Lisa Fittko, "The Story of Old Benjamin," (*The Arcades*, p. 946).
2 Walter Benjamin, *Pasaże*, ed. Rolf Tiedemann, polish trans. Ireneusz Kania, postface Zygmunt Bauman (Wydawnictwo Literackie: Kraków, 2005), p. 1136.
3 Theodor Wiesengrund Adorno, "Wstęp do *Pism* Benjamina," in: *O literaturze. Wybór esejów*, trans. Anna Wołkowicz, ed. Lech Budrecki (Warszawa: Czytelnik, 2005), p. 234.

I write about Benjamin, not about an arcade visitor or arcade-ologist, because the marginalia of Benjamin's *opus magnum* are equally interesting as the composition itself. I know I am touching only a small part of numerous identity particles of this intellectual who slips away of definitions mentioned and not mentioned by Geneviève Brisac: "Messianic and desperate, Jewish and not-Jewish, a poet rejecting intuition, a Godless theologian, a communist with no party, a flâneur, shock worker, a quotation hoarder without a library, obsessed with language but not with philology."[4]

Obviously, the simple fact that Walter Benjamin was born a Jew could not, by itself, lead to anything extraordinary, especially since he was not an orthodox Jew, a religious believer. However, was born in Europe late in the 19$^{th}$-century (the same year as Bruno Schulz, who was killed in 1942), and he shared the tragic face of European Jews (Simone Weil's suicide by hunger in 1943[5] is a notable example). He also shared the particularly tragic fate of German-speaking Jews (the case of Paul Celan for instance, who committed a deferred suicide in 1970). Last but not least, his plans for emigration to Jerusalem, as well as his efforts to learn Hebrew, competed with the grand undertaking of *The Arcades Project*.

The competition between the *Arcades* and Hebrew is described in letters from 1928–29 which create an impression – in the words by the polish volume's editor – "as if work with *The Arcades Project* were put a spoke in their wheel, a spoke of a simultaneous Benjamin's intention to learn Hebrew and to «make a future career among Jews» (Scholem, *Walter Benjamin – die Geschichte einer Freundschaft*, II, publ. Frankfurt a. M. 1976, p. 175)"[6]. In the letter from 30$^{th}$ of January 1928, addressed to Gershom Schodem, Benjamin mentions a very favourable moment "to devote myself to the study of Hebrew and to everything we think is connected with it" and adds that the moment is favourable "in terms of my being ready for the undertaking, heart and soul" (*The Correspondence of Walter Benjamin 1910–1940*, p. 322). The issue of learning Hebrew is mentioned in letters to Scholem until March 1929, when Benjamin informs his friend about a conversation with doctor Meyer, a Hebrew teacher. In June, he is still enthusiastic in a letter to Hugo von Hofmannsthal: "For the last two months, I have finally been putting my plan into practice: I am learning Hebrew. […] I was unable to leave Berlin. Yet I have found a really excellent teacher here, an older man with an admirable understanding for my situation yet with the necessary authority to force me to assimilate vocabulary

---

4 Geneviève Brisac, "Le Grain de blé de Benjamin," *Le Monde*, March 6 (1992), p. 25.
5 Relev. compare Ewa Bieńkowska, "Śmierć Simone Weil," in: *Spór o dziedzictwo europejskie. Między świętym a świeckim* (Warszawa: WAB, 1999), pp. 218–227.
6 Benjamin, *Pasaże*, p. 982.

and linguistic forms. On the whole, the only difficulty for me in my current situation is the constant switching between language learning and literary activity. I could imagine a series of the most beautiful days spent doing nothing but grammar. All the more so since at the moment I am unable to return to the Arcades project" (*The Correspondence of Walter Benjamin 1910–1940*, pp. 352–353). But already in the middle of September, again in a letter to Scholem, he complains that without the teacher (who was gone for holidays) he is "unable to force [himself] to work on Hebrew" (*The Correspondence of Walter Benjamin 1910–1940*, p. 356). Finally, at the beginning of 1930 the plan to learn Hebrew ultimately loses with his life's work, with the *Passagen-Werk* (see *The Correspondence of Walter Benjamin 1910–1940*, p. 359).

Why did Benjamin want to learn Hebrew? It is not necessary to know Hebrew in order to write about Kafka or to read *Le Juif errant* by Eugène Sue,[7] and Agnon's or Rosenzweig's readings were not really in the centre of Benjamin's research interests. I think that this undertaking, initiated, pursued, and finally abandoned, is related to Benjamin's two important qualities. Firstly, he reached culture through language. Hence, an excellent knowledge of French was for his a prerequisite for studies on Baudelaire. Secondly, his writing was a pendulum mechanism: he would abandon a theme and returning to it after a long intermission. Walter Benjamin never wrote one text at a time; 'notes and materials' piled up around his multiple and simultaneous readings, a working habit which is easily observed in *The Arcades Project*. Simultaneous readings and drifting reflection continuously triggered shifts from one theme to another. Some themes grew into separate studies, for example the fragments on 19th-century Paris or Baudelaire); perhaps the knowledge of Hebrew was supposed to strengthen the description of what Benjamin called "the Jewish contexts of history" (*The Arcades*, p. 462)[8], knowledge of this biblical language would enable him to take up studies in Cabbala and Messianism.

There is, however, another explanation. It was suggested by Theodor Wiesengrund Adorno in the introduction to Benjamin's *Schriften*, where he remarks:

> What Benjamin said and wrote sounded as if it came from depth of mystery. But its power came from obviousness. There was nothing esoteric or exclusive about what he thought and said; Benjamin never practiced 'privileged thinking'. Granted, he can be easily imagined

---

7   Compare *The Arcades*, p. 771: "Véron pays 100,000 francs for *Le Juif errant* before a line has been penned."
8   "In studying Simmel's presentation of Goethe's concept of truth, I came to see very clearly that my concept of origin in the *Trauerspiel* book is a rigorous and decisive transposition of this basic Goethean concept from the domain of nature to that of history. Origin – it is, in effect, the concept of *Ur*-phenomenon extracted from the pagan context of nature and brought into the Jewish contexts of history" (*The Arcades*, p. 462).

in a tall, pointed hat, and he would sometimes present a thought to friends as if it was a precious and delicate object, but all his thoughts, even the most alien and extravagant ones, had a sort of annotation, to the effect that an awakened consciousness could grasp this knowledge, provided that the consciousness is awakened for good[9].

Gershom Scholem, whose intention was to persuade Benjamin to 'convert' to Zionism and who wanted very much to believe in Benjamin's promise of coming to Jerusalem, learning Hebrew etc., cites a touching story telling that "in August 1927 he dragged me to the Musée Cluny in Paris, where, in a collection of Jewish ritual objects, has showed me with true rapture two grains of wheat on which a kindred soul had inscribed the complete *Shema Israel*."[10] A question poses itself, what was more important for Benjamin: was it the Jewish *credo*, the first prayer taught by fathers to their children and the last one said on deathbed, or was it the delight at the ability of containing such an important text in such a tiny space? Was it not Scholem himself, who admitted that "it was his never-realized ambition to get a hundred lines onto an ordinary sheet of notepaper"[11]?

Perhaps Benjamin wanted to learn Hebrew to interpret better, in order to create a more apt model of interpretation[12], and thus he kept returning to the starting point, to the Bible and to Hebrew. If there had been no other reason, he could do it in order to start an unavoidable dispute with the initial theological model.

Although Benjamin was "a heir of Jewish theological tradition,"[13] he was neither a Judaist, even though he was seriously occupied with studies on Judaism during the First World War and immediately afterwards, nor a Zionist, nor "an author from a Jewish camp" and he had an ability to refer critically to what he concerned to be a "Jewish fixation"[14] or "nationalistically Jewish"[15] sentiment. In his research notes

---

9   Adorno, "Wstęp do *Pism* Benjamina," p. 230.
10  Gershom Scholem, "Walter Benjamin," in: *On Jews and Judaism in Crisis*, ed. Werner J. Dannhauser (New York Schocken Books, 1976), p. 177.
11  Scholem, "Walter Benjamin," p. 177.
12  See Adorno, "Wstęp do *Pism* Benjamina," p. 237.
13  Adorno, "Wstęp do *Pism* Benjamina," p. 235.
14  "The problem is thus: to manage to relocate to America on time. For the time being, I have turned to Schocken. The what I could stake is a book about Kafka. However, taking into consideration his Jewish fixation as well as authors from Jewish camp whose huge offer puts pressure on him, the prospects for coaxing any sum from Schocken are poor" (Benjamin, *Pasaże*, p. 1107, from a letter to Gretel Adorno, the 20th of March, 1939).
15  "[…] in Jerusalem I have made Scholem a request to plead for me so that Schocken would become interested in the book about Kafka that I am intending to write. Unfortunately, Schocken is a gloomy autocrat. His financial might has grown immensely on Jews' destitution and his sympathies are directed towards nationalistically Jewish

he maintained complete impartiality, rarely commenting, and usually presenting somebody else's views. One might even risk a statement that Benjamin was more irritated with Jewish fixations than with anti-Jewish ones. A handful of examples:

> Fourier was a chauvinist: he hated Englishmen and Jews. He saw Jews not as civilized people but as barbarians who maintained patriarchal customs. (*The Arcades*, p. 647)

> Too many Jewish names appear on the membership rolls of the Saint-Simonian church for us to be surprised at the fact that the system of financial feudalism was established by the disciples of Saint-Simon. A Toussenel, *Les Juifs, rois de l'époque*, (Paris <1886>), ed. Gonet, p. 130–133. (*The Arcades*, p. 784)

> Maxims from James de Laurence, *Les Enfants des dieu, ou La Religion de Jesus réconciliée avec la philosophie*, Paris, June 1831): [...] The religion of the Jews was that of *paternity*, under which the patriarchs exercised their domestic authority. The religion of Jesus is that of *maternity*, whose symbol is a mother holding a child in her arms [...] (pp. 13–14). (*The Arcades*, p. 812)

Historical facts related to Jews he simply left without comment:

> "In 1852 the brothers Pereire, two Portugese Jews, founded the first great modern bank, Crédit Mobilier, of which one said that it was the biggest gambling hell in Europe. It undertook wild speculations in everything – railroads, hotels, colonies, canals, mines, theaters – and, after fifteen years, it declared total bankruptcy." Egon Friedell, *Kulturgeschichte der Neuzeit*, München vol. 3 (Munich, 1931), p. 187. (*The Arcades*, p. 585)

Testimonies of someone's views were similarly undiscussed:

> Militant representation of progress: "It was not error that is opposed to the progress of truth; it is indolence, obstinacy, the spirit of routine, everything that contributes to inaction. – The progress of even the most peaceful of arts among the ancient peoples of Greece and their republics was punctuated by continual wars. It was like the Jews' building the walls of Jerusalem with one hand while defending them with the other. Their spirits were always in ferment, their hearts always high with adventure; and each day was a further enlightenment." Turgot, *Oeuvres*, vol. 2 (Paris, 1844), p. 672 ("Pensées et fragments"). (*The Arcades*, p. 477)

---

creativity (Benjamin, *Pasaże*, p. 1105, letter to Horkheimer); compare words of Alexandre Koyré cited in a letter to Horkheimer dated the 18th of April 1939 and Benjamin's comment "«In vain do I use Koyré surname, everybody knows that my family name is Koire and that I am a Jew, naturalised to a French». Briefly speaking, no Jew in France is today allowed to engage in arranging anything for his or her «fellow believer» in an organisation another than Jewish" (Benjamin, *Pasaże*, p. 1110).

Occasionally, Benjamin would record an anecdote:

> "At the Stock Exchange, one Saint-Simonian is worth two Jews." "Paris-Boursier," *Les Petits-Paris: Par les auteurs des mémoires de Bilboquet* [Taxile Delord] (Paris, 1854), s. 54. (*The Arcades*, p. 591)

Only when some text was – to use a contemporary expression – an example of hatred speech, and when it touched on everyday life in Benjamin's times, he used to intervene ironically and defensively:

> *Gauloiserie* in Baudelaire: "To organize a grand conspiracy for the extermination of the Jewish race. / The Jews who are *librarians* and bear witness to the *Redemption*." Ch. B., *Oeuvres*, vol. 2, p. 222 ("Mon Coeur mis á nu"). Céline has continued along these lines. (Cheerful assassins!) (*The Arcades*, p. 300)

Thus, Gershom Scholem aptly pointed out that Jewishness in Benjamin's work is perceptible "only in overtones,"[16] but Scholem's conviction that Jewish identity constituted a foundation of Benjamin's thinking is hardly acceptable. However, it is Benjamin's correspondence with Scholem, as well as Scholem's book about Benjamin[17], that constitute the key to understanding of Benjamin's disputes with himself-as-a-Jew.

Adam Lipszyc describes Scholem as an independent (perhaps) thinker and a "witness of German Jews' history in the 20th century" as well as "a commentator of achievements of the most important thinkers of Jewish-German world at the outset of the 20th century,"[18] that is of Freud, Kafka, and Benjamin. Scholem wrote about them thus:

> Almost throughout their productive lives they shunned German phraseology, even the phrase "we Germans," and they wrote in full awareness of the distance separating them from their German readers. They are the most distinguished among the co-called German-Jewish authors, and it is as much their lives that bear witness the distance [...] as their writings in which things Jewish figure rarely if at all. They did not fool themselves. They knew that they were German writers – but not Germans. [...] Closely as they knew themselves tied to the German language and its intellectual world, they never succumbed to the illusion of being at home [...]. I do not know whether these men would have been

---

16 Scholem, "Walter Benjamin," p. 191.
17 See Gershom Scholem, *Walter Benjamin: The Story of a Friendship*, trans. Harry Zohn, introduction Lee Siegel (New York: NYRB, 2003).
18 Adam Lipszyc, *Introduction* to Gershom Scholem, *Żydzi i Niemcy: Eseje, listy, rozmowy*, ed. Adam Lipszyc, trans. Marzena Zawanowska and Adam Lipszyc (Sejny: Pogranicze, 2006), p. 5.

at home in the land of Israel. I doubt it very much. They truly came from foreign parts and knew it.[19]

The encounter between Scholem and Benjamin, and their friendship in letters, are events of the most unusual kind, since two great minds talk vividly here, one of which rebels against assimilative, middle class culture[20], and subsequently goes back to Jerusalem, Jewish mysticism and Kabbalah, while the other finds himself neither in Jerusalem nor in the Diaspora, but rather chooses to live between Berlin and Paris. Scholem's essays, as Adam Lipszyc remarks, recurrently express a conviction that Benjamin, did not stop using elements of Jewish tradition in his thought and writings, although he initially "playing with various motifs drawn from Jewish tradition"[21] and was inclined towards Communism and materialistic perspective in the thirties. According to the author of *On the Kabbalah and its Symbolism* "Benjamin has been someone of the kind of a Kabbalist who got astrayed to secular districts"[22]. And yet, Benjamin is also called a "Marxist rabbi"[23]. Scholem and Benjamin were joined by "apocalyptic messianic tradition,"[24] a Gnostic perception of the world as fallen creation; their paths parted when Benjamin started investing his hope in Marxism and (as Lipszyc says) joining the "belief in apocalypse with the belief in revolution."[25]

Scholem remarks that "two categories above all, and especially in their Jewish versions, assume a central place in his [Benjamin's] writings: on the one hand Revelation, the idea of the Torah and of sacred texts in general, and on the other hand the messianic idea Redemption"[26]. He also shows details. In 1916 and later in 1927 Benjamin devotes "pages of rare concentration and beauty" to the essence of "language in the first three chapters of Genesis"[27]; somewhere else he mentions about Jewish aspect of the person of Karl Kraus and "he will base his analysis of the world of Franz Kafka on the categories of the *halakhah* and *haggadah*"[28]. Brilliantly

---

19 Scholem, "Walter Benjamin," pp. 190–191.
20 See Lipszyc, *Introduction*, p. 7. Scholem called himself a "Post-assimilative Jew" (Scholem, *Żydzi i Niemcy*, p. 19).
21 Lipszyc, *Introduction*, p. 11.
22 Lipszyc, *Introduction*, p. 11.
23 Gershom Scholem, "Walter Benjamin and His Angel," in: *On Jews and Judaism in Crisis*, ed. Werner J. Dannhauser (New York: Schocken Books, 1976), p. 199.
24 Lipszyc, *Introduction*, p. 12.
25 Lipszyc, *Introduction*, p. 12.
26 Scholem, "Walter Benjamin," p. 193.
27 Scholem, "Walter Benjamin," p. 194.
28 Scholem, "Walter Benjamin," p. 194.

he describes Kafka's negative theology, intensive Judaism of a lost revelation; he talks about Kafka's characters that "his acolytes are beadles, but they have lost the house of prayer; his scholars are disciples, but they have lost the scripture."[29]

Benjamin's understanding of Kafka requires a little more attention, since, according to author of "One-Way Street," Kafkas's work "is an ellipse with foci that lie far apart and are determined on the one hand by mystical experience (which is above all the experience of tradition) and on the other by the experience of the modern city dweller" (letter to Scholem dated the 12th of June 1938 – *The Correspondence of Walter Benjamin 1910–1940*, p. 363). Benjamin's interest in arcades merges here with the desire to draw closer to Jewish tradition through learning Hebrew. When Benjamin states: "What is actually and in a very precise sense *folly* in Kafka is that this, the most recent of experimental worlds, was conveyed to him precisely by the mystical tradition" (*The Correspondence of Walter Benjamin 1910–1940*, p. 364; emphasis by Walter Benjamin). Thus, his seemingly distant interests meet. Moreover, in fragments such as the ones quoted below, written a year before the war that led to the Holocaust and Benjamin's tragic death, the philosopher wakes up from the 20th century (let me remind that in its essence, *The Arcades Project* had been intended to be an awakening from the 19th century):

> […] Kafka's world, frequently so serene and so dense with angels, is the exact complement of his epoch, an epoch that is preparing itself to annihilate the inhabitants of this planet on a massive scale. The experience that corresponds to that of Kafka as a private individual will probably first become accessible to the masses at such time as they are about to be annihilated. (*The Correspondence of Walter Benjamin 1910–1940*, p. 564)

> Kafka's real genius was that he tried something entirely new: he sacrificed truth for the sake of clinging to transmissibility, to its haggadic element. Kafka's writings are by their nature parables. But it is their misery and their beauty, that they had to become *more* than parables. They do not modestly lie at the feet of doctrine, as Haggadah lies at the feet of Halakah. When they have crouched down, they unexpectedly rise a mighty paw against it. (*The Correspondence of Walter Benjamin 1910–1940*, p. 565)

Among the Jewish categories applied by Benjamin – which might be, contrary to the ones mentioned above, questioned – Scholem names the idea of recalling ("We know that the Jews were prohibited from inquiring into the future: the Torah and the prayers instructed them in remembrance" – "On the Concept of History," in: *Selected Writings*, vol. IV, p. 397).

And the there is more; there are angels.

---

29 Scholem, "Walter Benjamin," p. 196.

Prophetic *Angesilaus Santander* was written in the year when Hitler came to power; it is an anagram of the angel-satan, although, as Scholem claims

> Everlasting angels like, say, the archangels or Satan, seen as the fallen angel of the Jewish and Christian tradition, were evidently less important for Benjamin than the talmudic theme of the formation and disappearance of angels before God [...]. To this, however, was added for Benjamin the further conception of Jewish tradition of the personal angel of each human being who represents the latter's secret self and whose name nevertheless remains hidden from him. In angelic shape, but in part also in the form of his secret name, the heavenly self of a human being man (like everything else created) is woven into a curtain hanging before the throne of God. This angel, to be sure, can also enter into opposition to, and a relation of strong tension with, the earthly creature to whom he is attached.[30]

The angel of history is not capable of fulfilling the messianic task, he is not able to "awaken the dead, and make whole what has been smashed" ("On the Concept of History," in: *Selected Writings*, vol. IV, p. 392). The painting by Paul Klee, its Benjaminian interpretation, and *Angelus Santander* are all filled with a special melancholy: *tikun* does not come true and the past "keeps piling wreckage upon wreckage [...] the sky" ("On the Concept of History," in: *Selected Writings*, vol. IV, p. 392). The Angels of Annihilation are coming.

Benjamin the Wandering Jew – "he found home in his own homelessness," despite he "throughout his life he tried strived to escape from wandering," wrote Zygmunt Bauman in his afterword to the Polish edition of *The Arcades Project*.[31] The outstanding European thinker takes morphine (a conduct worthy of Socrates), because deportation from Spain to France would mean death to him, and the deportation would mean death because he is a Jew. This is not a regular irony of fate.

As late as in 1936, already after Hitler came to power, Benjamin (pseudonymously) collected and published an anthology of letters (*Deutsche Menschen*) written between 1783 and 1883. Referring to the Biblical topics, he called this book "an ark [which] I built when the fascist deluge began to rise"[32]. Four years later, however, he too drowned in the flood. Perhaps Kafka's words were of greatest importance for him, then: "there is an infinite amount of hope, but not for us. This statement – Benjamin wrote to Scholem – really contains Kafka's hope; it is a source of his radiant serenity" (*The Correspondence of Walter Benjamin 1910–1940*, p. 565).

---

30 Scholem, "Walter Benjamin and His Angel," p. 213.
31 Zygmunt Bauman, "Posłowie," in: Benjamin, *Pasaże*, p. 1152.
32 Scholem, "Walter Benjamin," p. 183.

Benjamin himself wrote about fate as well, for example in *The Arcades Project*: "The intentional correlate of 'immediate experience' has not always remained the same. In the nineteenth century, it was 'adventure'. In our day, it appears as 'fate', *Schicksal*. In fate is concealed the concept of the 'total experience' that is fatal from the outset. War is its unsurpassed prefiguration. ('I am born German; it is for this I die' – the trauma of birth already contains the shock that is mortal. This coincidence <*Koinzidenz*> defines 'fate'.)" (*The Arcades*, p. 801).

It is an incomprehensible irony of fate, then, that must be irony of fate, unrevealed to each of us that in theses "On the Concept of History" Benjamin writes: "The Messiah comes not only as the redeemer; he comes as the victor one over the Antichrist" ("On the Concept of History," in *Selected Writings*, vol. IV, p. 391) and in history, which took Benjamin's life, another false Messiah would kill a whole "race" of Jewish "antichrists." It is sufficient to listen to Hitler's speeches and read Benjamin's essays. Scholem remarked on the perfection of Benjamin's German, which apparently takes the reader's breath away[33]; the man who sentenced Benjamin to death would probably not understand any of it.

Benjamin's rites of passage constitute a context necessary for understanding of his *Passagenwerk*, especially if "awakening from the nineteenth century" (*The Arcades*, p. 464) is its main topic. 'Rites de passage – this is the designation in folklore for the ceremonies that attach to death and birth, to marriage, puberty, and so forth" – Benjamin writes (*The Arcades*, p. 494), and adds: "The threshold must be carefully distinguished from the boundary. A *Schwelle* <threshold> is a zone. Transformation, passage, wave action are in the word *schwellen*, swell, and etymology ought not overlook these senses. (*The Arcades*, p. 494). Crossing the Pyrenees in September 1940 had exactly the sense of crossing a threshold, not only a border, similarly to crossing of the Alps by Julius Caesar, for Hölderlin[34], and for Rimbaud. When finally the manuscript with theses "On the Concept of History"

---

33  See Scholem, "Walter Benjamin," pp. 182–183.
34  See Adorno, "Wstęp do *Pism* Benjamina," p. 241; writing about Benjamin, he uses a periphrasis from the beginning of the *Pathmos* anthem: "What saves indeed appears in Benjamin's mind only in the presence of danger" ("Wo aber Gefahr ist, wächst, / Das rettende auch"). This parallel is a good topic for a separate essay. Both Adorno, writing about Benjamin (1955) and Heidegger, writing about Hölderlin (Martin Heidegger, *Elucidations of Hölderlin's Poetry*, trans. with an introduction by Keith Hoeller [New York: Humanity Books, 2000]), determine highest quality art of a philosopher and a poet as a restitution of sacred. Heidegger (p. 224): "What does Hölderlin's poetry say? Its word is: the holy"; Adorno (p. 246): "Each meeting with him restored what had been irretrievably lost: a holiday. In his presence one felt like a child on Christmas Eve […]."

had found itself on Spanish side it had escaped destruction and history showed the worst of its many faces.[35] What Zimmer's tower meant to Hölderlin, and what the return from Africa to Marseilles meant to Rimbaud, had its equivalent in the message to Benjamin that he must return to France. It was always death, but this time it was not even a reprieved death.

Translated by Jakub Drajerczak

## Bibliography

1. Theodor Wiesengrund Adorno, "Wstęp do *Pism* Benjamina," in: *O literaturze. Wybór esejów*, trans. Anna Wołkowicz, ed. Lech Budrecki (Warszawa: Czytelnik, 2005).
2. Zygmunt Bauman, "Posłowie," in: Walter Benjamin, *Pasaże*, ed. Rolf Tiedemann, polish trans. Ireneusz Kania, postface Zygmunt Bauman (Wydawnictwo Literackie: Kraków, 2005).
3. Walter Benjamin, "On the Concept of History," in: *Selected Writings*, ed. Michael W. Jennings and Marcus Bullock, Howard Eiland, Gary Smith, vol. IV (Cambridge, MA: Belknap Press of Harvard University Press, 2003).
4. Walter Benjamin, *Pasaże*, ed. Rolf Tiedemann, polish trans. Ireneusz Kania, postface Zygmunt Bauman (Wydawnictwo Literackie: Kraków, 2005).
5. Walter Benjamin, *The Arcades Project*, trans. Howard Eiland and Kevin McLaughlin, prepared on the basis of the German volume edited by Rolf Tiedman (Cambridge Mass.: The Belknap Press of Harvard University Press, 1999).
6. Ewa Bieńkowska, "Śmierć Simone Weil," in: *Spór o dziedzictwo europejskie. Między świętym a świeckim* (Warszawa: WAB, 1999).
7. Geneviève Brisac, "Le Grain de blé de Benjamin," *Le Monde*, March 6 (1992).
8. Adam Lipszyc, "Introduction," in: Gershom Scholem, *Żydzi i Niemcy: Eseje, listy, rozmowy*, ed. Adam Lipszyc, trans. Marzena Zawanowska and Adam Lipszyc (Sejny: Pogranicze, 2006).
9. Lisa Fittko, "The Story of Old Benjamin," in Walter Benjamin, *The Arcades Project*, trans. Howard Eiland and Kevin McLaughlin, prepared on the basis of

---

35 It is worth here to recall Adorno's words ("Wstęp do *Pism* Benjamina," p. 245): "It was mourning, not sadness that defined his nature, both as Jewish knowledge of the permanence of danger and catastrophe as well as a temperament of an antiquarian to whom even modern issues were accursed within a long bygone."

the German volume edited by Rolf Tiedman (Cambridge Mass.: The Belknap Press of Harvard University Press, 1999).
10. Martin Heidegger, *Elucidations of Hölderlin's Poetry*, trans. with an introduction by Keith Hoeller (New York: Humanity Books, 2000).
11. Gershom Scholem, "Walter Benjamin," in: *On Jews and Judaism in Crisis*, ed. Werner J. Dannhauser (New York Schocken Books, 1976).
12. Gershom Scholem, "Walter Benjamin and His Angel," in: *On Jews and Judaism in Crisis*, ed. Werner J. Dannhauser (New York: Schocken Books, 1976).
13. Gershom Scholem, *Walter Benjamin: The Story of a Friendship*, trans. Harry Zohn, introduction Lee Siegel (New York: NYRB, 2003).
14. *The Correspondence of Walter Benjamin 1910–1940*, ed. Gershom Scholem and Theodor W. Adorno, trans. Manfred R. Jacobson and Evelyn M. Jacobson (Chicago and London: The University of Chicago Press, 1994).

Roman Kubicki

# A Discourse of the Master Benjamin with Death and Life*

**Abstract:** In this essay, I describe the last moments of Walter Benjamin's life. I try to reconstruct the philosophical contexts of the choices he made at that time. The thesis I defend is: when Walter Benjamin decided to commit suicide, he argued for the necessity of death and, paradoxically, for a fully autonomous life.

**Keywords:** theory of biography; suicide; Witkacy; World War II

## I

If we are to believe Hannah Arendt, Benjamin's life was marked with a stigma of a pile of potsherd (*Scherbenhaufen*). Only there, objects with which he surrounded himself (relatively, which surrounded him) could find its appropriate and ultimate shape. He was fascinated with Proust who did not know how to light the fire or open a window.[1] The profound inability to move around "the things" made Proust live "beside" the world: according to the unanimous opinion of hagiographers, it was also a condition of all his writings.

It was the same clumsiness and awkwardness that governed Benjamin's life. Hannah Arendt writes that like a sleepwalker he was led to a place where the centre of his bad fate was placed, although – from any rational point of view – it was not there that it should have been placed. She adds that at the turn of 1939/1940, Benjamin decided to leave Paris due to the danger of its being bombarded. He went to Meaux. As it is known, not even one bomb fell on Paris; whereas Meaux – a place where soldiers were gathering – was one of the many seriously menaced towns in France.[2]

Benjamin was fascinated with things, although (or perhaps for this very reason) that their 'logic' was not fully conceivable to him. We will never know what was

---

\* The essay written on the basis of the article by Roman Kubicki; "Waltera Benjamina rozbieranie świata. Fascynacja i lęk," in: *Drobne rysy w ciągłej katastrofie. Obecność Waltera Benjamina w kulturze współczesnej*, ed. Anna Zeidler-Janiszewska (Warszawa: Instytut Kultury, 1993).
1 Hannah Arendt, *Water Benjamin, Bertold Brecht, Zwei Essayes* (München: R. Piper, 1971), p. 8.
2 Arendt, *Water Benjamin, Bertold Brecht*, pp. 8–9.

at the beginning: awkwardness in the face of constant challenges of details whose traces biographers could find in the darkness of his childhood or the challenges cast by importunities of fate, unfortunately, free from a flaw of any utility.[3]

## II

Amateurs of Benjamin's pure thought, disentangled from life, study it first at their own homes. Only steps of those who are fascinated with the philosopher's fate will be directed perhaps towards the cemetery in Portbou. They will stop on the place where, tens of years ago, the loftiness of thoughts once again met the pathos of the finished life, where it found its momentary motherland years before. On reading the inscription from 1970: "WALTER BENJAMIN/FOLOSOF ALEMANY/ BERLIN 1892 PORTBOU 1940", they will ask this not very sophisticated question: Who was the one who is not present here now and has never been present here?

Some people are convinced that the notion: "a German philosopher," in: the most appropriate way, sets Walter Benjamin's spiritual past and future in European culture. An eternal wanderer unexpectedly settled down in the household of "the great ancestors": Kant, Fichte, Hegel, Marks, Dilthey, Nietzsche and many, many other "German philosophers". A little known poet, in his poem dedicated to Benjamin, still mentions other philosophers – Erazm of Rotterdam and Teofrast, but the main advantage of these names – according to the principle *licencia poetica*, this time entering the sphere of interpretation and classification – seems to be, the guaranteed by them, appropriate number of syllables and the ability to find a rhyme: …Gast-…Theophrast.[4]

## III

In 1992, The Jewish Museum and The Film Society of Lincoln Center organized a festival in New York under the banner of: "Artists, Activists and Ordinary People: Jews in the 20th century Europe." Within the scope of the festival, they also presented a film *La ultima frontera* (The Ultimate Frontier) by a Spanish

---

3 See Walter Benjamin, "Paris, the Capital of the Nineteenth Century," in: *The Arcades*, p. 9.
4 This refers to a passage from a poem *Walter Benjamin* published in 1944 in *Exil*, a collection edited by Paul Mayer in Mexico: "Now you are wandering throung a different kingdom. \ You are guest of sould and minds in affinity. \ You are practicing the art of speech and accord \ With Erasmus and Theophrast". The text has been reprinted in: Momme Brodersen, *Spinne in eigenen Netz. Walter Benjamin. Leben und Werk* (Bühl-Moos: Elster Verlag, 1990), p. 269.

film director Manuel Casso-Ferrera. In the festival catalogue, we can read e.g.: "Walter, Benjamin, a German philosopher and critic of Jewish origin, who united late German Romanticism, Marxism and Kabala, was an intellectual secret agent fascinated with everything – from Baudelaire to the revolutionary possibilities of a popular and mass film."

52 years before, also in New York, a newspaper *Aufbau* published a short article. A Lisbon correspondent of the American Overseas News Agency reported that reliable sources informed about the suicidal death of a famous psychologist, Walter Benjamin. The journalist stated that according to the professor's four female friends, who claimed to have been the witnesses of the death, he had poisoned himself in the Spanish-French border town Portbou when the Spanish authorities had not permitted him to continue his journey to Lisbon and The United States. The correspondent added that although the professor had been a Jew, he had been buried on a Catholic cemetery in Portbou since officials found a letter about him from one of the prominent priests of the French Catholic Church, dedicated to prelates of the Spanish Catholic Church in which they had asked to help the professor continue the journey.[5]

## IV

It was not – if one may say so – "the best" time to commit a suicide. Europe did not miss death at that time. It suffices to mention that five months before, on the basis of Himmler's order of April 27, 1940, Rudolf Höss had begun to establish the Nazi concentration camp – Oświęcim-Brzezinka. When Walter Benjamin committed, the noted in the magazine, suicide, he joined the hundreds of thousands of war victims, who, according to the arithmetic governing the compassion of the world, most often became abstraction devoid of journalistic attractiveness and loftiness.

## V

Nevertheless, on Septemper 26, 1940, the 48-year-old Walter Benjamin committed a suicide.

At first, he tried to save himself. He was not condemned only to himself in these attempts. Friends – philosophers and intellectuals – remembered about him. They did everything – in Europe and The United States – to take Benjamin out of the European trap as quickly as possible. Only tiny formalities did not allow him to

---

5   "Scientist Suicide in Spain," *Aufbau*, 11 October (1940), p. 3.

leave France and go via Spain to Portugal from where it was possible to legally go to The United States.

## VI

Certainly, Benjamin did not know that a 54-year-old Polish artist, Witkacy, committed a suicide a year before on the path of war escape in a village Jeziory near Dąbrowica in Polesie region. Benjamin took his own life when, being convinced that "the worst had been over," he got to know suddenly that he had to come back to France, from where all roads, in case of a Jew, led to Auschwitz. Witkacy was looking for a shelter from Fascist executioners on the way to the east – on September 17, the road appeared unexpectedly to be a dead end blocked by a regiment of Soviet hangmen. It is not meant to look for relations and similarities between the tragic end of both of these lives. One remark comes to mind irrefutably: both of them could not afford a distance towards fascism and communism, the major danger for civilization and history, which they associated too rapidly "with the end of the world."

## VII

Unfortunately, resourcefulness of Walter Benjamin and his friends no longer kept up with the pace of events on the French scene. On September 24, a historical handshake between Hitler and Petaine took place in Montaire. According to the concluded agreement, German emigrants from the French part, not occupied by Fascists, were also forced to emigrate. Benjamin still did not have all the necessary papers. He decided to cross the border illegally together with some other people. The choice of place was excellent – two weeks before, Heinrich and Nelly Mann, Alma Machler, Franz Werfel and Golo Mann had crossed the border exactly in this area and it was where Hannah Ardent's *life-path* lead several months later. The director of the film *La Ultima Frontera* escaped from Franco's Spain also through Portbou but in the opposite direction. The escape took place without any serious complications. It was only Benjamin who caused the biggest trouble – he had to rest exactly every ten minutes due to his cardiac condition.[6] Nevertheless, the fugitives entered the Spanish Porbou in the afternoon with arranged plans to catch a train to Lisbon. Then they heard from a local gendarme that their transit visas to Spain were no longer valid since the Spanish authorities had introduced

---

6  Lisa Fittko writes on it in his work: *Mein Weg über die Pyrenäen. Erinnerungen, 1940/41* (München–Vienna: Carl Hanser, 1985), p. 137.

new regulations the night before and for that reason they would be extradited to France immediately.

## VIII

Walter Benjamin was exhausted. This exhaustion was begotten of fear. Walter Benjamin's fear of the return to France was justifiable. Even if the French did not deport him to Germany immediately, the officials of the Vichy government would certainly do so two years later. Yet in autumn, 1940 "The Register of the Jews of Paris and the Capital Region" was prepared on the Vichy government's initiative – Gestapo regarded it as an example to follow in other occupied countries. The officials from the General Commission for Jewish Affairs, ministers and the Vichy government officials took an active part in the organisation of the French part of *Solution Finale* (the so called Final Solution – in German called *Endlösung*).

## IX

The exhausted Walter Benjamin was unable to come to terms with the thought of return. He swallowed an overdose of morphine which, for some time, he had carried about him "just in case."[7] He was dying in the state of unconsciousness. He took to the grave a mystery of a black leather briefcase – he did not want it to get into the wrong hands. Hannah Arendt wrote that the day before he would have crossed the frontier without any problems, the day later it was known in Marseilles that it was impossible to go through Spain. Thus – she stated – the catastrophe could happen only on that particular day.[8]

A subjective intention which, for the first time in Benjamin's life revealed its pretension to extremes in 1931, forced its way to the world of facts. At that time, it only provoked him to make a will. Later, it was "an insuperable mistrust of the course of things and a readiness at all times to recognize that everything can go wrong" ("The Destructive Character," in: *Selected Writings*, vol. II, part 2, p. 542) and perhaps the hope that this time the suicide would compensate for the effort anyway related with it that won.

---

7   See: Hermann Deml, "Walter Benjamin von der Gestapo ermordet?," *Allgemeine jüdische Wochenzeitung*, 19 October (1984).
8   Arendt, *Water Benjamin, Bertold Brecht*, p. 27.

## X

Naturally, numerous legends and myths have arisen around Benjamin's suicidal death. According to Arnold Zweig, it was a consequence of some official's mistake who had received an order to halt another man with the same surname[9]; whereas a Spanish writer, Juan Goytisolo is convinced that Benjamin was murdered by the Spanish who collaborated with Gestapo[10]. Still Bertold Brecht wrote that Walter Benjamin had poisoned himself in some small Spanish border town and that the gendarmerie had stopped a little group to whom he had belonged. Before his fellow-travellers came to him next day to inform him that it was possible to continue the journey, he had already been dead.[11]

## XI

Walter Benjamin found himself in an extreme situation: he experienced restrictions which "immediately become the conditions of his freedom and the ground of his activity"[12] and thus he felt the state of his human freedom. Cast in the world, he deconstructed it with attention, however, he focused too much on the sources of its and his "tender defeats." Too late did he notice the announcement of a mantis's lascivious satisfaction in the world impudently stripped by the Angel of History and thus this time he called into being a moment which knew what would happen next. From the infinitely numerous hopes of the world, at last he chose the one for his death. Declaring for nothingness, he made the things which were to be an eternal source of activity within the borders of his finite life become the last moment of this life. Indeed, we do not know what to look for if any search is reasonable in this last decision. Shall we look for the boundlessly *hic et nunc* fulfilling absence of "the envy of the future," which – not having regard for the heroism of anyone's last moments – bears it cynically in the episodic act of creation from nothing (from nothing since it is purposeless to search for the participation of life which has resigned from its future voluntarily or under duress); the act of creation of present moments, which are unfamiliar as far as they are experienced only by others? Or on the contrary – should we extract from this decision a truly reliable testimony, a second which is,

---

9  See: Arnold Zweig, *Todesnachrichten* – a non published manuscript stored in the Litarary Achive of the former Academy of Arts, GDR in Berlin.
10  See: Deml, "Walter Benjamin von der Gestapo ermordet?".
11  The quotation of Brecht's statement from August 1941 included in *Arbeitsjournal* comes from: Karol Sauerland, "Waltera Benjamina rewizja materialistycznego pojmowania dziejów," *Studia Filozoficzne*, No. 1–2 (1986), p. 68.
12  Hannah Arendt, "What is Existenz Philosophy?," *Partisan Review*, No. 1 (1946), p. 55.

on the one hand, fairly short to ultimately end this life and, on the other hand, long enough to find oneself in the formed nothingness of history and thus of future?

## XII

One could expect that there is nothing in this death that could stand for any sort of testimony. Roughly speaking – this is just one of many deaths. Considering its time – of vary many indeed. It neither includes any proud gesture of Socrates who died despite the possibility of life that was given to him; nor the falseness of the late death of Hegesias of Cyrene who devoted a considerable part of his long life to convincing the others about the necessity of committing a suicide.

Benjamin's suicidal death did not make his life more reliable. It includes both a moment of escape – Hannah Arendt related that in fact there had been nothing in America that would have attracted Benjamin since, as he had admitted himself, there would have been nothing more to do with him than travel round the states and present him as "the last European"[13] – and of return – Brodersen stated that it had been the last chance for him to realise the thought that had accompanied him through all his life, namely to arrange the end of his physical existence which had become nearly worthless and nonsensical in those times.[14]

## XIII

Benjamin's last thought was free from dilemmas concerned with the complexity of literary style, it was deaf to the voice of ethics supervising the choice of appropriate quotations. Did he have to, however, ultimately deprive himself of the hope of thinking? Even if the quietus of thinking was already approaching, did not its very closeness deserve the perhaps impudent company of thinking given to him till the possibly far end? Walter Benjamin did not choose between sadness and nothingness. He chose rather between nothingness and fear, between the infinite – so infinite, of course, as what is inscribed in the finite life can be infinite – decision-making about himself and consent to the fact that all the settlements that were vital and ultimate in his life would be set without his participation – in the heads of blunt mercenaries, blind to the metaphysics of continuance, memory and history that he was constructing with exertion and rarely met patience with the world of details.

Translated by Barbara Komorowska

---

13 Arendt, *Water Benjamin, Bertold Brecht.*
14 Brodersen, *Spinne in eigenen Netz*, p. 266.

## Bibliography

1. Hannah Arendt, *Water Benjamin, Bertold Brecht, Zwei Essayes* (München: R. Piper, 1971).
2. Hannah Arendt, "What is Existenz Philosophy?," *Partisan Review*, No. 1 (1946).
3. Walter Benjamin, "Paris, the Capital of the Nineteenth Century," in: *The Arcades Project*, trans. Howard Eiland and Kevin McLaughlin, prepared on the basis of the German volume edited by Rolf Tiedman (Cambridge Mass.: The Belknap Press of Harvard University Press, 1999).
4. Walter Benjamin, "The Destructive Character," in: *Selected Writings*, ed. Michael W. Jennings and Marcus Bullock, Howard Eiland, Gary Smith, vol. II, part 2, (Cambridge, MA: Belknap Press of Harvard University Press, 1999).
5. Momme Brodersen, *Spinne in eigenen Netz. Walter Benjamin. Leben und Werk* (Bühl-Moos: Elster Verlag, 1990).
6. Hermann Deml, "Walter Benjamin von der Gestapo ermordet?," *Allgemeine jüdische Wochenzeitung*, 19 October (1984).
7. Lisa Fittko, *Mein Weg über die Pyrenäen. Erinnerungen, 1940/41* (München–Vienna: Carl Hanser, 1985).
8. Karol Sauerland, "Waltera Benjamina rewizja materialistycznego pojmowania dziejów," *Studia Filozoficzne*, No. 1–2 (1986).
9. "Scientist Suicide in Spain," *Aufbau*, 11 October (1940).
10. Arnold Zweig, *Todesnachrichten* (a non published manuscript stored in the Litarary Achive of the former Academy of Arts, GDR in Berlin).

# Textual Approach

Jerzy Kałążny
# In the Labyrinth of Benjamin's *Arcades Project*: The Flâneur, the Collector, and the Gambler as Readers of the Nineteenth Century

**Abstract:** The essay focuses on Benjamin's *Arcades Project* and the figures of the flâneur, the collector and the gambler who walk and interpret the urban space of Paris. The description of these figures is based, apart from the *Arcades Project*, on other essays, notes and reflections by Benjamin and on Franz Hessel's book *Spazieren in Berlin*.

**Keywords:** allegorical figures; phantasmagoria; urban space; cultural citation; Franz Hessel

Defined in the most general terms, the aim of Benjamin's *Arcades Project* is to read and remember the nineteenth century. The notes and materials for the *Arcades* include the following remark: "The expression «the book of nature» indicates that one can read the real like a text. And that is how the reality of the nineteenth century will be treated here. We open the book of what happened" (*The Arcades*, p. 464). Before we open the book, however, we must first wake up. It is hardly coincidental that the next note, which comments on Proust, speaks of awakening from the dream that was the nineteenth century:

> Just as Proust begins the story of his life with as awakening, so must every presentation of history begin with awakening; in fact, it should treat of nothing else. This one [*The Arcades Project*], accordingly, deals with awakening from the nineteenth century (*The Arcades*, p. 464).

The sequence of awakening and reading seems to encapsulate the dialectic of *The Arcades Project*. As Benjamin says, "The realization of dream elements in the course of waking up is the canon of dialectics. It is paradigmatic for the thinker and binding for the historian" (*The Arcades*, p. 464).[1]

The motifs of dreaming, awakening, and drowsing, as well as the metaphors of nineteenth-century space as text and labyrinth (according to Benjamin, "The city is the realization of the ancient dream of humanity, the labyrinth" – *The Arcades*,

---

1  In a letter to Siegfried Kracauer of 21 March 1929 Wlater Benjamin wrote: "I am working on The Arcades – »I feel as if it was a dream« »as if it was a part of me»" (Walter Benjamin, *Gesammelte Schriften*, ed. Rolf Tiedemann (Frankfurt am Mein: Suhrkamp Verlag, 1982), vol. V, p. 1091.

p. 429) recur throughout *The Arcades Project* and form the basis of Benjamin's inquiry into the various ways of reading the nineteenth century.

Benjamin saw Paris as a book and associated the reading of this book with the work of memory. In *The Arcades Project* the nineteenth century is experienced through "reading" and "remembering." The *flâneur*, the collector, and the gambler are the figures of nineteenth-century readers who walk and interpret the labyrinth of Paris streets. They are the protagonists of the present essay, which proceeds through a series of loosely related reflections rather than as a systematic argument.

## I. The *Flâneur*

Of the protagonists of Benjamin's *Arcades Project*, the *flâneur* is the best known and the most thoroughly described. He appears in Charles Baudelaire, Honoré de Balzac, Charles Dickens, Gustave Flaubert, E.T.A. Hoffmann, Victor Hugo, Joris Karl Huysmans, Edgar Allan Poe, Marcel Proust, Robert Walser, Eugène Sue, and Emile Zola. The *flâneur* as a figure of modernity is also discussed in the sociological works of Siegfried Kracauer, Georg Simmel, Franz Hessel, and Benjamin himself.[2]

Benjamin borrowed the figure of the Paris *flâneur* from Baudelaire, whose writings often feature a solitary artistic passer-by, a sophisticated aesthete who walks through the crowded streets and arcades of Paris. He maintains an ironic distance from reality, yet finds pleasure and joyous excitement in observing it. The Parisian origins and Baudelairean provenance of the *flâneur* are commonplaces in critical studies of Benjamin. However, the other literary contexts in which the *flâneur* appears are less well known in the Polish humanities, and will be discussed below in some detail.

Benjamin's review of Franz Hessel's *Spazieren in Berlin: Beobachtungen im Jahr 1929* can serve as a useful introduction to his theory of *flânerie* formulated in *The*

---

[2] Benjamin's reflections on the *flâneur* can be found in: *The Arcades Project* (file M [The Flâneur]); "Paris, the Capital of the Nineteenth Century," in: *Selected Writings*, vol. III; "The Paris of the Second Empire in Baudelaire," in: *Selected Writings*, vol. IV; and the review of Franz Hessel's *Spazieren in Berlin*: "The Return of the Flâneur," in: *Selected Writings*, vol. II, part 1. In addition, in Benjamin's radio talks about Berlin, broadcast in 1929–1930, the guide around the city is the Berlin "man of the street," a counterpart of the Paris *flâneur*. See Walter Benjamin, "Rundfunkgeschichten für Kinder," in: *Gesammelte Schriften*, ed. Tillman Rexroth (Frankfurt am Mein: Suhrkamp Verlag, 1991), vol. VII, pp. 68–145.

*Arcades Project*.³ Titled "The Return of the Flâneur," the review essay foregrounds those aspects of Hessel's book which manifest Hessel's affinity with Benjamin's own way of thinking about urban space. Hessel walking the streets of Berlin is a *flâneur* who simultaneously walks through the past as he remembers it. This experience is described by Benjamin: "The city as a mnemonic for the lonely walker: it conjures up more than his childhood and youth, more than its own history" ("The Return of the Flâneur," in: *Selected Writings*, vol. II, part 1, p. 262). It returns in *The Arcades Project*, in almost identical phrasing, as the key experience of *flânerie*:

> The street conducts the flâneur into a vanished time. For him, every street is precipitous. It leads downward – if not to the mythical Mothers, then into a past that can be all the more spellbinding because it is not his own, not private. Nevertheless, it always remains the time of the childhood. [...] In the asphalt over which he passes, his steps awaken a surprising resonance. The gaslight that streams down on the paving stones throws an equivocal light on this double ground. (*The Arcades*, p. 416)⁴

The allusion to Goethe's *Faust* refers to the *flâneur*'s experience of being immersed in the past, which is essentially a mythic past. The only adequate mode for expressing this experience, which concerns the past perceived as a whole, is storytelling. As Benjamin points out, Hessel does not describe things or events but tells a story he heard (see "The Return of the Flâneur," in: *Selected Writings*, vol. II, part 1, p. 262). Storytelling as a way of experiencing mythic totality is opposed to documenting the past, which is merely the registering of facts. For Benjamin, the substance of the past and the realm of fact are two different aspects of the *flâneur*'s experience of time past.

In his *Spazieren in Berlin* Hessel describes the perambulations of the *flâneur* as reading the text of the city:

> *Flânerie* is a sort of reading of the street in which people's faces, shop windows, coffee-house terraces, streetcars, automobiles, and trees become nothing but equally important letters composing the sentences and pages of an ever new book.⁵

Hessel's book seems to have inspired another important aspect of Benjamin's theory of *flânerie*. In *The Arcades Project* Benjamin argues that urban space forms a dialectical relation with the *flâneur* who navigates it: it opens before him as

---

3  Franz Hessel, *Spazieren in Berlin* (Wien\Leipzig: Verlag Hans Epstein, 1929); see also later editions, such as *Spazieren in Berlin: Beobachtungen im Jahr 1929* (Berlin: Morgen, 1979) and *Ein Flaneur in Berlin* (Berlin: Das Arsenal, 1984).
4  The quotation also appears in Benjamin's autobiographical "Berlin Childhood around 1900," in: *Selected Writings*, vol. III, pp. 352–354.
5  Hessel, *Spazieren in Berlin*, p. 130.

cityscape and closes around him as a domestic interior, a room.[6] This dialectic of outer and inner space is also of great significance to Benjamin's other protagonists, especially the collector.

The arcade is where the *flâneur* crosses the boundary between inside and outside. The arcade becomes an experiential space in which the city and cityscape, the street and the domestic interior are read as metaphors. "Arcades are midway between the street and the interior," Benjamin writes.[7] They are also a space of collective experience, unlike the domestic interior, which is the individual's private realm:

> Streets are the dwelling place of the collective. The collective is an eternally unquiet, eternally agitated being that – in the space between the building fronts – experiences, learns, understands, and ivents as much as individuals do within the privacy of their own four walls. For this collective, glossy enameled shop sings are a wall decoration as good as, if not better than, an oil painting in the drawing room of a bourgeois; walls with their «Post No Bills» are its writing desk, newspaper stands its libraries, mailboxes its bronze busts, benches its bedroom furniture, and the café terrace is the balcony form which it looks down on its hausehold. (*The Arcades*, p. 423)

The *flâneur* treats the street as a study room in which, in accordance with his traditional image as "physiognomist," he devotes himself to investigating human types and behaviors. The domestic interior, on the other hand, becomes a walking space, just like the city or the park. The description of a son and a father's walk in the son's own room, excerpted from early Kierkegaard (see *The Arcades*, p. 421), is strongly reminiscent of the walks taken by Felicjan Dulski in Gabriela Zapolska's play. However, Benjamin emphasizes the peripatetic aspect of this kind of *flânerie*, i.e. its combination of movement and thinking. Benjamin's peripatetic *flâneurs* include Dickens, who was unable to write outside of London, and Thomas de Quincey, who, according to Baudelaire, was "a sort of peripatetic, a street philosopher pondering his way endleslly through the vortex of the great city" (*The Arcades*, p. 436). Another peripatetic *flâneur* was Franz Hessel, whose dictum, "We see only what looks at us. We can do only... what we cannot help doing," Benjamin considered to be the quintessential expression of the philosophy of *flânerie* ("The Return of the Flâneur," in: *Selected Writings*, vol. II, part 1, p. 265).

The dialectic of inside and outside plays an important role in the *flâneur*'s functioning in urban space. The opening paragraph of the first chapter of *Spazieren in Berlin* describes walking through the busy streets of the city as pleasure,

---

6  See Benjamin, "The Return of the Flâneur," in: *Selected Writings*, vol. II, part 1, p. 264; see also *The Arcades*, 423.
7  Walter Benjamin, *Gesammelte Schriften*, ed. Rolf Tiedemann, Hermann Schweppenhäuser (Frankfurt am Mein: Suhrkamp Verlag, 1974), vol. I, p. 539.

heightened by the fact that the passer-by remains unnoticed by pedestrians. But in Berlin the leisurely passer-by arouses suspicion. "Whenever I try to walk amidst agitated people, they cast suspicious glances at me," Hessel observes. "I think they take me for a pickpocket."[8] This ironic remark brings into sharp relief the differences in relations between the individual and the crowd in different cities. Each of the three large cities of the nineteenth-century: Berlin, Paris, and London also presents different possibilities for simultaneously being on display and being invisible, an essential aspect of the *flâneur*'s condition. It is worth examining some of these differences in detail as they demonstrate how particular urban spaces shape the *flâneur*'s perception.

Describing Hessel's experiences in Berlin and Paris, Benjamin observes that what happened to Hessel in Berlin could not have happened in Paris. In Benjamin's view, Hessel's experience illustrates the *flâneur*'s evolution from the philosophizing passer-by, the Rousseauvian *promeneur solitaire* (see *The Arcades*, p. 805) and the kind-hearted "physiognomist" in E. T. A. Hoffmann's "The Cousin's Corner Window,"[9] to the confused werewolf in Edgar Allan Poe's "The Man of the Crowd":

> It is here [in Berlin], not in Paris, where it becomes clear to us how easy it is for the *flâneur* to depart from the ideal of the philosopher out for a stroll, and to assume the features of the werewolf at large in the social jungle – the creature of whom Poe has given the definitive description in his story "The Man of the Crowd". ("The Return of the Flâneur," in: *Selected Writings*, vol. II, part 1, p. 265)

The short stories by Hoffmann and Poe serve as paradigms for Benjamin's theory of *flânerie*. His *flâneur* must be situated somewhere in between Hoffmann's keen observer who takes pleasure in looking out from his corner window at the busy but hardly metropolitan market square and Poe's student of human fauna who, with merciless precision, attaches appropriate labels to individuals. The obsessive curiosity of the latter makes him follow one fascinating individual, whom he eventually identifies as "the man of the crowd," "the type and the genius of deep crime."[10] Clearly enough, Benjamin's *flâneur* displays a greater affinity to the narrator of Poe's story, who anticipates the figure of the detective, an investigator of crime in the city jungle. One reason for this lack of symmetry in the *flâneur* relationship to his two literary predecessors is the fact that Hoffmann's

---

8   Hessel, *Ein Flaneur in Berlin*.
9   Ernst Theodor Amadeus Hoffmann, "My Cousin's Corner Window," in: *The Golden Pot and Other Tales*, trans. Ritchie Robertson (New York: Oxford University Press, 2000).
10  Edgar Allan Poe, "The Man of the Crowd," in: *Poetry and Tales*, ed. Patrick F. Quinn (New York: Library of America, 1984), p. 396.

story, published in 1822, is probably set in Berlin, which in the 1820s was still a provincial city. "The Man of the Crowd," on the other hand, is set in London, one of the two modern European cities and the center of world capital, a city whose character was dramatically different from that of Paris. Perhaps no one captured the spirit of early capitalist London better than Heinrich Heine, whose account of his visit to England's capital city was published in 1828.[11] Only a few pages long, it documents the poet's impressions of the London metropolis and his reflection on how to convey them adequately. Heine concludes that London calls for a new aesthetics of perception and representation. He begins by describing his shock at the city's hugeness and incomprehensible strangeness:

> I saw the greatest curiosities that the world can show to an astonished spirit; I saw them and I am still astonished – still vivid in my memory is the stone forest of houses and, between them, the rapid flow of living people's faces with all their colorful passions, their horrifying haste in love, hunger, and hatred – it is London that I am speaking of.[12]

Who could describe all this? Certainly not a poet accustomed to an aesthetics of contrast and diversity. "Don't send a poet to London!" warns Heine.[13] The poet who sees beauty in what is original and unique and, in accordance with the classic aesthetic canon, perceives beauty as inseparable from goodness, is completely unprepared for the new experience and its overwhelming otherness. "The fearful solemnity of all things," Heine continues, "the colossal monotony, the mechanical movements, the surliness present even in joy – this exaggerated London suppresses the imagination and breaks the heart."[14]

## II. The Collector

Apart from *The Arcades Project* (see *The Arcades*, pp. 203–211), Benjamin talks about the collector in his long essay "Paris, the Capital of the Nineteenth Century,"[15] as well as in "Unpacking My Library: A Talk about Book Collecting,"[16] and the

---

11 Heinrich Heine, "London," quoted after Heinz Brüggemann: *"Aber schickt keinen Poeten nach London!" Großstadt und literarische Wahrnehmung im 18. und 19. Jahrhundert. Texte und Interpretationen* (Hamburg: Reinbek, 1985), pp. 254–258.
12 Heine, "London," p. 254.
13 Heine, "London," p. 254.
14 Heine, "London," p. 254.
15 Benjamin, "Paris, the Capital of the Nineteenth Century," esp. section "Louis-Philippe or the Interior."
16 See Walter Benjamin, "Unpacking My Library: A Talk about Collecting," in: *Selected Writings*, vol. II, part 2.

fragment on "Untidy Child" in "One-Way Street."[17] Throughout his life Benjamin had a passion for collecting, documented, for example, in his Moscow diary.[18] *The Arcades Project* is also the work of a collector: it is a sum of readings, painstakingly collected quotations, notes, and remarks which unquestionably can be described as a collection:

> Here, the Paris arcades are examined as though they were properties in the hand of a collector. (At bottom, we may say, the collector lives a piece of dream life. For in the dream, too, the, rhythm of perception and experience is altered in such a way that everything – even the seemingly most neutral – comes to strike us; everything concerns us. In order to understand the arcades from the ground up, we sink them into the deepest stratum of the dream; we speak of them as though they had struck us.) (*The Arcades*, pp. 205–206)

Quotations, which take up a large portion of *The Arcades Project*, function in exactly the same way as exhibits in a collection. The collector appropriates objects as he removes them from their original context to situate them in the new context that he creates:

> What is decisive in collecting – we can read in *The Arcades Project* – is that the object is detached from all its original functions in order to enter into the closest conceivable relation to things of the same kind. [...] It is the deepest enchantment of the collector to enclose the particular item within a magic circle, where, as a last shudder runs through it (the shudder of being acquired), it turns to stone. Everything remembered, everything thought, everything conscious becomes socle, frame, pedestal, seal of his possession. [...] Collecting is a form of practical memory, and of all profane manifestations of «nearness» it is the most binding. (*The Arcades*, pp. 204–205)

In *The Arcades Project*, an enormous collection in which the reader moves as in a labyrinth, the collector and the *flâneur* are presented as readers of the nineteenth century, even though the type of collector was also common in the twentieth. But unlike the *flâneur*, the collector is a private person who lives in a domestic interior, the sanctuary into which he withdraws from the external world.

The passionate collector resembles a child who stores all kinds of treasures, creating a peculiar collection valuable only to its owner. The child collector, Benjamin says, is like an Indian hunter on a track; he feeds his imagination on adventure novels, such as those of James Fenimore Cooper (see "One-way street," in: *Selected Writings*, vol. I, p. 465). The objects he collects become totems symbolizing the primitive aspects of the gatherer's existence.

---

17 See Walter Benjamin, "One-Way Street," in: *Selected Writings*, vol. I.
18 See a discussion of the *Moscow Diary* in the context of Benjamin's passion for collecting in *Benjamin Handbuch. Leben-Werk-Wirkung*, ed. Burkhardt Lindner (Stuttgart-Weimar: Metzler Verlag, 2006), p. 667.

According to Benjamin, the owner who reads his collection is excited and bewildered by the semblance and closeness of the objects. He has a dreamlike sense that everything, even the most immaterial incidents, "comes to strike us; everything concerns us" (*The Arcades*, p. 206). It is an allegorical interpretation: the objects collected have been torn out of their original web of meanings and functions, which enables the collector to see them with even greater clarity. The collector resembles an allegorist, another recurring figure in *The Arcades Project*.[19] His attitude is profoundly ambivalent: the careful preservation of objects, which he often saves from destruction, is predicated upon destroying their original context.

The collector's dual attitude as preserver and destructor is conspicuous in the essays "Unpacking My Library" and "The Destructive Character." The former is a humorous, largely autobiographical story of the troubles of the owner of a large library who continually has to move it from one place to another.

> Thus, the life of a collector manifests a dialectical tension between the poles of disorder and order. […] The most profound enchantment for the collector is the locking of individual items within a magic circle in which they are frozen as the final thrill, the thrill of acquisition, passes over them. ("Unpacking My Library: A Talk about Collecting," in: *Selected Writings*, vol. II, part 2, p. 487)

Benjamin explicitly contrasts the "destructive character" with the collector, whom the former seems to invalidate. "The destructive character," Benjamin argues, "knows only one watchword: make room. And only one activity: clearing away. His need for fresh air and open space is stronger than any hatred" ("The Destructive Character," in: *Selected Writings*, vol. II, part 2, p. 541). "The destructive character" is also an enemy of the "étui-man" [*Etui-Mensch*], whose natural environment is a velvet-lined interior. The collector is a type of "étui-man" as well, in a twofold sense. Firstly, as a private individual and user of a domestic interior, where he hides as in a protective casket:

---

19 The following passage defines the relationship between the collector and the allegorist: "Perhaps the most deeply hidden motiv of the person who collects can be described this way: he takes up the struggle against dispersion. […] The allegorist is, as it were, the polar opposite of the collector. He has given up the attempt to elucidate things through research into their properties and relations. He dislodges things from their context and, from the outset, relies on his profundity to iluminate their meaning. The collector, by contrast, brings together what belongs together; by keeping in mind their affinities and their succession in time, he can eventually furnish information about his objects. Nevertheless – and this is more important than all the differences that may exist between them – in every collector hides an allegorist, and in every allegorist a collector" (*The Arcades*, p. 211).

> The interior is not just the univers but also the étui of the private private individual. To dwell means to leave traces. In the interior, these are accentuated. Coverlets and antimacassars, cases and contrainers are devised in abundance; in these, the traces of the most ordinary objects of use are imprinted. In just the same way, the traces of the inhabitant are imprinted in the interior. (*The Arcades*, p. 9)

Modern architecture designed by Le Corbusier and others is not congenial to the collector or the *flâneur*. It becomes the realm of "the destructive character," who prefers air and open space to the safety and snugness of the étui. The new architecture with its prominent use of steel and glass destroys the collector's and the *flâneur*'s natural environment as it strips their space of intimacy and makes it impossible to leave traces. "Glass is generally hostile to mystery," Benjamin claims. "It is also hostile to ownership."[20]

The "étui-like" domestic interior described in the above-quoted passage can be seen as the city dweller's reaction to the shrinking of private space, and hence to the limited opportunity to leave traces, which he tries to compensate for in his own home. The brief essay "Spurlos wohnen" [Dwelling without trace] describes a domestic interior whose owner has not left a tiniest bit of space unfilled:

> As you entered a bourgeois room in the 1880s you experienced – despite its 'coziness' – a powerful feeling that "you had nothing to look for here." You had nothing to look for because there was not a single patch of space where the owner had not left his traces: as knick-knacks on the window sills, monogrammed coverlets on cushioned armchairs, stained-glass ornaments hung in windows, a screen in front of the fireplace.[21]

In those times, says Benjamin, dwelling was synonymous with leaving traces. Today, one is supposed to "dwell without trace." "Blot out your traces!" calls Brecht in a poem from *Lesebuch für Städtebewohner* [A Reader for City Dwellers], which Benjamin quotes in his essay. In late-nineteenth-century bourgeois interiors the traces are left to stay. It comes as no surprise that the bourgeois domestic interior provides the best setting for the detective stories of that period. This issue, however, remains outside the scope of the present essay. Let us close these remarks about the collector by pointing to another aspect of the "casket man's" existence. The collector is a casket man because he hides inside his collection as in a casket. As Benjamin says at the end of his essay about the library, "I have erected before you one of his dwellings, with books as the building stones; and now he is going

---

20 Walter Benjamin, *Gesammelte Schriften*, ed. Rolf Tiedemann, Hermann Schweppenhäuser (Frankfurt am Mein: Suhrkamp Verlag, 1977), vol. II, p. 217.
21 Walter Benjamin, "Spurlos wohnen," in: *Gesammelte Schriften*, ed. Tillman Rexroth (Frankfurt am Mein: Suhrkamp Verlag, 1972), vol. IV.1, p. 427.

to disappear inside, as is only fitting" ("Unpacking My Library: A Talk about Collecting," in: *Selected Writings*, vol. II, part 2, p. 492).

## III. The Gambler

Benjamin's whole oeuvre testifies to his keen interest in play and gambling. He talks about children's games and toys (e.g. in the Moscow diary) and discusses acting as imitation of reality.[22] The following description of the gambler is based on Benjamin's remarks in *The Arcades Project* (see *The Arcades*, pp. 489–515), the essay on Baudelaire,[23] and a number of notes and sketches, such as those in the collection *Denkbilder*.[24]

Benjamin's remarks about gambling in *The Arcades Project* begin with a fascinating question:

> Hasn't his eternal vagabondage [of the flâneur and the gambler – J.K.] everywhere accustomed him to reinterpreting the image of the city? And doesn't he transform the arcade into a casino, into a gambling den, where now and again he stakes the red, blue, yellow *jetons* of feeling of women, on a face that suddenly surfaces (will it return his look?), on a mute mouth (will it speak?). What, on the baize cloth, looks out at the gambler from every number – luck, that is – here, from the bodies of all the women, winks at him as the chimera of sexuality: as his type. […] For the gambling hall and bordello, it is the same supremely sinful delight: to challenge fate in pleasure. (*The Arcades*, p. 489)

The connection between gambling and prostitution is only one context in which Benjamin discusses games and the gambler in *The Arcades Project*. It is not only patrons of casinos who are gamblers; speculators on the stock exchange gamble as well. The novelty, in comparison with the *ancien regime*, is that in the nineteenth century the bourgeois become gamblers (see *The Arcades*, p. 490), while in the eighteenth century gambling was limited to the nobility.[25] A specifically nineteenth-century form of gambling is the stock exchange. The way capital circulates resembles the game of roulette, where one can bet on a number but cannot rationally calculate one's winnings. Through an apt selection of quotes Benjamin demonstrates the

---

22 See Benjamin, "The Work of Art in the Age of Its Technological Reproducibility," in: *Selected Writings*, vol. III, pp. 101–133.
23 See Benjamin, "On Some Motifs in Baudelaire," in: *Selected Writings*, vol. IV, pp. 313–355.
24 Benjamin, "Notes on a Theory of Gambling" and "The Path to Success, in Thirteen Theses," in: *Selected Writings*, vol. II, part 1; "Das Spiel," in: *Gesammelte Schriften*, vol. IV.1, pp. 426–427; "Die glückliche Hand. Eine Unterhaltung über das Spiel," in: *Gesammelte Schriften*, vol. IV.2, pp. 771–777.
25 Benjamin, *Gesammelte Schriften*, vol. I, p. 634.

"inexplicable" which "is enthroned in bourgeois society as in a gambling hall" (*The Arcades*, p. 497). In the economic sphere, the play of market forces strongly reminds him of the casino, where fortunes change owners as a consequence of totally unpredictable events (see *The Arcades*, p. 497).

Work also seems to have a lot in common with gambling. In section nine of "On Some Motifs in Baudelaire," which discusses work as a game of chance, Benjamin observes that "[t]he shock experience which the passer-by has in the crowd," an experience produced by his encounter with the mechanical movements and gestures of pedestrians, "corresponds to the isolated 'experiences' of the worker at his machine" ("On Some Motifs in Baudelaire," in: *Selected Writings*, vol. IV, p. 329). Benjamin stresses the seemingly paradoxical analogy between gambling and work, specifically the mechanized work in a factory. Although the work and wages of the factory worker do not depend on chance or a stroke of fate, they are also characterized by "futility, emptiness, an inability to complete something" ("On Some Motifs in Baudelaire," in: *Selected Writings*, vol. IV, p. 330) that are inherent in games of chance. In a lithograph by Alois Senefelder gamblers behave like pedestrians in Poe's "The Man of the Crowd": "They live their lives as automatons and resemble Bergson's fictitious characters who have completely liquidated their memories" ("On Some Motifs in Baudelaire," in: *Selected Writings*, vol. IV, p. 330). The gambler's memory is different from that of the *flâneur* and the collector because it is not grounded in mythical experience, although compulsive gamblers often resort to magical rituals that are supposed to bring them luck. Interestingly, Benjamin argues that chance as such is absent from gambling. In "Die glückliche Hand: Eine Unterhaltung über das Spiel" he concludes that if luck is present at all in a game of chance, it results from some intuitive knowledge of the future which resides in the gambler's unconscious. The gambler's body reacts to artificially produced danger, following instinct rather than reason. The gambler resembles a somnambulist whose "luck" lasts as long as he is asleep.[26] Just like the *flâneur* and the collector, the gambler lives and acts in a daze, in a state of exciting fear caused by the encounter with something unpredictable:

> The fascination of danger is at the bottom of all great passions. There is no fullness of pleasure unless the precipice in near. It is the mingling of terror with delight that intoxicates. And what more terrifying than gambling? It gives and takes away; its logic is not our logic. It is dumb and blind and deaf. It is almighty. It is a God. (citation from *Le Jardin d'Epicure* by Anatole France – *The Arcades*, p. 498)

Translated by Magdalena Zapędowska

---

[26] Benjamin, "Die glückliche Hand," pp. 775–776.

## Bibliography

1. *Benjamin Handbuch. Leben – Werk – Wirkung*, ed. Burkhardt Lindner (Stuttgart-Weimar: Metzler Verlag, 2006).
2. Walter Benjamin, "Berlin Childhood around 1900," in: *Selected Writings*, ed. Michael W. Jennings and Marcus Bullock, Howard Eiland, Gary Smith, vol. III (Cambridge, MA: Belknap Press of Harvard University Press, 2002).
3. Walter Benjamin, "Das Spiel," in: *Gesammelte Schriften*, vol. IV.1, ed. Tillman Rexroth (Frankfurt am Mein: Suhrkamp Verlag, 1972).
4. Walter Benjamin, "Die glückliche Hand. Eine Unterhaltung über das Spiel," in: *Gesammelte Schriften*, vol. IV.2, ed. Tillman Rexroth (Frankfurt am Mein: Suhrkamp Verlag, 1972).
5. Walter Benjamin, *Gesammelte Schriften*, vol. I, ed. Rolf Tiedemann, Hermann Schweppenhäuser (Frankfurt am Mein: Suhrkamp Verlag, 1974).
6. Walter Benjamin, *Gesammelte Schriften*, vol. II, ed. Rolf Tiedemann, Hermann Schweppenhäuser (Frankfurt am Mein: Suhrkamp Verlag, 1977).
7. Walter Benjamin, *Gesammelte Schriften*, vol. V, ed. Rolf Tiedemann (Frankfurt am Mein: Suhrkamp Verlag, 1982).
8. Walter Benjamin, "Notes on a Theory of Gambling," in: *Selected Writings*, ed. Michael W. Jennings and Marcus Bullock, Howard Eiland, Gary Smith, vol. II, part 1 (Cambridge, MA: Belknap Press of Harvard University Press, 1999).
9. Walter Benjamin, "One-Way Street," in: *Selected Writings*, ed. Michael W. Jennings and Marcus Bullock, Howard Eiland, Gary Smith, vol. I (Cambridge, MA: Belknap Press of Harvard University Press, 1996).
10. Walter Benjamin, "On Some Motifs in Baudelaire," in: *Selected Writings*, ed. Michael W. Jennings and Marcus Bullock, Howard Eiland, Gary Smith, vol. IV (Cambridge, MA: Belknap Press of Harvard University Press, 2003).
11. Walter Benjamin, "Paris, the Capital of the Nineteenth Century," in: *Selected Writings*, ed. Michael W. Jennings and Marcus Bullock, Howard Eiland, Gary Smith, vol. III (Cambridge, MA: Belknap Press of Harvard University Press, 2002).
12. Walter Benjamin, "Rundfunkgeschichten für Kinder," in: *Gesammelte Schriften*, vol. VII, ed. Tillman Rexroth (Frankfurt am Mein: Suhrkamp Verlag, 1991).
13. Walter Benjamin, "Spurlos wohnen," in: *Gesammelte Schriften*, vol. IV.1, ed. Tillman Rexroth (Frankfurt am Mein: Suhrkamp Verlag, 1972).
14. Walter Benjamin, *The Arcades Project*, trans. Howard Eiland and Kevin McLaughlin, prepared on the basis of the German volume edited by Rolf Tiedman (Cambridge Mass.: The Belknap Press of Harvard University Press, 1999).

15. Walter Benjamin, "The Destructive Character," in: *Selected Writings*, ed. Michael W. Jennings and Marcus Bullock, Howard Eiland, Gary Smith, vol. II, part 2, (Cambridge, MA: Belknap Press of Harvard University Press, 1999).
16. Walter Benjamin, "The Paris of the Second Empire in Baudelaire," in: *Selected Writings*, ed. Michael W. Jennings and Marcus Bullock, Howard Eiland, Gary Smith, vol. IV (Cambridge, MA: Belknap Press of Harvard University Press, 2003).
17. Walter Benjamin, "The Path to Success, in Thirteen Theses," in: *Selected Writings*, ed. Michael W. Jennings and Marcus Bullock, Howard Eiland, Gary Smith, vol. II, part 1 (Cambridge, MA: Belknap Press of Harvard University Press, 1999).
18. Walter Benjamin, "The Return of the Flâneur," in: *Selected Writings*, ed. Michael W. Jennings and Marcus Bullock, Howard Eiland, Gary Smith, vol. II, part 1 (Cambridge, MA: Belknap Press of Harvard University Press, 1999).
19. Walter Benjamin, "The Work of Art in the Age of Its Technological Reproducibility," in: *Selected Writings*, ed. Michael W. Jennings and Marcus Bullock, Howard Eiland, Gary Smith, vol. III (Cambridge, MA: Belknap Press of Harvard University Press, 2002).
20. Walter Benjamin, "Unpacking My Library: A Talk about Collecting," in: *Selected Writings*, ed. Michael W. Jennings and Marcus Bullock, Howard Eiland, Gary Smith, vol. II, part 2 (Cambridge, MA: Belknap Press of Harvard University Press, 1999).
21. Heinz Brüggemann, *"Aber schickt keinen Poeten nach London!" Großstadt und literarische Wahrnehmung im 18. und 19. Jahrhundert. Texte und Interpretationen* (Hamburg: Reinbek, 1985).
22. Franz Hessel, *Ein Flaneur in Berlin* (Berlin: Das Arsenal, 1984).
23. Franz Hessel, *Spazieren in Berlin* (Wien\Leipzig: Verlag Hans Epstein, 1929).
24. Franz Hessel, *Spazieren in Berlin: Beobachtungen im Jahr 1929* (Berlin: Morgen, 1979).
25. Ernst Theodor Amadeus Hoffmann, "My Cousin's Corner Window," in: *The Golden Pot and Other Tales*, trans. Ritchie Robertson (New York: Oxford University Press, 2000).
26. Edgar Allan Poe, "The Man of the Crowd," in: *Poetry and Tales*, ed. Patrick F. Quinn (New York: Library of America, 1984).

Lidia Banowska

# Paris in Walter Benjamin's *Arcades Project* – on the Threshold of Modernity

**Abstract:** In Benjamin's inspection Paris (an allegory of the center of the world and of modernity) is seen as a city of passages. It appears as a utopian (marked by the illusion of the permanence of civilization) and a melancholic space (marked by ruin), and is interpreted through images of an underworld or infernal metropolis. It is a modern city, the main features of its description being: interiorization, symbolic expressivity, oneiric phantasmagoricality and illusiveness.

**Keywords:** Paris; passages; modernity; oneirism; poetics of space

## The Inner City

"Each epoch dreams the one to follow" (*The Arcades*, p. 150) and, at the same time, each epoch deludes itself as to its absolute newness even as it contains its own prehistory whose archaic content comes alive – notes the author of *The Arcades Project*. Benjamin's nineteenth-century Paris dreams a dream about and foreshadows modernity. It is a border area, an area of ambiguity corresponding to the dialectical "yes" and "no". It is a many-aspected area characterized by, among other features, the suspension between the old and the new, between sleep and wakefulness, between the external and the internal. For example, Paris is at the same time old and new, not only in the sense of being divided into old and new districts, but also in that the new – embodied in arcades – entails the old. In the adopted perspective the newest and the most fashionable construction reveals its simultaneous antiquatedness.[1] The exemplarily mentioned coexistence of the old and the new also has a literal meaning: under the surface of the newly developed urban forms there exists the old subterranean city with its own, separate status and a parallel life. The underground area is a subsurface in both the abovementioned literal meaning and in the metaphorical meaning of the dark, nightmarish territory pushed beneath the communal subconscious. The phantasmagoric quality of the city, which is one of

---

1 See: "It is remarkable that constructions in which the expert recognizes anticipations of contemporary building fashions impress the alert but architecturally unschooled sense not at all as anticipatory but as distinctly old-fashioned and dreamlike" (*The Arcades*, p. 390).

the most important aspects of Benjamin's vision of Paris, is also one of the essential features of its inner landscape. This is because, even though the ambiguity of Paris is expressed – among other things – through the suspension of the city between the external and the internal, the proportions between the two spheres are not even: Paris is being absorbed by the inside, it is becoming an inner city.

The issue discussed here requires a few additional comments, or even explanations. A question may be asked whether Paris indeed has any existence beyond that of an inner city. It is a mythical city whose outer, architectural or any other, topography will always be tinged with mythology, and whose plans and maps will all, inevitably, depict imagined space. Perhaps, then, Paris was, is, and will be an inner city, and its topography – an inner topography. Having said that, however, it ought to be noticed that Benjamin's intuitions introduce a fundamental *novum*. Firstly, the reading of the city in *The Arcades Project* is based on the assumption of an "anthropocentrically conceived" topography.[2] Secondly, Benjamin's reading is a proposal for an unhurried, discerning observation which unveils a different city; it is a look inside, a look beneath the surface of phenomena as well as at the surface itself from the perspective of the interior (one example of such a view of Parisian architecture being the perception of façades as interiors, and of interiors as façades). Thirdly, and most importantly, the internalization of both the perspective and the object itself seems to function as one of the crucial signs-portents of modernity – as noted by Georg Simmel: "the essence of modernity as such is psychologism, the experiencing [*das Erleben*] and interpretation of the world in terms of the reactions of our inner life and indeed as an inner world."[3]

---

2   See: "A different topography, not architectonic but anthropocentric in conception, could show us all at once, and in its true light, the most muted *quartier*: the isolated fourteenth *arrondisement*. That, at any rate, is how Jules Janin already saw it a hundred years ago. If you were born into that neighborhood, you could lead the most animated and audacious life without ever having to leave it. For in it are found, one after another, all the buildings of public misery, of proletarian indigence, in unbroken succession: the birthing clinic, the orphanage, the hospital (the famous Santé), and finally the great Paris jail with its scaffold. At night, one sees on the narrow unobtrusive benches – not, of course, the comfortable ones found in the squares – men stretched out asleep as if in the waiting room of a way station in the course of this terrible journey" (*The Arcades*, p. 86).

3   Georg Simmel, "Philosophiche Kultur," in: *Gesamtausgabe*, ed. Rüdiger Kramme and Otthein Rammstedt, (Frankfurt: Suhrkamp, 1996), vol. XIV, p. 346. Quoted after Lourdes Flamarique, "From the Psychologization of Experience to the Priority of Emotions in Social Life," in: *The Emotions and Cultural Analysis*, ed. Ana Marta González (London and New York: Routledge, 2016), p. 56.

The question why it was Paris that became the object of Benjamin's scrutiny again directs us toward the interior: the city is an interior and it reveals an interior through its forms. In Benjamin's notes the city, which is the center of the world and of the nascent modern culture, functions as the inner house. The walls of the city mark the borders of that house, and everything within these walls becomes the interior.

It is a bird's-eye view of the city, in which perspective all architectural forms (buildings, for example), perceived in their entirety, are seen as interior decoration of the house; the eponymous arcades become its corridors, and the underground tunnels become its cellars. The inner Paris is also the Paris dreamed by Parisians, with forms of architecture expressing the inhabitants (the states of their different levels of consciousness: fears, aspirations, hopes, desires, illusions), and with interiors as carriers of traces of presence. The inner Paris is also the underground city of dark corridors functioning as a dark reverse of the gas-lit, and thus brightened, arcades. Such a way of looking at the city has its foundation in the thought that what is external for an individual can be internal for a community[4]; for example, fashion or architecture are treated as manifestations of the communal unconscious, a community's dream, its phantasmagoria, of how the community imagines itself.[5] Incidentally, the issue brings out one of the basic aspects of modernity, namely, the impossibility of direct expression, and the ambiguity or equivocation of the only available, symbolic expression through visual forms.

Parisian images of the internal implicate various sometimes mutually contradictory meanings. The luxurious novelty of the arcades may serve as an example of an exposed interior in which sacralization (imparting a sacred dimension to arcades) and profanation (the presence of prostitution) intertwine. Façades, the outermost parts of the buildings, are a paradoxical image of an interior exposed. What follows is that interiors of bourgeois houses, exposed to public view, are false interiors. Finally, the underground city is a hidden interior.

Paris as an image of an interior, then, is as much a sign of a sanctified as a sign of a profaned – revealed or hidden – center. It is simultaneously the heart or the core of and the bowels or a cesspit of civilization.

---

4  See: "The situation of consciousness as patterned and checkered by sleep and waking need only be transferred from the individual to the collective. Of course, much that is external to the former is internal to the latter: architecture, fashion – yes, even the weather" (*The Arcades*, p. 389).
5  Of the many examples which can be quoted here, one of the most prominent is the construction of the Triumphal Gate by Napoleon I dreaming of an imperial city.

## Paris, the city of arcades

The starting point of Benjamin's *exposé* about *Paris, Capital of the Nineteenth Century* is a discussion of the opinion that "the course of the world is an endless series of facts congealed in the form of things" which "appear as though identified for all time" (*The Arcades*, p. 14) and, as a result, always manifest as a phantasmagoria. Polemicizing with this reifying vision of cultural history, the author of the volume emphasizes:

> This conception of history minimizes the fact that such riches own not only their existence but also their transmission to a constant effort of society – an effort, moreover, by which these riches are strangely altered. (*The Arcades*, p. 14)

Asking why arcades become the central allegory of nineteenth-century Paris in Benjamin's reflection, voice should be given to the author again. The following note is placed in the notes grouped under the heading [*Dream City and Dream House, Dreams of the Future, Anthropological Nihilism, Jung*]: "[e]very epoch has such a side turned toward dreams, the child's side. For the previous century, this appears very clearly in the arcades" (*The Arcades*, p. 388). Thus, an arcade functions as a metonymy of dreamed, phantasmagoric and illusory Paris which becomes the focal point of the imaginings the community has about itself.

Through images a dream expresses the unconscious of the community which in the nineteenth century – as the author notes – "through the arcades, communes with its own insides" (*The Arcades*, p. 389):

> The nineteenth century a spacetime <*Zeitraum*> (a dreamtime <*Zeit-traum*>) in which the individual consciousness more and more secures itself in reflecting, while the collective consciousness sinks into ever deeper sleep. But just as the sleeper […] sets out on the macrocosmic journey through his own body […] so likewise for the dreaming collective, which, through the arcades, communes with its own insides. We must follow in its wake so as to expound the nineteenth century – in fashion and advertising, in buildings and politics – as the outcome of its dream visions. (*The Arcades*, p. 389)

"The *passage* is a city, a world in miniature" (*The Arcades*, p. 3) – this quote from the *Illustrated Guide to Paris* which describes the capital city around the year 1852, reveals the multiplicity of meanings inscribed in the arcades. Parisian "streets-galleries", as they were called, are depicted as "a recent invention of industrial luxury"[6] (*The Arcades*, p. 31), as well as a "a street of lascivious commerce" (*The Arcades*,

---

6   It is worth noting here that among the voices of the epoch which characterized the arcades as a luxurious *novum* an ironic voice which uncovered the presumptuousness of the contemporaries could also be found: See: "I hear they want to roof all the streets

p. 42) which, however, lacks movement. The street, being a phantasmagoric image of modernity, also evokes phantasmagoria in the *flâneur* who deludes himself as to his knowledge of the human mind (*The Arcades*, pp. 21–22).

In the Parisian allegories of modernity the attention of Benjamin is drawn to the ambiguity inscribed in them, which is "Ambiguity is the manifest imaging of dialectic, the law of dialectics at a standstill. This standstill is utopia and the dialectical image, therefore, dream image. Such an image is afforded by the commodity per se: as fetish. Such an image is presented by the arcades, which are house no less than street. Such an image is the prostitute – seller and sold in one" (*The Arcades*, p. 10). In the arcades she is "incorporated" in their very construction (glass and steel) as well as, so to speak, condensed through the ambiguity of the space they occupy (house-street) and through the fact that they are the selling place for products ("fetish" – *The Arcades*, p. 10) and the space of thriving prostitution, that equivocal "love market" (*The Arcades*, p. 360).[7]

The ambiguity of the construction itself turns out to be of especial importance, considering that, as Benjamin writes, quoting Sigfried Giedion, "[i]n the nineteenth century [...] construction plays the role of the subconscious" (*The Arcades*, p. 391)[8]. Arcades are suspended between the house and the street, between an open space and a hall. The ambiguity of arcades has its source in their internalization, in the closing up of the space that used to be open. "Parisians make the street an interior" (*The Arcades*, p. 421), "[s]treets are the dwelling place of the collective" (*The Arcades*, 423). There, signboards function as paintings hung up on the walls, the walls are the writing desk, kiosks are libraries, and the arcade itself – a salon (*The Arcades*, pp. 423–425) in which "the street reveals itself in the arcade as the furnished and familiar interior of the masses" (*The Arcades*, p. 423).

The phantasmagoria of that ambiguous space is perceived, among other things, in the note that the "[a]rcades are houses or passages having no outside – like the dream" (*The Arcades*, p. 406). It is difficult, as has been stressed already by

---

of Paris with glass. That will make for lovely hothouses; we will live in them like melons" (*The Arcades*, p. 56).

7  See: "Glass before its time, premature iron [...]. And today, it is the same with the human material on the inside of the arcades as with the materials of their construction. Pimps are the iron bearings of this street, and its glass breakables are the whores" (*The Arcades*, pp. 873–874).

8  Benjamin gives further details: "Attempt to develop Giedion's thesis: 'In the nineteenth century,' he writes, 'construction plays the role of the subconscious.' Wouldn't it be better to say 'the role of bodily processes' – around which 'artistic' architectures gather, like dreams around the framework of physiological processes?" (*The Arcades*, p. 391).

Baudelaire, to notice entrances to the arcades (see *The Arcades*, p. 60). The internalization of arcades and their luxurious character, given to them by the gas lighting and iron elements of construction, are seen by Benjamin as invested with a prophetic value (the technique, beams and girders, iron construction). The arcades and the magazines within them are the first heralds of department stores whose architectural principle is the possibility of "tak[ing the floors] in, so to speak, 'at a glance'" (*The Arcades*, p. 40).

"God be praised, and my shops too" (*The Arcades*, p. 36) – is a saying ascribed to Louis Philippe. With time, arcades start to put on the character of sacred space[9]. Seeing in them one of the images of a dream house, Benjamin describes their architectural form as "nave with side chapels" (*The Arcades*, p. 37). In another passage he notes:

> The arcade as iron construction stands on the verge of horizontal extension. That is a decisive condition for its 'old-fashioned' appearance. It displays, in this regard, a hybrid character, analogous in certain respects to that of the Baroque church. (*The Arcades*, p. 160)

And, quoting Alfred Gotthold Meyer's work, adds that the analogy is built on the predominance of height over width (see *The Arcades*, p. 160).

> On the other hand, it may be said that something sacral, a vestige of the nave, still attaches to this row of commodities that is the arcade. From a functional point of view, the arcade already occupies the field of horizontal amplitude; architecturally, however, it still stands within the conceptual field of the old "hall". (*The Arcades*, p. 160)

On the other hand there exists a phenomenon with an opposite vector, that is, borrowing elements of style from everyday architecture for sacral one (see *The Arcades*, p. 408). Due to that practice "[t]he dream house of the arcades is encountered again in the church" (*The Arcades*, p. 408). Recalling Baudelaire's concept of "religious intoxication of great cities" Benjamin notes: "the department stores are temples consecrated to this intoxication" (*The Arcades*, p. 61). Needless to say, arcades are the simultaneous embodiment and prefiguration of those "temples of commodity capital" (*The Arcades*, p. 36)[10].

The arcades, seen as internalized, ambiguous, oneiric, and phantasmagoric space, become for Benjamin also the sign of the utopian character of the epoch. That feature is exemplified in the primary assumption of the temporariness of

---

9   Benjamin even quotes a fragment of Joseph Girard's 1801 work which offers the following depiction of an arcade: "is paved in part with funerary stones, on which the Gothic inscriptions and the emblems have not yet been effaced" (*The Arcades*, p. 56).
10  See: "The arcade as temple" (*The Arcades*, p. 406).

the arcades which, as time went on, was replaced with the essentially paradoxical dream of living in the passage.[11]

The arcades, being "centers of commerce in luxury items" (*The Arcades*, p. 15), were seen by the contemporaries as a threshold of the new, better world. They were the object of desire and admiration, as well as an attraction for tourist, with their portents of the new which has already been mentioned: gas lighting, metal construction. In the floral inspiration of the arcades (recalling the thought of "glass houses" or "orangeries") one can perceive humanity's "aspir[ation to] after a purer, more innocent, more spiritual existence than it has been granted" (*The Arcades*, p. 331), a better world, and a better life. Similar impressions are raised with the music in the arcades[12]. The arcades can also be viewed through on other Benjamin's image: the image of a plant owner as a "the factory owner as a quaint figurine in the landscape of machines, dreaming [...] of [...] future greatness" (*The Arcades*, p. 226). The arcades will then appear to be one version of dreams of power – dreams of the greatness, affluence, prestige, as well as permanence, indestructibility, and even the eternity of civilization.

> Balzac was the first to speak of the ruins of the bourgeoisie. [...] The development of the forces of production shattered the wish symbols of the previous century, even before the monuments representing them had collapsed. [...] All these products are on the point of entering the market as commodities. But they linger on the threshold. From this epoch derive the arcades and *intérieurs*, the exhibition halls and panoramas. They are residues of a dream world. (*The Arcades*, p. 13)

The arcades, then, being one of the examples of "dreamed ideals" of the nineteenth century, had been a ruin from the very beginning, from the moment of their coming into existence, long before they started to fall into oblivion. The extract quoted above draws attention with the passage which says that the arcades (among other things) have their origin in the transitory period just before the entry of goods which will become products to the market: they "are on the point of entering" and "linger on the threshold." An arcade as a dialectical image in which time is

---

11  See the remarks on Fourier's utopia: "In the arcades, Fourier recognized the architectural canon of the phalanstery. This is what distinguishes the 'empire' character of his utopia [...]. The arcades, which originally were designed to serve commercial ends, become dwelling places in Fourier" (*The Arcades*, pp. 16–17).
12  See: "Music seems to have settled into these spaces only with their decline [...]. Nevertheless, there was music that conformed to the spirit of the arcades" (*The Arcades*, p. 204).

stopped is revealed as the figure of threshold, of passage[13], and of the prevarication that accompanies a passage. This transitoriness, the structural and functional element of an arcade, becomes important especially in the metaphorical meaning. Benjamin emphasizes:

> [r]emarkable propensity for structures that convey and connect – as, of course, the arcades do. And this connecting and mediating function has a literal and special as well as figurative and stylistic bearing. (*The Arcades*, p. 125)

It was not accidental that the "passage points" placed in front of the entry to the passage are named "penates", a word which initially pertained to the Roman deity taking care of the household, and later to domestic objects and personal belongings.[14] The entry to the passage is the entry to the mythical space of the "dream house":

> At the entrance to the arcade [...]: *penates*. The hen that lays the golden praline-eggs, the machine that stamps our names on nameplates and the other machine that weighs us [...], slot machines, the mechanical fortuneteller – these guard the threshold. They are generally found, it is worth noting, neither on the inside nor truly in the open. They protect and mark the transitions [...]. (*The Arcades*, p. 88)

It is the space of magic, dreaming, it is the crossing of the threshold of the longed-for paradise in which one can taste entertainment but also play with fate with the view of winning a better future or a lottery prize.

---

13 A similar statement was made by Ryszard Różanowski in *Pasaże Waltera Beniamina. Studium myśli* (Wrocław: Wydawnictwo Uniwersytety Wrocławskiego, 1997), p. 97: "the arcade is simultaneously a threshold, passage, and motionlessness", which posits the passage as a crucial term for understanding Benjamin's thought. See p. 42: "The most important figurative device for a description of 19th century, the symbol of modernity, the arcade, is also a passage; as a passage it is a city, or even a world on a small scale, an audience crystalizing in 'dialectic images' of historical movement. The notion of the present, central for Benjamin philosophy of history, is a passage, as is the image of the awakening."

14 See: Pierre Grimal, "Penates," in: *A Concise Dictionary of Classical Mythology*, ed. Stephen Kershaw, trans. A.R. Maxwell-Hyslop (Oxford: Basil Blackwell, 1990), p. 336; "Penaty," in, *Mała encyklopedia kultury antycznej* (Warszawa: PWN, 1988), p. 580; "Penaty," in, *Słownik wyrazów obcych*, ed. Jan Tokarski (Warszawa: PWN, 1972), p. 561 and *Wielki słownik wyrazów obcych*, ed. Mirosław Bańko (Warszawa: PWN, 2003), p. 959 (also here: the information about the etymological relationship between the words 'penaty' ('penates') and 'wnętrze' ('interior'): Latin *penates*, from *penus* 'food reserves', related to *penes* 'inside').

"Penates," as the author writes, "protect [...] the transitions" (*The Arcades*, p. 88). An arcade is as much a passage as a threshold of modernity.

> These gateways – the entrances to the arcades – are thresholds. No stone step serves to mark them. But this marking is accomplished by the expectant posture of the handful of people. Tightly measured paces reflect the fact, altogether unknowingly, that a decision lies ahead. (*The Arcades*, p. 89)

Writing about the "mythological topography of Paris" Benjamin draws attention to "the character given [Paris] by its gates. Important is their duality: border gates and triumphal arches. [...] Out of the field of experience proper to the threshold evolved the gateway that transforms whoever passes under its arch" (*The Arcades*, pp. 86–87). Passing under a gate always means crossing a border – the inner and the outer border. Apart from the most obvious spatial boundary it can also be the boundary of time or, defining it more broadly, of cultural formation, as in the note from 1856, quoted by Benjamin: "[u]ntil the moment you saw the toll collector appear between two columns, you could imagine yourself before the gates of Rome or of Athens" (*The Arcades*, p. 91). The author emphasizes the liminal and sacral[15] character of the triumphal arch, and argues marches through the arch were treated as a "*rite de passage* [...] to which the significance of a rebirth attaches" (*The Arcades*, p. 97). Crossing a threshold or a boundary in physical space appears as a symbolic sign of transformation of identity – of reaching an important stage in the inner journey (of a subject or of a community).

The hardly perceptible, symbolically charged beginning/ending of an arcade – "the threshold of the threshold", "the entrance to the arcade" – becomes a specific abbreviation, a *pars pro toto* of the figure itself, and allegory squared. Benjamin even writes about "the magic of the threshold" which marks the moment of change and sets the border between the past and the future. A doorbell also draws power from that magic; its sound is accompanied by two emotions: "melancholy" when it "heralds departure," or anxiety when it announces that someone is "about to cross the threshold" (*The Arcades*, p. 88). Thus, the doorstep as the figure of the beginning and the end evokes the situations of welcoming and saying goodbye. One of the pictures of leave-taking in the poetic volume of Benjamin's notes is the mailbox: "At the entrance to the arcade, a mailbox: a last opportunity to make some sign to the world one is leaving" (*The Arcades*, p. 88). The threshold, however, may just as well signify "a step into the void":

---

15 Benjamin writes: "Noack mentions that [...] there was operative for the... Romans a conception of the sacred as boundary or threshold" (*The Arcades*, p. 97).

> The city is only apparently homogenous. [...] Nowhere, unless perhaps in dreams, can the phenomenon of the boundary be experienced in a more originary way than in cities. [...] As threshold, the boundary stretches across streets; a new precinct begins like a step into the void – as though one had unexpectedly cleared a low step on a flight of stairs. (*The Arcades*, p. 88)

The future pointed to by – among other things – the arcades, appears as the great unknown, not accidentally described with the help of metaphors of a way and of an interior: "a step in the void", "a low step on a flight of stairs". The exclusive arcades, the showpieces of the upcoming epoch, invite to a saunter which once more unfolds as the inner journey, more dangerous than it at first appears. The stroll turns out to lead downward, toward the darkness, toward the emptiness.

## Looking under the skin. The underground city

Benjamin looks at the arcades from many points of view. He takes into consideration the flow of time which makes him observe them now from the perspective of the time of their birth and stunning career, now from the perspective of their demise or even their fall. The future of so promising constructions turned out to be an ossified ruin. The question how it was possible to ascribe stability to the primarily temporary constructions returns repetitively in the text:

> The first structures made of iron served transitory purposes: covered markets, railroad stations, exhibitions. Iron is thus immediately allied with functional moments in the life of the economy. What was once functional and transitory, however, begins today, at an altered tempo, to seem formal and stable. (*The Arcades*, p. 154)

The sober remarks are juxtaposed with oneiric visions of the epoch which, as dreams of the future, prove to be one of the versions of dreams of power. One example is the description of Charles Fourier's system in which an arcade was to be an "architectural canon of the phalanstery" (*The Arcades*, p. 5)[16], and the phalanx itself was designed as a city made up of arcades (see *The Arcades*, p. 5). This way of seeing the city sometimes assumes the character of a futuristic vision, like in the socialistic dream of Paris in 2000:

> "Once the socialist government had become the legitimate owner of all the houses of Paris, it handed them over to the architects with the order … to establish *street-galleries*.

---

16  Benjamin includes a detailed description from an anthology of Fourier's writings: "The Phalanx has no outside streets or open roadways exposed to the elements. [...] The street-galleries of a Phalanx wind along just one side of the central edifice and stretch to the end of each of its wings" (*The Arcades*, p. 44).

> ... [The street-galleries] constitute[d] a network ... embracing the whole city. [...] a person could stroll through the entire city without ever being exposed to the elements. ... As soon as the Parisians had got a taste of the new galleries, they lost all desire to set foot in the streets of old – which, they often said, were fit only for dogs." Tony Moilin, *Paris en l'an 2000*, (Paris 1869), pp. 9–11. (*The Arcades*, p. 53)

The image of Paris as a city of arcades, drawn in the quoted extract, is a quintessence of oneiric illusoriness, of a communal vision. It is also the most distinct, because literal, realization of the metaphor of Paris as the inner house.

The author of *The Arcades Project* offers a different, non-naïve perspective on the Parisian interior. He proposes looking under the surface, and one of the fragments quoted by Benjamin seems to hold the key to that outlook:

> The beauty of the body is only skin-deep. For if, like the legendary lynx of Boeotia, men were to see what lies beneath the skin, they would recoil with disgust at the sight of a woman. That well-known charm is nothing but mucus and blood, humors and bile. Just stop to consider what is hidden away in the nostrils, the throat, or the belly: everywhere filth. And if, in fact, we shrink from touching mucus or dung with even the tip of our finger, how could we ever wish to embrace the sack of excrements itself? (*The Arcades*, p. 402)

That emphatic excerpt on looking at the inside of the body can be seen in relationship to the viewpoint of sharp-seeing Benjamin, the more so as in *The Arcades Project* the writer frequently recalls Baudelaire's vision of Paris in which the image of a woman merges with the image of death. The quotation also finds its ironic completion in the anthroponymic perception of Paris in which the city is compared with human body. Such process can be found, for example, in projects made by Barthélemy Enfantin "who developed plans for the city of the future with the aid of the anatomical charts" (*The Arcades*, p. 398). Enfantin's idea found a continuation in Saint-Simonists' schemes:

> We wanted to give a human form to the first city inspired by our faith. [...] It is there that the head of my city will repose. ... The palaces of your kings will be its brow [...]. From the top of that head I will sweep away the old Christian temple, ... and in this clearing I will arrange a headdress of trees. ... Above the breast of my city, in that sympathetic foyer where the passions all diverge and come together, where sorrows and joys vibrate, I will build my temple, ... solar plexus of the giant. [...] My city is in the posture of a man about to set off. (*The Arcades*, p. 398)

Similarly, it was not by accident that Benjamin placed Paul Valéry's thought in the notes devoted to the city of dreams:

> Man is himself, is man, only at the surface. Lift the skin, dissect: here begin the machines. It is then you lose yourself in an inexplicable substance, something alien to everything you know, and which is nonetheless the essential. (*The Arcades*, p. 404)

Inner Paris manifests itself also as the underground city. The image is not unambiguous. For example, it includes wine cellars which form "as it were, a city in which the streets bear the names of the most important wine regions of France" (*The Arcades*, p. 91). For the most part, however, the space is not high-class, it is primitive, and the substance of the description of the "preponderance of [...] underground passages" is well phrased in Roger Caillois's expression: "*roman noir*" (see *The Arcades*, pp. 97–98).[17] Benjamin is inspired with a dream to:

> construct the city topographically – tenfold and a hundredfold – from out of its arcades and its gateways, its cemeteries and bordellos, its railroad stations and its …, just as formerly it was defined by its churches and its markets. And the more secret, more deeply embedded figures of the city: murders and rebellions, the bloody knots in the network of the streets, lairs of love, and conflagrations. (*The Arcades*, p. 83)

Indeed, "few things in the history of humanity are as well known as the history of Paris" (*The Arcades*, p. 82). Benjamin tracks "topographic traces of the prehistoric: the old bed of the Seine. The subterranean waterways. The catacombs. Legends of subterranean Paris." (*The Arcades*, p. 895)[18]. To that list one may add: quarries, dungeons, cemeteries – all analyzed by the author in other parts of the text. The meaning of the discovery and understanding of Parisian underground is highlighted by the comparison to Vesuvius, both as the allegory of revolution and as the allegory of the unconscious:

> "There is nothing on the surface of the earth that was not once subterranean (water, earth, fire). Nothing in the intellect that has not been digested and circulated in the depths." (Dr. Pierre Mabille, "Préface à l'*Eloge des préjugés populaires*"). (*The Arcades*, p. 397)

The way to the interior opens at night:

> One knew of places in ancient Greece where the way led down into the underworld. Our waking existence likewise is a land which, at certain hidden points, leads down into the underworld – a land full of inconspicuous places from which dreams arise. [...] By day, the labyrinth of urban dwellings resembles consciousness; the arcades (which are galleries leading into the city's past) issue unremarked onto the streets. At night, however [...] their denser darkness protrudes like a threat. (*The Arcades*, p. 84)

---

17  See: Roger Caillois, "Paris, a Modern Myth," trans. Camille Naish, in: *The Edge of Surrealism: A Roger Caillois Reader*, ed. Claudia Frank (Durham, NC: Duke University Press, 2003), p. 189.
18  Here it is worth noting again the ambiguity of the arcades: the corridors of underground Paris constitute the reverse of the overground arcades, but the arcades themselves are compared with underwater landscape and so become subterranean (see *The Arcades*, p. 10).

Parallel to that overground net of streets is the underground labyrinth: the underground whose corridors are described by Benjamin as "misshapen sewer gods" or "catacomb fairies" (*The Arcades*, p. 84), and the underground itself becomes a metaphor of hell, of medieval genealogy:

> Paris is built over a system of caverns from which the din of Métro and railroad mounts to the surface, and in which every passing omnibus or track sets up a prolonged echo. And this great technological system of tunnels and thoroughfares interconnects with the ancient vaults, the limestone quarries, the grottoes and catacombs which, since the early Middle Ages, have time and again been reentered and traversed. Even today, for the price of two francs, one can buy a ticket of admission to this most nocturnal Paris, so much less expensive and less hazardous than the Paris of the upper world. The Middle Ages saw it differently. [...] there were clever persons who, now and again [...] undertook to guide their fellow citizens underground and show them the Devil in his infernal majesty. (*The Arcades*, p. 85)

The underground was a condemned space also in the literal meaning of the legend-enwrapped prison whose dungeons formed complicated galleries divided into streets (see *The Arcades*, p. 89). A shocking description of those dungeons was left by Victor Hugo in *Les Misérables* where the darkness of The Grand Châtelet was compared to a tomb-hell (see *The Arcades*, p. 93). Hugo also recalls that Paris of canals used to be called "the Stink-Hole" (*The Arcades*, p. 412) which is just a small step from calling the capital of Paris "a sewer and the emptying pot of all sewers" (*The Arcades*, p. 98).

## The city of ruins

Among Benjamin's notes there is the following Marcel Proust's thought: "a mere excursion does not suffice for a visit to the dead city – excavation is necessary also" (*The Arcades*, p. 404). The quotation is an excellent comment on the vision of Paris sketched above. A sewer, a hell, a tomb – it is a vision of a city infected with death. It is close to Baudelaire's vision, although Baudelaire's socially conditioned diagnosis lacks a natural basis:

> The Paris of his poems is a sunken city, and more submarine than subterranean. It is the city of a death-fraught idyll. Yet the substrate of this idyll is nothing natural, and consists in neither the subterranean channels of Paris nor its catacombs and the legends that have grown up around them. It is, rather, a social, and that is to say, a modern substrate. But precisely the modern, *la modernité*, is always citing primal history. Here, this occurs through the ambiguity peculiar to the social relations and products of this epoch. The twilight of the arcades, which contemporaries compared to an undersea landscape, lies over the society that built them. (*The Arcades*, p. 896; see also *The Arcades*, p. 10)

Viewed by Benjamin, Paris appears as the space of social experience which is lived through as an inner personal experience. The city functions as, simultaneously, a metonymy and a personification of the nascent modern civilization whose greatness is a pretence, and whose marginality and destitution are pushed beyond the border of consciousness, and also –literally – under the ground.

What is unwanted is also sometimes removed mechanically, destroyed methodically so that the ground is prepared for the desired 'new,' as in the case of the enormous amount of demolitions made in the nineteenth-century Paris, which had turned to dust many an ancient building, and even the whole alleys, streets, or districts, before they forever changed the appearance of the city which had been formed through centuries. In the words of the contemporaries (including Hugo) Paris – "the capital of the nineteenth century" looked like a city of ruins at that time. In the ruins one can see the ruins of the old world which was becoming the past. However, one can also see them – and this vision seems to be an equally, if not more justified – as the ruins of the nascent modernity built on the debris. Modernity itself can be viewed as a ruin[19] – as a form infected with death from its very birthday.

The demolitions did not encompass everything: "[l]et the old houses collapse, so long as the old monuments remain" (*The Arcades*, p. 126). That remark contains a trace of the attitude of modernity toward antiquity[20] – antiquity was to be a point of reference for the new. The novelty loving formation sought a foundation and ennoblement at the sources of culture, in the myths of its youth, through which process, however, the "new" inevitably turned out to be "eternally the same." That is the reason why so many nineteenth-century notes include comparisons with

---

19  A ruin can – looking at the subject from a broader perspective – be treated as a central figure for Benjamin's understanding of history. See the famous remark about the Angel of History: "Where a chain of events appears before *us, he* sees one single catastrophe, which keeps piling wreckage upon wreckage and hurls it at his feet" ("On the Concept of History," in: *Selected Writings*, vol. 4, p. 392). See also Różanowski, *Pasaże Waltera Beniamina*, p. 12.

20  See Różanowski, *Pasaże Waltera Beniamina*, p. 85: "When Christianity took advantage of classical antiquity, in order to destroy the pagan world, the paradoxical and undesired outcome was that antiquity was saved. Thus, antiquity is treated as an antithesis of Christianity, but the antithesis itself becomes one of the most influential elements of modern culture."

the antiquity: descriptions of gates, taverns[21], and even beggars on the streets[22]. Benjamin notes that

> the modern, with Baudelaire, appear not only as the signature of an epoch but as an energy by which this epoch immediately transforms and appropriates antiquity. Among all the relations into which modernity enters, its relation to antiquity is critical. (*The Arcades*, p. 236)

Attempting "to give a form to modernity" is compared by the author to "the task of the ancient hero" (*The Arcades*, p. 322). Finally, Benjamin states that "with Baudelaire, modernity is nothing other than the 'newest antiquity'" (*The Arcades*, p. 336). The following comment on Baudelaire's works seems to build an important context for these reflections:

> But to become obsolete means: to grow strange. Spleen lays down centuries between the present moment and the one just lived. It is spleen that tirelessly generates 'antiquity'. And in fact, with Baudelaire, modernity is nothing other than the 'newest antiquity'. Modernity, for Baudelaire, is not solely and not primarily the object of his sensibility; it is the object of a conquest. Modernity has, for its armature, the allegorical mode of vision. (*The Arcades*, p. 336)

The common denominator for this analogy seems to be an outlook in which the old culture, homely and familiar, appears at the same time to be distant and foreign due to the lapse of time, which creates a play of closeness and distance, specific to the distant attitude, and even to the estrangement of a modern inhabitant from the space he or she no longer identifies with.

The key to the understanding of the attitude of modernity toward antiquity are the ideas of time[23] and of greatness. In the modern phantasmagorias antiquity

---

21 See also the quotation from Hugo: "The wine shops of the Faubourg Antoine resemble those taverns on Mount Aventine, above the Sibyl's cave" (*The Arcades*, p. 92).

22 Among the notes Benjamin makes in reference to the topic is Charles Péguy's note: "Rest assured that when Hugo saw a beggar on the road, … he saw him for what he is, for what he really is in reality: the ancient mendicant, the ancient supplicant, … on the ancient road" (*The Arcades*, p. 92). See also the note on Baudelaire who "[i]n the guise of a beggar […] continually put the model of bourgeois society to the test" (*The Arcades*, p. 338).

23 See: "The figure of the 'modern' and that of 'allegory' must be brought into relation with each other: 'Woe unto him who seeks in antiquity anything other than pure art, logic, and general method! By plunging too deeply into the past, … he renounces the … privileges provided by circumstances; for almost all our originality comes from the stamp that *time* imprints upon our feelings <*sensations*>.' Baudelaire, *L'Art romantique* (Paris), p. 72 ('Le Peintre de la vie moderne'). But the privilege of which Baudelaire

functions as an allegory of dreams about greatness and immortality (lasting forever in culture and through culture), and the allegory helps dismiss the recollection of the inevitability of the passing of time. Paradoxically, however, "[i]t is in transitoriness that modernity shows itself to be ultimately and most intimately akin to antiquity" (*The Arcades*, p. 332). The essence of the modern reception of antiquity can be caught through a look at the role of mirrors in the construction of an arcade:

> doors and walls are made of mirrors, there is no telling outside from in, with all the equivocal illumination. Paris is a city of mirrors. […] Let two mirrors reflect each other; then Satan plays his favorite trick and opens here in his way (as his partner does in lovers' gazes) the perspective on infinity. […] In the arcades, the perspective is lastingly preserved as in the nave of a church. […] Ambiguity of the arcades as an ambiguity of *space*. […] The outermost, merely quite peripheral aspect of the ambiguity of the arcades is provided by their abundance of mirrors, which fabulously amplifies the spaces and makes orientation more difficult. […] The space that transforms itself does so in the bosom of nothingness. (*The Arcades*, pp. 877–878)

The space becomes the image of halted time which seems to extend endlessly into the great past and the dreamed-of future. In this perspective, antiquity surfaces as a projection of the desire for eternity. The pride of the civilization which wants to be confirmed in its illusions of its own uniqueness examines itself in the reflected mirages of Parisian arcades. However, the mirrors lie. Their reflections are unfaithful, and the game is lined with irony: greatness (of splendor, luxury, prestige) finds a reflection in mediocrity and in destitution, while death looks eternity in the eye and laughs at modern hopes, dreams, and fears.

The tunnel of mirrors is a paradoxical road to self-knowledge also through its fragility. It is not by accident that "the infirmity and decrepitude of a great city" (*The Arcades*, p. 332), present in Baudelaire's poetry, is chosen to be an illustration of modern civilization described by the poet as half transitory, half eternal (see *The Arcades*, p. 234). The fragility of the city in its literal meaning was made obvious with the ruins which raised fears of continuing demolitions and, in a broader sense, of the fall of the city. The fears were a smokescreen for the fear of changes and, as Benjamin aptly noted, they testified to "the fact that technology was not accepted" (*The Arcades*, p. 97) and proved the awareness that "along with the great cities have evolved the means to raze them to the ground" (*The Arcades*, p. 97).

---

speaks also comes into force, in a mediated way, vis-à-vis antiquity: the stamp of time that imprints itself on antiquity presses out of it the allegorical configuration" (*The Arcades*, p. 239). See also: "The key to the emancipation from antiquity – which (see in the Guys essay, *L'Art romantique*, p. 72) can furnish only the canon of composition – is for Baudelaire allegorese" (*The Arcades*, p. 240).

Fantasies about the fall of Paris sometimes reached the very foundations of the urban space they occupied; they were a version of pictures of nature, like in one of the notes quoted by the author: "[t]his recently deposited limestone – the bed on which Paris rests – readily crumbles into a dust" (*The Arcades*, p. 107). However, it was not the only sign of the end: the next one is the illness resulting from the dust floating around, and finally "the unprepossessing bleached gray of the houses, which are all built from brittle limestone mined near Paris" (*The Arcades*, p. 108).

The vision of the fall of the city, however, would be incomplete, if the images of ruins – even those resulting from the demolitions – were not compared to ancient ruins: "In a long series of classical writers from Polybius onward, we read of old, renowned cities in which the streets have become lines of empty, crumbling shells" (*The Arcades*, p. 100). The excerpt was taken by Benjamin from Oswald Spengler's significantly titled *Le Déclin de l'Occident*. The decline of the western civilization, whose symbolical expression is the fall of the city, is sometimes described in more dramatic terms:

> Léon Daudet on the view of Paris from Sacré Coeur. 'From high up you can see this population of palaces, monuments, houses, and hovels, which seem to have gathered in expectation of some cataclysm, or of several cataclysms – meteorological, perhaps, or social. ... [...] at a certain moment I heard in myself something like a tocsin, a strange admonition, and I saw these three magnificent cities ... threatened with collapse, with devastation by fire and flood, with carnage, with rapid erosion [...]. At other times, I saw them preyed upon by an obscure, subterranean evil, which undermined the monuments and neighborhoods, causing entire sections of the proudest homes to crumble. ... From the standpoint of these promontories, what appears most clearly is the menace. [...] Hence, [...] what astounds us is that Paris, Lyons, and Marseilles have endured. (*The Arcades*, p. 100)

In the quoted passage the reader is struck with the multiplicity of images of decline: a cataclysm, bells tolling, a threat of a ruin, damages, massacres, dying, a hidden disease consuming the body of the city; similarly prominent is the emphasis on their twofold origins: the natural (floods, fires) and the social one. Besides, in the end the former root turns out to only be a mask for the latter. The dangers awaiting the city and the death of its architecture are described in Victor Hugo's *A Bird's-eye View of Paris*[24].

While the journey through the Parisian *inferno* makes possible the discovery of the secrets of the underground city, the "demolitions reveal the mysteries of the upper world of Paris" (*The Arcades*, p. 98). In his work, Benjamin quotes Victor

---

24 See *The Arcades*, p. 164. Also, compare with the fragments of Victor Hugo's *À l'arc de triomphe* (*The Arcades*, pp. 93–95).

Fournel, the author of the book *Paris nouveau et Paris futur* (1868) which, in the chapter on the ruins of contemporary Paris, points to the causes and consequences of Haussmann's demolitions:

> Modern Paris is a parvenu that goes back no further in time than its own beginnings, and that razes the old palaces and old churches to build in their place beautiful white houses with stucco ornaments and pasteboard statues. In the previous century, to write the annals of the monuments of Paris was to write the annals of Paris itself, from its origins up through each of its epochs; soon, however, it will be … merely to write the annals of the last twenty years o four own existence. (*The Arcades*, p. 146)

It seems that Fournel managed to describe an essential feature of modernity which wanted to be "the only point of reference" for itself. The city which "razes to the ground" old churches destroys its vertical axis that had been pointing to another dimension, and renounces the sacred space. At the same time, the city continues to grow and becomes "a cosmopolitan crossroads" (*The Arcades*, p. 129):

> The centralization, the megalomania, created an artificial city, in which the Parisian […] no longer feels at home. […] The Parisian, in his own town, which has become a cosmopolitan crossroads, now seems like one deracinated. (*The Arcades*, p. 129)

The inhabitant of Paris becomes a figure of a modern man: an uprooted denizen of a big city who experiences emptiness, alienation, and loneliness in a crowd of strangers. Benjamin assumes impotence to be the key figure of loneliness in Baudelaire's works[25]; he also writes about the social basis for the poet's conviction of the "the unavoidable necessity of prostitution for the poet" (*The Arcades*, p. 337):

> in view of the limited success of his work, Baudelaire more and more threw himself into the bargain. He flung himself after his work, and thus, to the end, confirmed with his own person what he had said about the unavoidable necessity of prostitution to the poet. (*The Arcades*, p. 337)

Impotence and prostitution, in other words: incapability and sale, pertain to the very foundations of life: to love, creativity, passion, man's attitude toward other things and himself. The meaning of the two figures is explained with another one: "The whore is the most precious booty in the triumph of allegory – the life which signifies death" (*The Arcades*, p. 336). Life which means death: this accurate formula synthetically describes much more than the phenomenon of prostitution in modern Parisian arcades. Mourning alive: this is the state which defines the situation of the capital of the nineteenth century: "The new dreariness and

---

25 See: "Impotence is the key figure of Baudelaire's solitude. An abyss divides him from his fellow men. It is *this* abyss of which his poetry speaks" (*The Arcades*, p. 337).

desolation of Paris [...] comes on the scene together with the dreariness of men's attire, as an essential moment in the image of modernity" (*The Arcades*, p. 335). A similar statement is made in Benjamin's note on "Allegorical interpretation of modern clothing for men, in the *Salon de 1846*" (*The Arcades*, p. 285):

> As for the garb, the outer husk, of the modern hero, ... is it not the necessary garb of our suffering age, which wears the symbol of perpetual morning even on its thin black shoulders? [...] We are all of us celebrating some funeral. (*The Arcades*, p. 285)

"We are all of us celebrating some funeral" (*The Arcades*, p. 285). Life at the cemetery, life which bemoans a loss, life which is death – all these meanings are contained in the allegorical picture of Paris as a city of ruins.

## Melancholy and Death

In this context, Benjamin's attention to allegory[26] comes as less than a surprise. In allegory, the author of *The Arcades Project* saw a figure which "views existence, as it does art, under the sign of fragmentation and ruin" (*The Arcades*, p. 380), and which is characterized by "the renunciation of the idea of harmonious totality" (*The Arcades*, p. 380). Allegory must have seemed the most adequate means for the description of the nineteenth century which had lost the concept of the city (world) as a whole (see e.g. *The Arcades*, p. 148). Repeatedly recalling Baudelaire's vision of Paris, at a certain point Benjamin summons the figure of the poet himself and, trying to understand "the Golgotha-way of impotence trod by Baudelaire" (*The Arcades*, p. 334) the author of *Les fleurs du mal*, employs "the coin of allegory, with the scythe-wielding skeleton on one side, and, on the obverse, the figure of Melancholy plunged in meditation" (*The Arcades*, p. 334). Skeleton and Melancholy: it seems that the picture of this inseparable couple is an accurate image of not only Baudelaire's problem but also the problem of his city. Dying and death, disintegration, and old age touching man as well as the products of his culture are recurring motifs in Benjamin's work, along with pictures of melancholy. In one of the passages the motifs appear in a condensed and multiplied manner. The passage the more interesting as it describes the birth of an idea of writing a book about a dying city:

---

26  As regards this topic see, among others: Grzegorz Dziamski, "Rehabilitacja alegorii. Baudelairowski motyw w refleksji nad sztuką współczesną," in: *"Drobne rysy w ciągłej katastrofie". Obecność Waltera Benjamina w kulturze współczesnej*, ed. Anna Zeidler-Janiszewska (Warszawa: Wydawnictwo Instytutu Kultury, 1993) oraz Michał Głowiński, "O kilku motywach u Benjamina," *Literatura*, No. 41 (1975).

It was, for the writer, one of those moments when a man who is about to leave youth behind thinks of life with a resigned gravity that leads him to find in all things the image of his own melancholy. The minor physiological decline which his visits to the optician had just confirmed put him in mind of what is so quickly forgotten: that law of inevitable destruction which governs everything human. ... Suddenly, he began [...] to envision a day when this town, too, [...] would itself be dead, as so many capitals of so many empires were dead. The idea came to him that it would be extraordinarily interesting for us to have an exact and complete picture of an Athens at the time of Perides, of a Carthage at the time of Barca, of an Alexandria at the time of Ptolemies, of a Rome at the time of the Ceasars. ... By one of those keen intuitions he clearly perceived the possibility of writing about Paris this book which the historians of antiquity had failed to write about their towns. (*The Arcades*, p. 91)

The gradual loss of sight as old age approached made Maxime Du Camp[27] see in a different, deeper way: the glimmer of intuition allowed his melancholy look to embrace the pictures of not only his own biography but also of the biography of the city. The eye disease, consciously accepted as the symptom of aging and of the probably near end of life, facilitated the discovery of Paris as a space which also undergoes the process of aging and death. "[T]his town [...] would itself be dead" (*The Arcades*, p. 90), and the signs of the dissolution can already be perceived by the person who knows how to look; this city has started dying – Benjamin concretizes.

In the writer's notes, the images of melancholy return with greater frequency when he describes the arcades. For example, during the reading of August Strindberg's *The Pilot's Trials*, the attention of the author of *The Arcades Project* is caught by the "unfathomability of the moribund arcades" (*The Arcades*, p. 205), and in the shell shop in the arcades, described in the story, Benjamin notices "[e]xtinct nature" (*The Arcades*, p. 205). The shell, as an outer and beautiful but dead form in which once life thrived, becomes the sign of death, emptiness, and stagnation, corresponding with the thought-provoking absence of any sort of people – customers, owners, passers-by – from the arcades. The theme of "the death of the Paris arcades", seen as "the decay of a type of architecture" (*The Arcades*, p. 204), is also brought about by the reflection on Émile Zola's *Thérèse Raquin*. The semidarkness prevalent in the streets-galleries, which Benjamin associates with "submarine landscape", is yet another symbol of demise: "the gloomy light" (*The Arcades*, p. 204), fragility of construction, dummies' heads substituting for real people, the

---

[27] Maxime Du Camp, the author of a monumental work on Paris (*Paris, ses organes, fonctions et sa vie dans la seconde moitié du XIXème siècle*, 6 vol., [Paris: Hachette, 1893–1896]), was the hero of the story told above.

symbolic sale (betrayal) of fossilized figures, are all elements which frequently occur together in the text of *The Arcades Project*:

> Often these inner spaces harbor antiquated trades, and even those that are thoroughly up to date will acquire in them something obsolete. They are the site of information bureaus and detective agencies, which there, in the gloomy light of the upper galleries, follow the trail of the past. In hairdressers' windows, you can see the last women with long hair. […] they have been betrayed and sold, and the head of Salome made into an ornament […]. And while these things are petrified, the masonry of the walls above has become brittle. Brittle, too, are ▪ mirrors ▪. (*The Arcades*, p. 204)

The arcades are here seen as a fossil, fragile like a mirror, in which modernity – having fallen into lethargy – reflects itself. "The arcades are dying" (*The Arcades*, p. 121). In one of his notes Benjamin laconically enumerates the "[r]easons for the decline of the arcades: widened sidewalks, electric light, ban on prostitution, culture of the open air" (*The Arcades*, p. 88). Immediately after that, he interprets those direct causes. The stuffiness of the arcades gains the status of a symbol of confinement, lifelessness, death through suffocation:

> "In Paris … they are fleeing the arcades, so long in fashion, as one flees stale air. The arcades are dying. From time to time, one of them is closed, like the sad Passage Delorme, where, in the wilderness of the gallery, female figures of a tawdry antiquity used to dance along the shopfronts, as in the scenes from Pompeii interpreted by Guerinon Hersent. […] The arcades have one great defect for the Parisians: you could say that, just like certain paintings done from stifled perspectives, they're in need of air." Jules Claretie, *La Vie à Paris, 1895*, (Paris, 1896), pp. 47ff. (*The Arcades*, p. 121)

Attention should be paid to the comparison of arcades with panoramas. Max Brod's remark ("[i]nteriors of churches, or of palaces or art galleries, do not make for beautiful panorama images. They come across as flat, dead, obstructed" – *The Arcades*, p. 124) is met with the following comment from Benjamin: "[a]n accurate description, except that it is precisely in this way that the panoramas serve the epoch's will to expression" (*The Arcades*, p. 124). "Paris is musty and close" (*The Arcades*, 122), Paris is suffocating (see *The Arcades*, p. 101), and the lack of air also becomes a sign of the epoch of despotism, pomp, and hurry. After the Restoration the European situation was as stated below:

> Typically, Corynthian columns are used almost everywhere. … This pomp has something oppressive about it, just as the restless bustle accompanying the city's transformation robs native and foreigners alike of both breathing space and space for reflection. … Every stone bears the mark of despotic power, and all the ostentation makes the atmosphere, in the literal sense of the words, heavy and close. … One grows dizzy with this novel display; one chokes and anxiously gasps for breath. The feverish haste with which the work of several centuries is accomplished in a decade weighs on the senses. (*The Arcades*, p. 125)

The new, proudly entering and expected to be a symbol of luxury and good taste, very soon turned out to be second-rate:

> The arcade that for the Parisians was a sort of salon-walk, where you strolled and smoked and chatted, is now nothing more than a species of refuge which you think of when it rains. Some of the arcades maintain a certain attraction on account of this or that famed establishment still to be found there. (Jules Claretie's words, *The Arcades*, p. 121)

The transformation of the drawing-room into a shelter-house is a picture of degeneration, of sinking into destitution and oblivion, of shifting from the center to the margin. All these melancholy pictures – of death, ruin, demise – describe the streets which quite recently have been considered to be symbols of greatness, luxury, splendor, and fashion. In this way, Benjamin's reflection on the aging of allegory is confirmed: "[a]llegories become dated because it is part of their nature to shock" (*The Arcades*, p. 325). The repeated use of vanitas, funereal, and elegiac motifs is intended to awaken from the nineteenth century: "Baudelaire's allegory bears traces of the violence that was necessary to demolish the harmonious façade of the world that surrounded him" (*The Arcades*, p. 329). It seems that while writing about Baudelaire's allegory Benjamin describes his own views:

> That which the allegorical intention has fixed upon is sundered from the customary contexts of life: it is at once shattered and preserved. Allegory holds fast to the ruins. Baudelaire's destructive impulse is nowhere concerned with the abolition of what it falls to. (*The Arcades*, p. 329)

In another place Benjamin specifies: "allegory has to do […] with dispelling […] illusion" (*The Arcades*, p. 331). One of the pretences is bestowing the value of eternity on transitory objects. In a fragment of the volume the author, quoting Edgar Allan Poe's work, recalls the character of Charles Meryon, a Parisian etcher "whose work gives us the sensation of persistent nostalgia." His pictures:

> seem to be the image, despite being drawn directly from life, of things that are finished, that are dead or about to die. […] There was something of the visionary in Meryon, and he undoubtedly divined that these rigid and unyielding forms were ephemeral […]. [H] is evocative poetry […] radiates eternal melancholy through the vision of immediate appearances. (*The Arcades*, p. 96)

Also in this fragment Melancholy meets Death, and the dream of eternal life is tainted with the (un)consciousness of death: the stiffness of forms designed to mask the truth about their transience, fleetingness, impermanence, turns out to be cadaverous rigidity. Progress, forward movement, leaning toward the future, everything that falls under the description of programmatic progressiveness and the dynamism of modernity – all these are put under suspicion. Benjamin asks rhetorically about the progress of the world which is dying or maybe already has died, only that fact has not been brought to consciousness yet. "What good is talk of progress to a world sinking into rigor mortis? Baudelaire found the experience of such a world set down with incomparable power in the work of Poe" (*The Arcades*, pp. 233–234). The arcades which are a (market) street pretending to be a (public) house, with no movement going on within them, emerge as a metonymy of a world immobilized and stagnant, palsied with agony. A saunter through the interiors of Parisian arcades, a stroll along the streets of the dead city may turn out to be a walk among cadavers:

> "Those who have traveled in Sicily will remember the celebrated convent where, as a result of the earth's capacity for drying and preserving bodies, the monks at a certain time of year can deck out in their ancient regalia all the grandees to whom they have accorded the hospitality of the grave [after which] they allow the public to pass between these rows of skeletons. … Well, this Sicilian convent gives us an image of our society. Under the pompous garb that adorns our art and literature, no heart beats – there are only dead men, who gaze at you with staring eyes, lusterless and cold, when you ask the century where the inspiration is, where the arts, where the literature." (Alfred Nettement's words, *The Arcades*, p. 92)

Once more, Paris looms as a graveyard space: a corpse-conserving, gigantic sepulcher:

> the cemeteries of Paris, these three other cities within the larger one – cities smaller in appearance than the city of the living, which seems to contain them, but in reality how much more populous, with their closely packed little compartments arranged in tiers under the ground. (François Porché's words, *The Arcades*, p. 99)

The special aspect, however, seems to be less important than the symbolical meaning: the Parisian cemetery is an inner city not only in the architectural or urban-planning sense – it is Paris that is a cemetery, a city of the dead, and a dead city, the capital of the nascent, modern Europe which reveals its cadaverous face. To the face one can apply the note about Chodruc-Duclos: "[w]e are haunted with what was perhaps the remains of some rugged old citizen of Herculaneum who, having escaped from his underground bed, returned to walk again among us […] living in the midst of death" (*The Arcades*, p. 109).

Benjamin's recognition that "[b]aroque allegory sees the corpse only from the outside; Baudelaire evokes it from within" (*The Arcades*, p. 329) can obviously be applied to himself as well, as the stunning kaleidoscope of images of modern Paris, which emerges from the book, is in large part but anatomic pathology which serves to unmask pretence.

## "To turn the lining of time to the outside"

The death-marked illusions of modernity are one of the keys to the understanding of the epoch, so Benjamin's Paris, built of a thousand of notes, extracts, and author's comments, reveals itself before the reader as a phantasmagoric city. "The world dominated by its phantasmagorias – this, to make use of Baudelaire's term, is 'modernity'" (*The Arcades*, p. 26). Modern Paris is also infernal Paris because modernity is "the time of hell" (*The Arcades*, p. 544) in which "[t]he punishments of hell are always the newest thing going in this domain" and which "never alters" (*The Arcades*, p. 544). Modernity assumes its phantasmagoric character as it is raised to the rank of the absolute and considered to be a value in itself. One example Benjamin gives is:

> [the fact that culture] is marked with the fatality of being one day antiquity, and it reveals this to whoever witnesses its birth. Here we meet the quintessence of the unforeseen, which for Baudelaire is an inalienable quality of the beautiful. The face of modernity itself blasts us with its immemorial gaze. Such was the gaze of Medusa for the Greeks. (*The Arcades*, pp. 22–23)

The Paris of arcades is gone – there is no longer the gas-lit aura of passage between what has been and what is approaching, i.e. modernity which has foretold its own demise at the time of its birth. The Paris of arcades is gone, and the arcades themselves have become "an ideal panorama of a barely elapsed primeval age" (*The Arcades*, p. 874) "a past become space" (*The Arcades*, p. 871):

> All this is the arcade in our eyes. And it was nothing of all this. [...] It was not decline but transformation. All at once, they were the hollow mold from which the image of "modernity" was cast. Here, the century mirrored with satisfaction its most recent past. (*The Arcades*, p. 874)[28]

For a *flâneur*, entering an arcade is like entering a "through a vanished time [...] if not to the mythical mothers, then into the past" (The Arcades, pp. 879–880), the past of the youthful age or even of the childhood of his ancestors. Entering an arcade is like falling asleep:

---

28 See the extract of Louis Aragon's *Le Paysan de Paris*, quoted in *The Arcades Project*: "It is only today, when the pickaxe menaces them, that they have at last become the true sanctuaries of a cult of the ephemeral, the ghostly landscape of damnable pleasures and professions. Places that yesterday were incomprehensible, and that tomorrow will never know" (*The Arcades*, p. 87).

"It is the obscurely rising dream of northerly streets in a big city [...]. The streets grow narrow and the houses right and left draw closer together; ultimately it becomes an arcade with grimy shop windows, a gallery of glass. To the right and left: Are those dirty bistros, with waitresses lurking in black-and-white silk blouses? It stinks of cheap wine. Or is it the garish vestibule of a bordello?" (Franz Hessel's words, *The Arcades*, p. 87)

Therefore, telling about the arcades is like telling one's dreams:

> Boredom is a warm gray fabric lined on the inside with the most lustrous and colorful of silks. In this fabric we wrap ourselves when we dream. We are at home then in the arabesque of its lining. But the sleeper looks bored and gray in his sheath. And when he later wakes and wants to tell of what he dreamed, he communicates, by and large, only his boredom. For who would be able at one stroke to turn the lining of time to the outside? Yet to narrate dreams signifies nothing else. And in no other way can one deal with the arcades – structures in which we relive, as in a dream, the life of our parents and grandparents, as the embryo in the womb relives the life of animals. (*The Arcades*, p. 881)

The aim of Benjamin's stroll through Parisian arcades is the telling of the story about the pictures of the "dream- and wish-image of the collective" (*The Arcades*, p. 905) so that he can experience wakefulness through the shock of awakening:

> Every epoch, in fact, not only dreams the one to follow but, in dreaming, precipitates its awakening. It bears its end within itself and unfolds it [...] by cunning. With the destabilizing of the market economy, we begin to recognize the monuments of the bourgeoisie as ruins even before they have crumbled. (*The Arcades*, p. 13)

In his passion of preserving the "ruins of ruins" Benjamin renounces the attitude of a conservator who glues together what has been broken, and assumes the stance of a romantic who desires to discover the face of the epoch in the cracks of the "cracking wall":

> What are phenomena rescued from? Not only, and not in the main, from the discredit and neglect into which they have fallen, but from the catastrophe represented very often by a certain strain in their dissemination, their 'enshrinement as heritage'. – They are saved through the exhibition of the fissure within them. – There is a tradition that is catastrophe. (*The Arcades*, p. 473)

Thanks to that, while remembering the phantasmagoric greatness of the arcades and displaying the history of their transformation, Benjamin manages to preserve the sense of their existence through revealing the inner split inscribed in their very structure ("construction"). The split, when interpreted, is deprived of the mythical power over the present. In other words, it enables the awakening from the nineteenth century.

## Bibliography

1. Walter Benjamin, "On the Concept of History," in: *Selected Writings*, ed. Michael W. Jennings and Marcus Bullock, Howard Eiland, Gary Smith, vol. IV (Cambridge, MA: Belknap Press of Harvard University Press, 2003).
2. Walter Benjamin, *The Arcades Project*, trans. Howard Eiland and Kevin McLaughlin, prepared on the basis of the German volume edited by Rolf Tiedman (Cambridge Mass.: The Belknap Press of Harvard University Press, 1999).
3. Roger Caillois, "Paris, a Modern Myth," trans. Camille Naish, in: *The Edge of Surrealism: A Roger Caillois Reader*, ed. Claudia Frank (Durham, NC: Duke University Press, 2003).
4. Maxime Du Camp, *Paris, ses organes, fonctions et sa vie dans la seconde moitié du XIXème siècle*, 6 vol. (Paris: Hachette, 1893–1896).
5. Grzegorz Dziamski, "Rehabilitacja alegorii. Baudelairowski motyw w refleksji nad sztuką współczesną," in: *"Drobne rysy w ciągłej katastrofie". Obecność Waltera Benjamina w kulturze współczesnej*, ed. Anna Zeidler-Janiszewska (Warszawa: Wydawnictwo Instytutu Kultury, 1993).
6. Lourdes Flamarique, "From the Psychologization of Experience to the Priority of Emotions in Social Life," in: *The Emotions and Cultural Analysis*, ed. Ana Marta González (London and New York: Routledge, 2016).
7. Michał Głowiński, "O kilku motywach u Benjamina," *Literatura*, No. 41 (1975).
8. Pierre Grimal, *A Concise Dictionary of Classical Mythology*, ed. Stephen Kershaw, trans. A.R. Maxwell-Hyslop (Oxford: Basil Blackwell, 1990).
9. *Mała encyklopedia kultury antycznej* (Warszawa: PWN, 1988).
10. Ryszard Różanowski, *Pasaże Waltera Benjamina. Studium myśli* (Wrocław: Wydawnictwo Uniwersytetu Wrocławskiego, 1997).
11. Georg Simmel, "Philosophiche Kultur," in: *Gesamtausgabe*, vol. XIV, ed. Rüdiger Kramme and Otthein Rammstedt, (Frankfurt: Suhrkamp, 1996).
12. *Słownik wyrazów obcych*, ed. Jan Tokarski (Warszawa: PWN, 1972).
13. *Wielki słownik wyrazów obcych*, ed. Mirosław Bańko (Warszawa: PWN, 2003).

Jerzy Borowczyk

# The Poet of Awakening

**Abstract:** The paper addresses the problem of Benjamin's attitude towards the 19th century perceived as the domain of two kinds of consciousness – individual (reflective) and collective (which falls into sleep). In his *Arcades Project* the German philosopher aimed at developing a method of awakening from this kind of sleep. The paper analyses Benjamin's observations and interpretations concerning oneiric objects located in Paris – railway station and elements of city arcades. In these passages one can observe lyrical elements resulting from Benjamin's strong attachment to Baudelaire's poetry and to the works of surrealists. In this way the author of the *Arcades Project* himself becomes, as it were, a poet, which protects him from intellectual schematism and dogmatism.

**Keywords:** history of the 19th century; oneirism; Baudelaire; city in culture

## 19th Century's Dream Book

Because this is going to be a discussion of the poetic aspect of *The Arcades Project*, I want to quote several lines from a Polish poem which, like the *Project*, is set in a big city:

> Jest coś wśród wielkich miast i naokoło,
> Zwłaszcza pod wieczór, zwłaszcza dla pielgrzyma,
> Co wypogadza lub zachmurza czoło,
> Ziejąc nań niby westchnienie olbrzyma –
> Jest coś w tym szmerze, co pierwszy dolata,
> Skoro się miejskich bram rozemknie krata[1].

> [There is something in big cities, and around them, / Especially in the evening, especially for a pilgrim, / That brightens or darkens the face, / Breathing at it like a giant – / There is something in that murmur, that is heard at first, / When the bars of a city gate open.]

The lines come from the initial stanza of Cyprian Kamil Norwid's *Quidam*. The twilight and the beginning; a day is ending in the city's murky gateway. The first delicate *murmur*, as strong as that of a predatory beast. Norwid's pilgrim hero is exposed to the potentiality, the life-giving force, but at the same time to the deathly horror breathing through the new space. All that is juxtaposed with the impending

---

1 Cyprian Norwid, "Quidam. Przypowieść," in: *Pisma wszystkie*, ed. Juliusz Wiktor Gomulicki (Warszawa: PIW, 1971), vol. III, p. 82.

twilight. As the traveller is recovering from weariness, he falls into a reverie, which is as piercing and elusive as a dream can be. Everything is possible. Both Norwid and Benjamin never ceased in their search for manifestations and essence of that *thing*. That is why they were so sensitive to the illuminating quality of the delicate *murmur*. The *murmur's* epiphanic quality, however, can have long-lasting effects; it falls into memory and demands a studied explanatory method, an interpretation.

Norwid places his anonymous hero in the bowels of the ancient city of Rome, but the poet's aim is a critical scrutiny of his own time. The quotation from *Quidam* can be interpreted as an initiation of a stranger from Epirus into forms of a different civilization, but the stranger is also a representative of the 19th century. Benjamin probes into "the nineteenth century a spacetime <*Zeitraum*> (a dreamtime <*Zeit–traum*> in which the individual consciousness more and more secures itself in reflecting, while the collective consciousness sinks into ever deeper sleep. [...] through the arcades, communes with its own insides" (*The Arcades*, p. 389). He wants to "expound the nineteenth century – in fashion and advertising, in buildings and politics – as the outcome of its dream visions" (*The Arcades*, p. 389).

The author of the *Arcades Project* is conscious of the fact that his task is extremely complicated, because he is undertaking it in the age when traditional ways of interpreting dreams were becoming exhausted. In the 20th century there is no place for explanation "in terms of tradition, of religious doctrine." Thus, the German critic peeks Marcel Proust's way, Proust being a "unprecedented phenomenon," that can "emerge [...] only a generation that had lost all bodily and natural aids to remembrance and that, poorer than before, was left to itself to take possession of the worlds of childhood in merely an isolated, scattered, and pathological way."

Then, Benjamin clearly marks his intended goal: to make "an experiment in the technique of awakening" from the 19th century's dream (*The Arcades*, p. 388). It is very telling that he supports his words with writers, with people. Proust, on many occasions, is one of those people, but the surrealists are used even more frequently, and above all it is Baudelaire. Benjamin treats works of these artists not as a raw material for interpretation, but rather as handbooks of methodology, of gold-mining, of mining for the ore from which he extracts the meaning of time: the one he lost, and the one he lives in.

## The Train Station – "A Factory of Dreams"

An interesting passage can be found in the L file of the *Arcades*, entitled "Dream House, Museum, Spa":

> The Gare Saint-Lazare: a puffing, wheezing princess with the stare of a clock. 'For our type of man,' says [in 1927 – JB] Jacques de Lacretelle, 'train stations are truly factories of dreams' […]. To be sure: today, in the age of automobile and airplane, it is only faint, atavistic terrors that still lurk within the blackened sheds; and that stale comedy of farewell and reunion, carried on before a background of Pullman cars, turns the railway platform into a provincial stage. Once again we see performed the timeworn Greek melodrama: Orpheus, Eurydice, and Hermes at the station. Through the mountains of luggage surrounding the figure of the nymph, looms the deep and rocky path, the crypt into which she sinks when the Hermaic conductor with the signal disk, watching for the moist eye of Orpheus, gives the sign for departure. Scar of departure, which zigzags, like the crack on a Greek vase, across the painted bodies of the gods. (*The Arcades*, pp. 405–406)

The passage contains anthropomorphizations (the station is a princess, the clock looks, fears sleep), metaphors (the scar of parting), similes, epithets, visionary images (the pile of suitcases as a corridor leading to the land of the dead), and it all ends with a sad punch line (the parting and cracks on a Greek vase). The image of St. Lazare station, once discussed by Queneau, is composed of enough elements to make a good poem, such is the wide scale of impressions and key notes in the passage. Nobility mixed with anatomy in the figure of princess-like station. The look of her clock eye: is it ruthless? Compassionate? Piercing? Defenseless? The look is juxtaposed with a trivialized, mawkish, modern repetition of an ancient story of Orpheus and his beloved. The image reaches its closure when the scene of parting is touchingly compared to a frail but irremovable crack on the doubly symbolic figure of beauty: gods' bodies and a Greek vase. The ancient canon of beauty is so frail that it almost disappears on the modern scene, where the mass comedy of hellos and goodbyes is set against the primitive backdrop of Pullman carriages. This is the train station where the 19th century dreams its dream. Those who woke up from the dream must still remember something of it, because the scar of the parting is still hurting.

The passage on the train station, that dream factory, follows a remark which is the key to the L file of *The Arcades Project*: "Dream houses of the collective: arcades, winter gardens, panoramas, factories, wax museums, casinos, railroad stations" (*The Arcades*, p. 405). Source quotations follow, but they are interlaced with a number of observations and interpretations by Benjamin himself, more numerous and longer than in most sections of the project. The author comments on train stations, those structures of communal dreams. Interestingly, dreams of a community often assume the form of a homestead, a space which is tamed and internalized, a shelter and a sanctuary.

Thus, arcades are defined as "houses or passages having no outside," which makes them similar to the dream (*The Arcades*, p. 406). A wax figure turns out to be a "setting wherein the appearance <Schein> of humanity outdoes itself" (*The Arcades*, p. 409). City gates and thresholds are subjected to similar treatments. Basic elements of the urban teritory, as well as its smallest portions, are all rooted in a dream. Another passage, in the chapter on the house made of dreams, describes Benjamin's prospective method of presenting a city which has been merely designed, a city which had a place only in the dreams of architects and city planners: "To set up, within the actual city of Paris, Paris the dream city – as an aggregate of all the building plans, street layouts, park projects, and street-name systems that were never developed" (*The Arcades*, p. 411). The passage opens up a great space for verbal construction, a visionary, lyrical act of creation. There is no indication that any of the two cities should be deemed more important that the other. The real Paris and the imaginary one are combined into one, poetically coherent metropolis. A city made of dreams is also (or perhaps above all) made of words.

However, all this poetic machinery is not supposed to bring a dreamlike, self-contained beuty into this world. The machinery, together with two Benjamin's favourites: theology and dialectic materialism, will be employed in a reverse process, a task of "The compelling – the drastic – experience, which refutes everything 'gradual' about becoming and shows all seeming 'development' to be dialectical reversals, eminently and thoroughly composed, is the awakening from dream." The stake to be won is a "new, dialectical method of doing history [...] as the art of experiencing the present as waking world, a world to which that dream we name the past refers in truth. To pass through and carry out *what has been* in remembering the dream!" The following sections of this essay will try to determine, how poetic images of matter in the *Arcade Project* become a medium through which a subject's voice can be finally heard (*The Arcades*, p. 389).

Adam Lipszyc claims that Benjamin's inhabitants of 19th century Paris, together with all people of that age, dreamt world exhibitions, fashion, arcades, city architecture, and dreamt it despite their commonsensical sobriety. Their phantasms, "made independent from human beings, close them in a vicious circle that resembles a dream."[2] Benjamin adopted this dreamlike concept from surrealists. It is well known that one of inspirations behind *The Arcades Project* was Louis Aragon's surrealist fantasy (1926), whose opening scene is an imaginary, dreamlike walk through the Passage de l'Opera. According to the Introduction by Rolf Tiedeman, Benjamin wanted to adopt the surrealist view of empirical reality as "mere content of dreams."[3] In 1929 the author of the *The Arcades Project* made the following remark on surrealism:

---

2   Adam Lipszyc, "Księga Benjamina," *Gazeta Wyborcza*, 18–19 February (2006).
3   Rolf Tiedemann, "Dialectics at a Standstill," in: *The Arcades*, p. 933.

"Life seemed worth living only where the threshold between waking and sleeping was worn away in everyone as by the steps of multidinous images flooding back and forth; language seemed itself only where sound and image, image and sound, interpenetrated with automatic precision and such felicity that no chink was left for the penny-in-the-slot called 'meaning'. Image and language take precendence" ("Surrealism: The Last Snapshot of the European Inteligentsia," in: *Selected Writings*, vol. II, part 1, p. 208). This precedence is visible in Benjamin's authorial comments which sometimes, though quite rarely, crop out among the thousands of quotations in *The Arcades Project*. For the author it was a way of bringing out the "concealed, latent thoughts, slumbering" in the 19th century[4].

There is another important observation that Benjamin made about surrealism. It is similar to the passage on awakening, which has already been invoked here: "The trick by which this world of things is mastered ... consists in the substitution of a political for a historical point of view" ("Surrealism: The Last Snapshot of the European Inteligentsia," in: *Selected Writings*, vol. II, part 1, p. 210). In this procedure, or trick, Benjamin saw a chance of waking up from the 19th century nightmare. At the same time he expected that "this motif of awakening separated him from the Surrealists."[5] Thus, *The Arcades Project* includes numerous masterpieces of description of dreams, which are only subsequently interpreted and denounced in a theological or historiosophic way. As an interpreter of dreams, Benjamin is also a poet. In 1916 he wrote to Martin Buber: "I can understand writing as such as poetic, prophetic, objective in terms of its effect, but in any case only as *magical*, that is as un-*mediated*" (*The Correspondence of Walter Benjamin 1910–1940*, p. 80). In many discussions of Benjamin's work, critics point out that Benjamin shared this approach to language with his German predecessors (poets and philosophers) of the 18th and 19th centuries.[6] Apart from the artists mentioned above (Baudelaire, Proust, surrealists), those predecessors could be described as patrons of the lyrical fragments by Benjamin.

Returning to the surrealist supremacy of the image, in *The Arcades Project* Benjamin extensively discusses the method of retrieval of the past through images. "It's not what is past casts its light on what is present, or what is present its light on what is past; rather, image is that wherein what has been comes together in a flash with the now to form a constellation" (*The Arcades*, p. 462). The past is entangled with the poetic now, for example by means of phantasmagoric images

---

4   Tiedemann, "Dialectics at a Standstill," p. 933.
5   Tiedemann, "Dialectics at a Standstill," p. 934.
6   Hamann, Jacobi, Schleiermacher, Novalis and Friedrich Schlegel.

of St. Lazare station as a princess, arcades as "pump rooms," "hot springs," a place for "therapeutic walks" or as "hot spring room in a ravine." *Pastness* has been entirely permeated, it intruded into the present.

## Diligence of Method

> To great writers, finished works weigh lighter than those fragments on which they work throughout their lives. For only the more feeble and distracted take an inimitable pleasure in closure, feeling that they lives have thereby been given back to them. To the genius each caesura, and the heavy blows of fate, fall like gentle sleep itself into his workshop labor. Around he draws a charmed circle of fragments. "Genius is application." ("One-way Street," in: *Selected Writings*, vol. I, p. 446)

So far, the discussion of *The Arcades Project* was limited to the chapters on city and houses made of dreams. These links, together with the chapter on Baudelaire which preceeds them, were placed in the middle of Benjamin's tome. They constitute a sort of core, to which other "convolutes" collected in the *Project* have been attached. Or perhaps, it is the present author's own, hypothetical axis of it.

What Benjamin found in Baudelaire's work, allowed him to look deeper into the birth of modernity. What is, then, the composition of the hypothetical axis of Benjamin's arcade world, the "J" folder entitled simply with the name of the poet? A tangle of quotations, sparsely adorned with authorial comments. This is scarcely an opportunity for a discussion of poetics. It cannot be found, certainly, on the level of Benjamin's style, since this arcade (unlike other ones) contains questions of sparing, is not ascetic, rhetoric. It seems that Benjamin restrains his poetic and subjective creativity. His voice, however, is not silenced, his images do not disappear, and the speaking "I" does not sink in the abyss of quotations from other voices. Everything is subjected to the goal of multifaceted, precise recreation of Baudelaire's poetic and intellectual activity. Referring back to the passage on diligence, quoted above, it is possible to infer that Benjamin's diligence is aimed at recreating Baudelaire's one.

The efforts of the author of *The Arcades Project* are focused on weaving a tapestry of quotations, arranging them into constellations whose meanings are often so multilayered that their finesse can be described as poetic. Selection and arrangement of fragments from Baudelaire, and from a host of his critics, is reinforced with comments which, in spite of being apothegmatic, are not devoid of imaginary potential or interpretative momentum. In the course of successive readings of the Baudelaire book,[7] the reader, already introduced in the micro- and macrocosm

---

7   In the German encyclopedia of Benjamin (*Benjamin – Handbuch. Leben – Werk – Wirkung*, ed. Burkhardt Lindner, Thomas Küpper and Timo Skrandies [Stuttgart –

of the arcades, captures more manifestations, camouflaged of clearly open, of the author's subjectivity. Benjamin managed to achieve this effect, while retaining what Gershom Scholem called the style "meticulously pointed, shining with a contemplative luster."[8]

A few examples of the poetic arrangement of quotations and comments can be provided now. In a selection of quotations about the key questions of the *Project*, one could include the fragments on the arcane craft of poetry, or on the secrets of the big city (its aura and inhabitants), and on the condition of "modern man." On the level details, time and again there are remarks about the image of stars (both their poetic and philosophical implications) or about editing and typography of different editions of *The Flowers of Evil*.

As for poetic images of the big city, Benjamin is fond of juxtaposing Baudelaire's fragments with remarks on Balzac's fiction and Victor Hugo's poetry. In Hugo, he points out the "element of passivity in Hugo's experience of the crowd," where the individual turns out to be a "solitary animal" (*The Arcades*, p. 269). *The Flowers of Evil* are also a source of observations on metropolitan scares (e.g. images of cathedrals juxtaposed with wild woods), but the fear is harmoniously contrasted with with the remark on the pivotal, for Benjamin, poem in Baudelaire's great cycle: *Morning Twilight* (*Le Crépuscule du matin*), thus described by Benjamin: "The morning wind disperses the clouds of myth" (*The Arcades*, p. 268). Which justifies a long quotation from the poem:

> Reveille rang thinly from across a barrack square,
> And a breath of morning troubled the street lamp's stare.
> [...]
> The extra pinch of cold, amid that of penury,
> Added, for women in labour, its insult to injury.
> Slitting the fogged air, the cry of a distant cock
> Broke like a jet of blood through the spasm of a cough.
> Buildings still swam in vague tides of mist;
> And in silenced hospitals, with a last
> Convulsive rattle, the dying gave up breath,

---

Weimar: Metzler J.B., 2006], pp. 567–584) there is even a suggestion to intruduce the term Baudelaire Book (*Das Baudelaire-Buch*) which would denote the entirety of Benjamin's work on the French poet.

8   Gershom Scholem, "Walter Benjamin," in: *On Jews and Judaism in Crisis*, ed. Werner J. Dannhauser (New York: Schocken Books, 1976), p. 182.

> – While night revellers staggered home, tired to death.
> Morning, shivering in her robe of rose and green,
> Made her hesitant way along the deserted Seine,
> While Paris, rubbing tired eyes in its dark,
> Woke like an ancient drudge to another day's work.[9]

Repeating Benjamin's words, "The morning wind disperses the clouds of myth. Human beings and their affairs are exposed to view" (*The Arcades*, p. 268). Demythization must be painful, and ambiguous, sice in the poem's title there is both twilight and morning. In *The Arcades Project*, Benjamin searched for such momens in individual lives, but above all, in the life of society. This time, the process of awakening, full of ambivalence and suffering, was not shown through poetic-theological inquiry, but through comment on Baudelaire's lyric poetry, the place of ritual of "religious inebriation of big cities."[10] A striking quality of the stanzas is their inseparable clasp of ecstatic night and rough morning. The birth is accompanied by agony. Baudelaire turned out to be a poet of awakening, that is of the state in which the content of a dream is still alive and becomes almost tangible. The dream contributes to creation of a new content; it opens a new epoch.[11]

This religious enchantment, however, is very ambiguous in Benjamin's interpretation. Baudelaire's words about the bliss of dissolving in the crowd are accompanied by a curt comment: "Extract the root of the human being!" (*The Arcades*, p. 290). Equally interestingly, in the peculiarly primitive images of Paris from Balzac's fiction "human figures are larger than the streets they move in," and "Baudelaire is the first to have conjured up the sea of houses, with its multistory waves" (*The Arcades*, p. 244). The maritime metaphor can be associated with ancient (e.g. Hebrew or Biblical) connotations of sea abyss as the abode of powers adverse to human beings, destroying human subjectivity. Benjamin pursues this direction, and shows a number of links in *The Flowers of Evil* that are devoid of the word "I," or links where the word was relegated to the background. By digression, in this part of *The Arcades Project*, the same thing happens to the "I" who arranged and commented on the poetry.

And yet, the poets Baudelaire and Benjamin continue in their search for subjectivity's sanctuary. Benjamin searches for the sanctuary in images of the sky and stars (not only from Baudelaire), whose constellations are sprinkled throughout

---

9   Charles Baudelaire, "Morning Twilight," trans. David Paul, in: *The Flowers of Evil*, ed. Marthiel and Jackson Mathews (New York: New Directions, 1955), pp. 131–132.
10  Baudelaire's term quoted by Benjamin in the *The Arcades*, p. 289.
11  There is not reference to Benjamin's essays on Baudelaire, because it seems that awakening in *The Flowers of Evil* is discussed only in *The Arcades Project*.

the Baudelaire chapter of the *Project*. He repeats, after Elizabeth Schnizel, that Baudelaire's constellations symbolize the "the ardor and energy of the human imagination" (*The Arcades*, p. 251). Benjamin meticulously copies the stellar and celestial fragments of *The Flowers of Evil*, only to admit that Baudelaire's cosmic space is a starless void, whose sky can be indifferent and ironic for the human being immersed in history. Benjamin, however, did include these images in *The Arcade Project*, and they are the answer to his heart piercing question, a question asked by the author lost in readings, in the world, and in the universe, a question asked unexpectedly, a question poetically ambiguous: "Where in Ovid is the passage in which he said that the human face was made to mirror the stars?" (*The Arcades*, p. 262).

Scattered stars, dispersed work, and two diligent prodigies in their poetic observatories. One of them, Benjamin, copies from work of the other one, a fragment about sculptures encountering the the *flaneur* of greath metropolies: "You are passing through a great city that has grown old in civilization – one of those cities which harbor the most important archives of universal life – and your eyes are drawn upward [...].the stone phantom takes possession of you for a few minutes and commands you, in the name of the past, to think of things which are not of the earth" (*The Arcades*, pp. 289–290). Benjamin confesses that there is something "in the highest degree prophetic" (*The Arcades*, p. 290) in this image. From roaming in the past, straight into the future.

According to Agata Bielik-Robson: "For Benjamin, culture is not a 'triumph of mind over matter,' but precisely the opposite: a deepening triumph of matter over human subjectivity, which, sliding into objects, gradually becomes one of them."[12] And yet, for a brief moment multiplied by the time of their reader's meditation, the lyrical flashes of *The Arcades Project* make it possible for a subject to become present in the world, to rise from the fall. This happens in spite of the oppressively melancholic condition of the individual. Thanks to poetic alertness and diligence, subject remains faithful to itself: as a poet of detail, of still image, of imaginary medium. This, if nothing else, seems to give *The Arcades Project* some sort of coherence.

---

12  Agata Bielik-Robson, "Gnostyk w wielkim mieście. O *Pasażach* Waltera Benjamina," *Europa*, 8 February (2006), p. 13.

## *Postscript*

> We know that the Jews were prohibited from investigating the future. The Torah and the prayers instruct them in remembrance, however. This stripped the future of its magic, to which all those succumb who turn to the soothsayers for enlightenment. This does not imply, however, that for the Jews the future turned into homogeneous, empty time. For every second of time was the street gate through which the Messiah might enter.
>
> Walter Benjamin[13]

The above is a quotation from the (chronologically) last paragraph of Benjamin's work. In this statement, Gershom Scholem sees a reflection of the idea of remembering, an idea of essential importance for Benjamin. The confession is markedly related to his comment on Baudelarie, quoted in the previous section of this paper. Another relation is to the passages in "One-Way Street" (1928), where Benjamin depreciates auguring and appraises independent creation of the future from past things. Referring to memories is also the formula of *Berlin Childhood around 1900*, which was the outcome of Benjamin's work in the early 1930s. Scholem commented on the childhood sections of "One-Way Street" and on the Berlin memories: this "works dedicated to the as yet undistorted world of the child and its creative imagination, which the metaphysician describes with reverent wonder and at the same time seeks conceptually to penetrate. […] The philosopher and his outlook is present behind every one of these, but under the gaze of memory his philosophy is transmuted into poetry."[14]

A fragment of the Berlin confession (*The Mummerehlen*) brings something of an *ars poetica* derived from the epoch of childhood:

> Early on, I learned to disguise myself in words, which really were clouds. The gift of perceiving similarities is, in fact, nothing but a weak remnant of the old compulsion to become similar and to behave mimetically. In me, this compulsion acted through words. Not those that made me similar to models of good breeding, but those that made me similar to dwelling places, furniture, clothes. Never to my own image, though. And that explains why I was at such a loss when someone demanded of me similarity to myself.[15]

These sentences may be considered to be the source of Benjamin's practice of charging material objects with poetry, a practice which would be essential for the reifying visions of *The Arcades Project*. One cannot forget that in the *Project* there is an explanation of awakening as a gradual process, "that goes on in the

---

13 Quoted by Scholem, "Walter Benjamin," p. 197.
14 Scholem, "Walter Benjamin," pp. 175–176.
15 Walter Benjamin, *Berlin Childhood around 1900*, trans. Howard Eiland (Cambridge: Harvard University Press, 2006), p. 131.

life of the individual as in the life of generations. (...) Its historical configuration is a dream configuration. Every epoch has such a side turned toward dreams, the child's side" (*The Arcades*, p. 388).

From "One-Way Street," fragments of the small essay on auguring seem to be equally relevant:

> He who asks fortune-tellers the future unwittingly forfeits an inner intimation of coming events that is a thousand times more exact than anything they may say. [...] Omens, presentiments, signals pass day and night through our organism like wave impulses. [...] For before such prophecy or warning has been mediated by word or image, it has lost its vitality, the power to strike at our center and force us, we scarcely know how, to act accordingly. [...] Like ultraviolet rays, memory shows to each man in the book of life a script that invisibly and prophetically glosses the text. ("One-way Street," in: *Selected Writings*, vol. I, p. 482–483)

In all these texts, the struggle between personal memory and its imaginary recollection becomes the basic pattern, the source of poetic flashes, of Benjamin's small lyrical essays in *The Arcade Project*. In an evocative, no matter how cryptic, way he suggests what awakening could be, and what is the role of verbal art in it. In the *Project*, they explore dreamlike remembrance of the entire community, not only of an individual. Poetry, or verbal art in general, is an ever present component of Benjamin's intellectual activity. The lyrical element intrudes into his game between theology and materialism. Scholem himself points this out, when he writes about the "undogmatic manner of thinking" of his friend, and relating this to "felicitous metaphors and striking images saturated with meaning," which "he had an effortless command."[16] When I am calling Benjamin a poet of awakening, I do it by writ of metaphor, which allows me to capture, as I believe, an important, artistic element of his strolls through the arcades of Paris, crowded and cluttered with extracted quotations.

Translated by Paweł Stachura

## Bibliography

1. Charles Baudelaire, "Morning Twilight," trans. David Paul, in: *The Flowers of Evil*, ed. Marthiel and Jackson Mathews (New York: New Directions, 1955).
2. *Benjamin – Handbuch. Leben – Werk –Wirkung*, ed. Burkhardt Lindner, Thomas Küpper and Timo Skrandies (Stuttgart – Weimar: Metzler J.B., 2006).

---

16 Scholem, "Walter Benjamin," p. 174.

3. Walter Benjamin, *Berlin Childhood around 1900*, trans. Howard Eiland (Cambridge: Harvard University Press, 2006).
4. Walter Benjamin, "One-Way Street," in: *Selected Writings*, ed. Michael W. Jennings and Marcus Bullock, Howard Eiland, Gary Smith, vol. I (Cambridge, MA: Belknap Press of Harvard University Press, 1996).
5. "Surrealism: The Last Snapshot of the European Inteligentsia," in: *Selected Writings*, ed. Michael W. Jennings and Marcus Bullock, Howard Eiland, Gary Smith, vol. II, part 1 (Cambridge, MA: Belknap Press of Harvard University Press, 1999).
6. Walter Benjamin, *The Arcades Project*, trans. Howard Eiland and Kevin McLaughlin, prepared on the basis of the German volume edited by Rolf Tiedman (Cambridge Mass.: The Belknap Press of Harvard University Press, 1999).
7. Agata Bielik-Robson, "Gnostyk w wielkim mieście. O *Pasażach* Waltera Benjamina," *Europa*, 8 February (2006).
8. Adam Lipszyc, "Księga Benjamina," *Gazeta Wyborcza*, 18–19 February (2006).
9. Cyprian Norwid, "Quidam. Przypowieść," in: *Pisma wszystkie*, vol. III, ed. Juliusz Wiktor Gomulicki (Warszawa: PIW, 1971).
10. Gershom Scholem, "Walter Benjamin," in: *On Jews and Judaism in Crisis*, ed. Werner J. Dannhauser (New York: Schocken Books, 1976).
11. *The Correspondence of Walter Benjamin 1910–1940*, ed. Gershom Scholem and Theodor W. Adorno, trans. Manfred R. Jacobson and Evelyn M. Jacobson (Chicago and London: The University of Chicago Press, 1994).
12. Rolf Tiedemann, "Dialectics at a Standstill," in: Walter Benjamin, *The Arcades Project*, trans. Howard Eiland and Kevin McLaughlin, prepared on the basis of the German volume edited by Rolf Tiedman (Cambridge Mass.: The Belknap Press of Harvard University Press, 1999).

Wiesław Ratajczak

# Photography and *The Arcades Project*

**Abstract:** The essence of photography, and its place in culture, are some of Benjamin's most important themes. The German critic commented on the influence of the invention of photography on transformations in art, and predicted its outcome in a sort of epidemic habit of image-collecting. He was particularly interested in the social role of photography, in particular its influence on the extension of range of commodity economy. The author of Arcades project demonstrated how pictures have assumed, with astonishing rapidity, the position of the most common commodity.

**Keywords:** photography; flâneur; theory of art; production and market; voyeurism

## I

There is an intriguing relationship between photography and *The Arcades Project*. And as in any relationship, it is fascinating to observe what the two parties think about each other, how they perceive each other, how they unwittingly imitate each other. This essay discusses Walter Benjamin's views on the invention of photography and its influence on the transformation of art as well as his predictions about the consequences of the epidemic of collecting paintings. It also examines *The Arcades Project* from the vantage point of photography: does it shape the poetics of Benjamin's book? Does *The Arcades Project* resemble a photographic album?

Benjamin's reflection on photography begins, predictably enough, at the beginning. He talks about Daguerre's invention of daguerreotypy, presented at the meeting of the French Academy of Sciences in January 1839, and contrasts photography with the traditional plastic arts. But soon afterwards he adds: "The effort to launch a systematic confrontation between art and photography was destined to founder at the outset. It could only have been a moment in <the> confrontation between art and technology – a confrontation brought about by history" (*The Arcades*, p. 675). As this statement suggests, Benjamin tends to approach cultural change as a process which ominously leads to the triumph of technology over art.

As a cultural historian studying photographs and a viewer of the Paris shop windows, the German thinker concludes that the modern world increasingly presents itself as an exhibition that demands to be admired. This change is epitomized by the great world expositions, and Benjamin could not have ignored the fact that the Paris exposition of 1855 was the first to include "a special display called «Photography»" (*The Arcades*, p. 6). Among the objects displayed at the world's largest marketplace were reproductions of paintings: "The social role of photography becomes apparent during the Exhibition of 1855. Photography dramatically expands the range of commodity economy, in that it exploited, on the market, the figures, landscapes, events, which could not be useful for a customer in any way other than as images. To increase trade volume, photography renews its objects through fashionable modifications, which are characteristic in later history of photography"[1]. The rapidly developing new industry transformed the social elite into celebrities. The powerful and wealthy remain distant and untouchable but can be seen or even purchased; they become part of the "universe of commodities" (*The Arcades*, p. 8) brought into being by world expositions. Benjamin underscores the connections between photography and commerce, connections as old as photography itself. Photographs quickly became the commonest, cheapest, and hence the most accessible commodity. The example of Marseilles illustrates the industrialization of photography and the new industry's demand for an army of professionals: about 1850 the city had four or five painters of miniatures who were barely able to earn a living. Several years later it had forty or fifty photographers running very successful shops (see *The Arcades*, p. 676). A host of amateurs appeared almost simultaneously, following François Arago's public presentation of the results of his experiment. Perhaps photography, as a fashion and an art, is a manifestation of the nineteenth century's characteristic "fusion of individualistic and collectivist tendencies," (*The Arcades*, p. 390) as Benjamin suggests after Sigfried Giedion. By nature, photography is simultaneously mine and someone else's.

Always a keen observer of the relations between culture and economy, Benjamin planned "Excursus on the later development: extension of the commodity world through the photo" (*The Arcades*, p. 915). He also discussed the parallel development of mass media and distinguished several spheres of their influence, ascribing different products to different consumer groups: "On information, advertisements, and feuilletons: the idler must be furnished with sensations, the merchant with customers, the man in the street with a worldview" (*The Arcades*, p. 383). Although readers seem to expect objective and complete knowledge about the world, their appetite is satisfied by utterly superfluous facts: "The press brings into play an overabundance of information, which can be all the more provocative the more it is exempt form any use" (*The Arcades*, p. 447). Not surprisingly, this paradox also pertains to photography. This is how Benjamin describes the contemporary news hunters: "News service and idleness. Feuilletonist, reporter,

---

[1] Walter Benjamin, "Das Passagen-Werk," in: *Gesammelte Schriften*, ed. Rolf Tiedemann (Frankfurt am Main: Suhrkamp Verlag, 1982), vol. V, p. 1227.

photographer constitue a gradation in which waiting around, the «Get ready» succeeded by the «Shoot,» becomes ever more important vis-à-vis other activities" (*The Arcades*, p. 802).[2]

The combination of commodity, information, and image is an explosive planted at the heart of culture, whose strength and substance have always derived from making, listening to, telling and retelling stories. The ancient ideal of wisdom surrendered under the attack of immaterial scraps of reality. Benjamin brilliantly describes this process: "Just as the industrial labor process separates off from handicraft, so the form of communication corresponding to this labor process – information – separates off from the form communication corresponding to the artisanal process of labor, which is storytelling. [...] This connection must be kept in the mind if one is to form an idea of the explosive force contained within information. This force is liberated in sensation. With the sensation, whatever still resembles wisdom, oral tradition, or the epic side of truth is razed to the ground" (*The Arcades*, p. 804). Acutely aware of the revolutionary character of his era, Benjamin notices the subversive potential of trick photographs as an effective instrument of political campaigning.

If writing disburdens our memory and reduces the need to remember, a need fundamental to storytelling, photography is even more conducive to forgetting. Why should we remember anything – landscapes, cities, family reunions – if we can store the whole world in neat stacks of pictures and have it there forever. The lack of memory is characteristic of modern culture, which resorts to a trivial remedy: "Fashions are a collective medicament for the ravages of oblivion. The more short-lived a period, the more susceptible it is to fashion" (*The Arcades*, p. 80). Here again photography plays an ambiguous role. On the one hand, it is the most powerful ally of fashion; on the other, it becomes fashion's greatest enemy. Photography is a servant of fashion in catalogues and posters but it simultaneously discredits fashion because there is no better proof of how imitative the newest look is than a similar picture from a previous season.

*The Arcades Project* presents the photograph as a defense against the rapid acceleration of the pace of life. Photographic images performed an important function during Haussmann's great renovation of Paris, when he cut through the old city panoramas to mark out straight, wide boulevards. The city's disappearing old forms could only survive in pictures. But while the photograph resists transience,

---

[2] Susan Sontag's classic book also associates the camera with the gun: "Like a car, a camera is sold as a predatory weapon – one that's as automated as possible, ready to spring." Susan Sontag, *On Photography* (New York: Delta, 1982), p. 14.

it is also an embodiment of transience. An engraving captures a timeless situation, achieves a certain synthesis, whereas the photograph captures a fleeting moment and, taken at the same site a month or an hour later, will reveal the passage of time. Fragments recorded on a light-sensitive medium testify to the transitoriness of the world, provoking us to intervene in the process of change, for if nothing can arrest this process, it may at least be worth trying to manipulate its pace. Inventions related to photography or preceding it, such as the myriorama, a moving panorama first presented in London in 1802, force us to rethink our concepts of time, the past, the present, and the future: "Careful investigation into the relation between the optics of the myriorama and the time of the modern, of the newest. They are related, certainly, as the fundamental coordinates of this world. It is the world of strict discontinuity; what is always again new is not something old that remains, or something past that recurs, but one and the same crossed by countless intermittences" (*The Arcades*, p. 843).

The camera is an instrument which measures time and tries to arrest it. Benjamin quotes Baudelaire's remarks about the passage of time: "I assure you that the seconds are now strongly accented, and rush out of the clock crying, «I am Life, unbearable and implacable Life!»" (*The Arcades*, p. 317). People who experience life at an accelerated pace share the temptation which was "Baudelaire's deepest intention": "To interrupt the course of the world" (*The Arcades*, p. 318) Does photography make it possible? Half-jokingly, we may say that the history of Baudelaire's photographic image suggests it does. Although his contemporaries mention an extraordinary changeability of his face (Benjamin brings it up several times), it is only the one, unchanging photograph taken by Etienne Carjat that Baudelaire is now associated with. The following passage from Lemercier quoted in *The Arcades Project* also conveys the dream of immortality which photography confers on people and events:

> The image imprisoned within the glass plate,
> Preserved from all threatening contact,
> Retains its bright life […] (*The Arcades*, p. 675)

Although photography may able to preserve and immortalize any object, it hardly ever gets beneath the surface (the work of artist photographers is an exception to the rule). Benjamin's remark about "Hollowing out of inner life" (*The Arcades*, p. 348) captures this superficiality. Benjamin knew that it was difficult to point the lens at the inside and was convinced that photography destroyed sublimity. His reading of *Mariés de la tour Eiffel* occasioned the comment that Cocteau's work "can perhaps be considered a «critique of the snapshot,» insofar as in this piece the two aspects of shock – its technological function in the mechanism and its sterilizing function in the experience – both come into play" (*The Arcades*, p. 692).

Beginning with Emile Zola's novels, culture does not know any forbidden realms, it reaches everywhere. Browsing through Benjamin's notes we may conclude that photography preceded literature in its disregard for the taboo as it recorded, with equal fascination, the Paris sewers, dissection rooms, and bedrooms. Photographs escalate the voyeurism characteristic of city life. They also contribute to the development of the prostitution market. Brochures targeted at the male clientele appeared even before photography became popular: "Eduard Fusch mentions «the appearance of an illustrated catalogue of prostitutes, which could date from 1835–1840. The catalogue in question consists of twenty erotic litographs in color, each one of which has printed at the bottom the addresses of a prostitute»" (*The Arcades*, p. 507). Nonetheless, photography certainly stimulated the market of sexual services. In his note about the year 1861, Benjamin mentions an illustrator who made available the addresses of his models posing for "obscene photographs" (*The Arcades*, p. 508). Such images were unabashedly placed in the windows of photographers' shops.

Photography's ability to abet desire links it with the modern traveling mania. Benjamin writes about a legion of photographers making long journeys to supply their customers with views of faraway places. Just like pornographic images, picture postcards are meant to arouse desire and give a promise of satisfaction.

Benjamin's remarks about photography's participation in cultural change, scattered throughout *The Arcades Project*, can be recapitulated in one word: "ferment." It is in the chapter on photography that the German writer discusses this concept, borrowed from Alfred Gotthold Meyer. "«Fermenters» are catalytic agents which provoke or accelerate the decomposition of relatively large quantities of other organic substances. [...] These «other organic substances,» however, in reaction to which the fermenting agents manifest their destructive power, are the historically transmitted stylistic forms. The fermenters [...] are the achievements of modern technology. They [...] can be grouped according to three great material divisions: (1) iron, (2) the art of machinery, (3) the art of light and fire" (*The Arcades*, p. 672). Since Benjamin leaves this fragment without comment, photography's exact contribution to the decline of culture must be deduced by the reader. *The Arcades Project*, however, provides ample evidence of this process.

Photographs in general, and especially those which have sentimental value because they represent people or places that are of personal importance to the owner, can be usefully approached in terms of Benjamin's concepts of the aura and the trace: "The trace is appearance of a nearness, however far removed the thing that left it behind may be. The aura is appearance of a distance, however close the thing that calls it forth. In the trace, we gain possession of the thing; in the aura, it takes possession of us" (*The Arcades*, p. 447). This passage reveals the ambiguous position of the owner of the photograph/object, especially with regard to portraits.

Photography is intimately associated with one particular aspect of *flânerie*. Benjamin regarded "category of illustrative seeing" as being of "fundamental for the flâneur" (*The Arcades*, p. 419). This attitude is often assumed by people who look at pictures as random, decontextualized fragments of somebody else's life, the history of a place, etc. Looking means creating plots out of conjectures, scraps of memories, fantasies, splinters of "the mirror with a memory,"[3] to use Oliver Wendell Holmes's well-known phrase.

## II

The *flâneur* is a peculiar, sentient camera. Collecting images is one of his vital functions. One could even talk about rivalry between this sentient being who absorbs the views of the city and the cold, unfeeling machine. It is difficult to imagine the *flâneur* with a camera in hand because he would certainly despise being considered a supplement to technology (as Benjamin writes: "What makes the first photographs so incomparable is perhaps this: that they present the earliest image of the encounter of machine and man" – *The Arcades*, p. 678).

The passer-by thinks of the streets as a "great interior" (*The Arcades*, p. 422); stores remind him of wardrobes; he feels just as much at ease in a coffeehouse as he does in his own room. The photographer behaves in a similar fashion, unabashedly seizing every object that catches his eye, as if it belonged to him. Like the *flâneur*, the photographer is indecisive (see *The Arcades*, p. 425); he can have anything (especially today, when taking and storing images is so easy), only later will he decide later which shots should be printed or developed. The photographer is insatiable, he never seems to have enough pinned specimens; like for the *flâneur*, "there is always something more to see" (*The Arcades*, p. 806). But where the protagonist of *The Arcades Project* is by nature an idler oriented toward "unlimited duration," (*The Arcades*, p. 806) tourists and photojournalists work dutifully with the camera in hand. They will not experience the great pleasure which, after

---

[3] "But this other invention of *the mirror with a memory* and especially that application of it which has given us the wonders of the stereoscope, is not so easily, completely, universally recognized in all the immensity of its applications and suggestions" – Oliver Wendell Holmes, "The Stereoscope and the Stereograph," *The Atlantic Monthly*, June (1859), pp. 738–748: 22 June 2017 https://www.theatlantic.com/magazine/archive/1859/06/the-stereoscope-and-the-stereograph/303361/

Baudelaire, Benjamin described as the desire to "set up hause in the heart of the multitude, amid the ebb and flow" (*The Arcades*, p. 443).

The invention of photography is a voyeur's dream come true. The camera, more and more advanced technologically, enables him to spy on others while remaining unseen. He appropriates other people's privacy and then admires his trophies in solitude or circulates them, exchanging pictures for jingling change. As a matter of fact, Benjamin, like the authors of realistic novels, also indulges in voyeurism. He wants to spy on modernity, to catch it red-handed without losing sight of anything, not even that which is embarrassing or seemingly unimportant. *The Arcades Project* is a huge photographic album – an unfinished collection composed of fragmented pictures which have a certain function within the whole and are meaningful within particular chapters, according to the author's intentions, but which can also be (and often are) taken out of the collection to begin a new, more limited life as quotations. The popularity of photographs and quotations is a symptom of the aphoristic quality of contemporary life: when haste precludes listening to long stories and the end of grand narratives has become a truism, the fragment is our only resort.

Amateur, home photographic albums – I am still trying to describe this genre, which is quickly disappearing in the computer era – combine privacy and its negation in a peculiar way. The albums are the individual or collective work of people who assembled them, updated them over the years, changed the order of photographs, sometimes adding brief descriptions, and protected the albums during times of familial or historical unrest. At the same time, the albums would not exist if it had not been for the artists or artisans who either took the images or, in their darkrooms, performed a series of alchemical operations on the material with which they were entrusted. Old photographs are marked with the names of those photographers or their workshops, just as the fragments in *The Arcades Project* are identified by their bibliographic source. The photographic album is a more or less well thought-out montage of what its maker wants to show, what she thinks is worth keeping, remembering, and sharing with a select audience. Benjamin described his book as follows: "Method of this project: literary montage. I needn't *say* anything. Merely show" (*The Arcades*, p. 460 and p. 860). The difference between these two compilers, the imagined author of a family photo album and the author of *The Arcades Project*, is that the former is emotionally involved in her project, while the latter approaches his material with a scholar's reserve. But not really: rather, he carefully assembles what others have rejected, the scraps of culture: "I shall appropriate no ingenious formulations, purloin no valuables. But the rags, the refuse – these I will not describe but put on display" (*The Arcades*, p. 860).

The structure of a photographic album often remains unclear, especially for someone who is not part of the family or the circle of friends. The structure of *The Arcades Project* is not self-evident, either. Nor is it static, since in every reading, whether linear or random, one notices different quotations which subjugate the neighboring ones. Every fragment, like every photograph, is an autonomous entity, and simultaneously acquires meaning in the context of other fragments or photographs. Benjamin writes: "Notes on montage in my journal. Perhaps, in this same context, there should be some indication of the intimate connection that <existe> between the intention making for nearest nearness and the intensive utilization or refuse – a connection in fact exhibited in montage" (*The Arcades*, p. 861).

*The Arcades Project* seems to suggest a reading that is similar to looking at pictures in an album. The reader lingers over something that seems familiar, recognizing the features of a writer, painter, or politician, and perhaps seeing him in an unusual situation or a strange company. Then, intrigued by the figures never encountered before, he resorts to encyclopedias to find out who they are. He looks at page after page, trying to pay sustained attention, but soon gives up and just begins to drift among the fragments. He feels tired, but after a while experiences a Barthesian punctum. He knows that it is impossible to see or read everything. As he absent-mindedly turns the pages, he is worried about missing something important or irrevocably losing something. There are a plethora of notes, just as there are a plethora of commodities in a shop window or photographs in an album. The reader realizes that he will not comprehend or systematize this excess; there is no storyline that could help in this task. Although the maker of this huge storehouse of human documents is thorough and meticulous, the reader who enters it finds himself at the mercy of chance. He may think that the book accumulates evidence of the modern rupture of cultural continuity, for the past suddenly appears to him as a lumber room.

As I mentioned above, Benjamin imagined photojournalists as hunters waiting for game. Benjamin himself is also keeping watch, not with a camera, but with a pen that is ready to shoot: "Necessity of paying heed over many years to every casual citation, every fleeting mention of a book" (*The Arcades*, p. 470). The photographer collects fragments of the world: pretty, exotic, eccentric, related to certain feelings or capable of evoking them later. Benjamin is also a great collector, and the Paris arcades, as well as his own *Arcades Project*, can be seen as collections. Benjamin observed of collecting that it was "a form of practical memory, and of all the profane manifestations of «nearness» it is the most binding" (*The Arcades*, p. 205). He saw gathering as one of the biological functions ("it should not be overlooked that, with the nest-building of birds, collecting acquires a clear biological function" – *The Arcades*, p. 210) and the foundation of knowledge ("Collecting is a primal phenomenon of study: the student collects knowledge" – *The Arcades*, p. 210). Photography, just like the collection, confers importance and value on the object. As a collection, the photographic album is never complete: it attempts to reconstruct a certain order (that of someone's biography, family history, a journey) but never fully succeeds because the photographer has always overlooked something or missed some event, or a photograph has been lost. The surplus cannot be mastered. Every author of a photographic album and every collector, including the author of *The Arcades Project*, seem to pursue the same goal. "Perhaps the most deeply hidden motive of the person who collects can be described this way: he takes up the struggle against despersion. Right from the start, the great collector is struck by the confusion, by the scatter, in which the things of the world are found" (*The Arcades*, p. 211). In addition, the photographer, the collector, and Benjamin all desire to stop the passage of time. "The deepest enchantment of the collector: to put things under a spell, as though at a touch of the magic wand, so that all at once, while a last shudder runs over them, they are transfixed" (*The Arcades*, p. 852). Referred to photography, this sentence from *The Arcades Project* again reveals its ambiguity, especially in the case of portrait photographs: a loved face is frozen and framed, torn out of the context of the past and the future, presented outside of time, and hence in death.[4]

It seems appropriate to conclude the above remarks about the analogies between photography and *The Arcades Project* with a warning: Both are addictive!

Translated by Magdalena Zapędowska

## Bibliography

1. Roland Barthes, *Camera Lucida: Reflections on Photography*, trans. Richard Howard (New York: Hill and Wang, 1981).
2. Walter Benjamin, "Das Passagen-Werk," in: *Gesammelte Schriften*, vol. V, ed. Rolf Tiedemann (Frankfurt am Main: Suhrkamp Verlag, 1982).
3. Walter Benjamin, *The Arcades Project*, trans. Howard Eiland and Kevin McLaughlin, prepared on the basis of the German volume edited by Rolf Tiedman (Cambridge Mass.: The Belknap Press of Harvard University Press, 1999).

---

4 See Roland Barthes, *Camera Lucida: Reflections on Photography*, trans. Richard Howard (New York: Hill and Wang, 1981).

4. Oliver Wendell Holmes, "The Stereoscope and the Stereograph," *The Atlantic Monthly*, June (1859): 22 June 2017 https://www.theatlantic.com/magazine/archive/1859/06/the-stereoscope-and-the-stereograph/303361/
5. Susan Sontag, *On Photography* (New York: Delta, 1982).

Piotr Śniedziewski

# *The Arcades Project*, or the Melancholy of "Editing"

**Abstract:** Benjamin's frequent critical remarks about wandering, endless quoting, and departing from the main topic, obsessive classifying and meticulous attention to detail which blurs the line of argument can all be applied to his unfinished magnum opus. This "philological" aspect of *The Arcades Project*, dominated by an experience of melancholy, will be the main focus of the present essay.

**Keywords:** melancholy; *écriture mélancolique*; library; labyrinth; ruin

> Bear in mind that commentary on a reality
> (for it is a question here of commentary, of interpretation in detail)
> calls for a method completely different from that
> required by commentary on a text. In the one case,
> the scientific mainstay is tehnology;
> in the other case, philology.
> (*The Arcades*, p. 460)

To describe Benjamin's *Arcades Project* or define its subject matter seems an impossible task. It is a book full of internal tension, a curious blend of theology and historical materialism. Gershom Scholem wrote that *The Arcades Project* "appeared to him a self-liquidating ventuure"[1] because it tried to marry Marxist philosophy of history and the philosophy of language understood as the interpretation of literary texts in their social and historical contexts. But *The Arcades Project* is also a moving, sometimes lyrical Baedeker written by the *flâneur*, a guide to a Paris as the capital of the nineteenth century that no longer exists. Finally, it is one of the "fat books" so mercilessly ridiculed in "One-Way Street" ("One-Way Street," in: *Selected Writings*, vol. I, p. 457). Benjamin's frequent critical remarks about wandering, endless quoting, and departing from the main topic, obsessive classifying and meticulous attention to detail which blurs the line of argument can all be applied to his unfinished magnum opus. This "philological" aspect of *The Arcades Project* will be the main focus of the present essay. I am primarily

---

1 Gershom Scholem, "Walter Benjamin," in: *On Jews and Judaism in Crisis*, ed. Wrner J. Dannhauser (New York: Schocken Books, 1976), p. 189.

interested in Benjamin as writer,[2] less so in the philosopher, sociologist, or tourist guide, although all those roles are closely connected and are only separated for the purposes of this argument.

Benjamin himself foregrounds the role of the writer in *The Arcades Project*. The chapter "On the Theory of Knowledge, Theory of Progress," which is of crucial importance for understanding the book, contains many references to the act of writing, or "editing," as Benjamin prefers to call it. One particularly revealing passage defines "editing" as, firstly, the idea which is the germ of the writing, secondly, the implementation of this idea, and thirdly, the final result. (The German term *Redaktion* means both "editing," i.e. the process of working on the text, and "edition," i.e. the text which is the result of this process.)

> Say something about the method of composition itself: how everything one is thinking at a specific moment in time must at all costs be incorporated into the project then at hand. Assume that the intensity of the project is thereby attested, or that one's thoughts, from the very beginning, bear this project within them as their telos. So it is with the present portion of the work, which aims to characterize and to preserve the intervals of reflexion, the distances lying between the most essential parts of this work, which are turned most intensively to the outside. (*The Arcades*, p. 456)

Let us have a closer look at Benjamin's assumptions. First of all, his plan is staggeringly ambitious. Benjamin demands that the edited text include everything that comes to the author's mind. There is no selection, hierarchization, or evaluation at this stage. What has been thought should be carefully and accurately recorded. Benjamin does say a word about any ordering principle, nor does he allude to the difficulty of writing, so vividly depicted in "One-Way Street": "If the smoke from the tip of my cigarette and the ink from the nib of my pen flowed with equal ease, I would be in the Arcadia of my writing" ("One-Way Street," in: *Selected Writings*, vol. I, p. 463). *The Arcades Project* displays none of this nonchalance; it is marked by a nervous uncertainty, primarily because the author wants to give evidence of "the intensity of the project." In a way, *The Arcades Project* is an autobiographical work, a reminiscence of "[…] the milions of leaves that were visited by the fresh breeze of diligence, the stertorous breath of the researcher, the storm of youthful zeal, and the idle wind of curiosity" (*The Arcades*, p. 457) – which is how Benjamin describes the countless hours spent at the Bibliothèque Nationale in Paris. The nervousness of "editing" is also caused by the fact that whatever has been thought

---

[2] Benjamin actually described his work on *The Arcades Project* as "literary activity." See his letter to Hugo von Hofmannsthal, 26 June 1929 (*The Correspondence of Walter Benjamin 1910–1940*, p. 353).

ought to find its way into what is being written. The assumption that ideas can be recorded without any prior selection and that the resulting work ("turned most intensively to the outside") will communicate the author's intentions in a coherent manner is the most utopian aspect of Benjamin's project. The triadic sequence of the idea, its implementation, and the text, also mentioned in "One-Way Street,"[3] underlies the overambitious goal and the melancholy failure of *The Arcades Project*.

The above three stages of "editing" correspond to three metaphors borrowed from architecture. Benjamin's preference for catachresis – here, the use of architectural concepts to refer to successive stages of working on a text – reveals an important aspect of his imagination. Susan Sontag observes that Benjamin thought in spatial terms and that his imagination was governed by the desire to convert time into space and to capture movement in a spatial image.[4] Accordingly, "editing" is thought of as library (at the stage of the idea, when Benjamin strives for totality and is obsessed with the catalogue), a labyrinth (at the stage of implementation, which is marked by delay, wandering, and an obsession with quoting), and a ruin (at the final stage, when *The Arcades Project* ceases to be a completed work and is swallowed by its own material: references, quotations, allusions).

## The Library

Unlike the metaphors of the labyrinth and the ruin, which recurred in Benjamin's works beginning with *The Origin of German Tragic Drama* (1928) and which have been widely discussed by critics,[5] the metaphor of the library has attracted little

---

3   "Work on good prose has three steps: a musical stage when it is composed, an architectonic one when it is built, and a textile one when it is woven" ("One-Way Street," in: *Selected Writings*, vol. I, p. 455) and "Stages of composition: idea – style – writing. The value of the fair copy is that in producing it you confine to calligraphy. The idea kills inspiration; style fetters the idea; writing pays off style" ("One-Way Street," in: *Selected Writings*, vol. I, p. 459).

4   Susan Sontag, "Under the Sign of Saturn," in *Under the Sign of Saturn* (London: Vintage, 1996), p. 116. This quality of Benjamin's imagination is also revealed in the following passage from "One-Way Street": "[…] feeling is not located in the head, […] we sentiently experience a window, a cloud, a tree not in our brains but rather in the place where we see it" ("One-Way Street," in: *Selected Writings*, vol. I, p. 449). The statement is a hidden quotation from Baudelaire.

5   See Ryszard Różanowski, *Pasaże Waltera Benjamina. Studium myśli* (Wrocław: Wydawnictwo Uniwersytetu Wrocławskiego, 1997), pp. 79–80, 99. Różanowski often cites *Allegorie und Melancholie*, ed. Willem van Reijen (Frankfurt am Main: Suhrkamp, 1992) – esp. Bryan S. Turner's "Ruine und Fragment. Anmerkungen zur Barockstil,"

critical attention even though it is just as significant and intriguing. The figure of the library played an essential role in Benjamin's conception of *The Arcades Project* and is of key importance in much of his writing. The library was also Benjamin's true obsession. As Scholem eloquently reminisces,

> His most enduring personal passion was the collecting of books. In him the author and the collector were combined in rare perfection [...]. His own library, which I knew quite well, clearly mirrored his complex character. The great works which meant much to him were placed in highly baroque patterns next to the most out-of-the-way writings and oddities, of which – both as an antiquarian and as a philosopher – he was no less fond[6].

Benjamin's library was a bizarre collection in which classic works stood next to "curiosities," including children's books or books written by madmen (as Scholem further recalls). Its diversity reveals the owner's respect for tradition and concern for its continuity as well as his sensitivity to what has been excluded, forgotten, or neglected. No wonder that Scholem's reminiscence blends admiration for Benjamin's acute literary sense with friendly bemusement about his collecting mania.[7] For Benjamin the library was a world in miniature where an ancient hero meets a seventeenth-century burgher and a harlot converses with a poet. The library thus encapsulates the situation of the writer, determined on the one hand by the social and economic conditions of his time and on the other hand, by the past which is constantly shaping those conditions. More importantly for the purposes of this essay, the library owner becomes a writer-as-collector and the library, a model of his text.

The book collector or "the bibliophile" (*The Arcades*, p. 207) mentioned in *The Arcades Project* is a curious figure. He does not use books as a source of knowledge or as professional tools but, as Sontag points out, as "contemplative objects, stimuli for reverie."[8] However, before a book is transformed into a "contemplative object," before it finds its place on the shelf, the librarian collector searches for it madly. Even if he knows perfectly well what he wants to find, he is always at the mercy

---

pp. 202–223, and Willem van Reijen, "Labyrinth und Ruine. Die Wiederkehr des Barock in der Postmoderne," pp. 261–291.
6  Scholem, "Walter Benjamin," p. 175.
7  The obsession with collecting, which also affects book lovers, is discussed in "One-Way Street": "Each stone he [child] finds, each flower he picks, and each butterfly he catches is already the start of a collection, and every single thing he owns makes up one great collection. In him this passion shows its true face, the stern Indian expression that lingers on, but with a dimmed and manic glow, in antiquarians, researchers, bibliomaniacs" ("One-Way Street," in: *Selected Writings*, vol. I, p. 465).
8  Sontag, "Under the Sign of Saturn," p. 120.

of chance. Benjamin admits that the progress of *The Arcades Project* depended on his accidental discoveries: "How this work was written: rung by rung, according as chance would offer narrow foothold" (*The Arcades*, p. 460). Forcing his way through piles of books in second-hand bookstores, the librarian collector can never be certain to find the one book he is desperately looking for. Consequently, he cannot go hunting with only one title in mind but has to think about each and every title all the time, which means that he never looks just for one particular book but browses through shelves, hoping to find a book that will fit his collection. He thus resembles a documentary writer, who knows the subject of his work (just as the collector knows the topic of his collection) but whose knowledge does not lessen the chaos of his archival research or curb his mania for copying down anything that is even remotely related to his topic. As the author of *The Arcades Project*, Benjamin remained a collector and documentalist. To search, gather, copy everything down – this was the principle of his preliminary research on the book. Less than a year into the project, when he still hoped to complete it, Benjamin complained in a letter to Scholem: "In any case, it gives me no respite" (*The Correspondence of Walter Benjamin 1910–1940*, p. 335). But the consequences of his passion were perfectly clear to him.

First of all, like every collector, a book collector and a writer who collects quotations strip the desired objects of their usefulness: "What is decisive in collecting is that the object is detached from all its original functions in order to enter into the closest conceivable relation to things of the same kind" (*The Arcades*, p. 204). In Benjamin's case, the countless quotations copied from books at the Bibliothèque Nationale in Paris and the Staatsbibliothek in Tiergarten become important not by virtue of the whole to which they used to belong but by virtue of the new whole created by the writer-as-collector, namely, his collection. This brings us to another consequence of the collector's habit of hoarding and insatiable desire for completeness. Stripping the object of its past uses, the collector wants to invest it with a new meaning and situate it in the system he is creating. This pursuit is melancholy in nature, which prompts Benjamin to identify the collector with the allegorist (see *The Arcades*, p. 206). The melancholy results from stripping the object (the quotation) of its primary meaning and clothing it in phantasmagoria, an illusion of novelty. But the collection is not a new quality; it is merely another form, a camouflaged repetition of existing forms. It does not produce any new unifying meaning but exposes a procession of empty forms, according to Benjamin's account of the mechanisms of melancholy and allegory in *The Origin of German Tragic Drama* (see *The Origin of German Tragic Drama*, pp. 138–158). The collector and the allegorist, as well as the librarian and the writer assembling quotations, wage a "struggle against dispersion" (*The Arcades*, p. 211). The fight, however, is illusory. This brings us to a third consequence of the destructive habit of hoarding: "As far as the collector is concerned, his collection is never complete; for let him discover just a single piece missing, and everything he's collected remains a patchwork" (*The Arcades*, p. 211). There is no new whole or a unifying meaning. There is only the idea of totality, which is impossible to implement because the collector cannot gather everything. The librarian wants to possess all books and the writer tries to accumulate all quotations. Both are misled: to achieve his dream, the librarian would have to convert the whole world into a library, and the writer would have to copy all existing books instead of writing his own. To hold those absurdities in check, both the librarian and the writer have to develop a system which will create at least an appearance of order, namely, a catalogue.

The library catalogue, or card index, can be seen as a figure of the text. It has the advantage of passionlessness and objectivity, making it possible to inventory great and important works next to the most surprising and bizarre writings. The catalogue gives us an illusive sense of mastering chaos as it promises a victory over what is dispersed. Simultaneously, however, the catalogue tends to become a collection in its own right, a self-contained book of index cards which detaches us from the texts it classifies. As Benjamin pointedly remarks in "One-Way Street," "And today the book is already, as the present mode of scholarly production demonstrates, an outdated mediation between two different filing systems. For everything that matters is to be found in the card box of the researcher who wrote it, and the scholar studying it assimilates it into his own card index" ("One-Way Street," in: *Selected Writings*, vol. I, p. 456). Those ironic comments can be applied to Benjamin's own *Arcades Project*. Most likely contrary to the author's intention,[9] the "fat books" ("One-Way Street," in: *Selected Writings*, vol. I, p. 457) asks to be read precisely as a catalogue. For it is first and foremost a subject catalogue, an overly detailed table of contents in which "the whole composition must be permeated with a protracted and wordy exposition of the initial plan" ("One-Way Street," in: *Selected Writings*, vol. I, p. 457), to quote Benjamin one more time, and against his intentions. It does not mean that the text disintegrates, becomes disorganized, or lacks an author. Rather, *The Arcades Project* suffers from an excess of organization, as if the author had used all his energy to prepare the index. Of course, we must remember that it is an unfinished work and that, as

---

9   As Benjamin observes in "One-Way Street," "The typical work of modern scholarship is intended to be read like a catalogue" ("One-Way Street," in: *Selected Writings*, vol. I, p. 457).

Scholem reminds us, in the late 1920s and early 1930s Benjamin grappled with serious methodological problems which led him from theology and systematic philosophy to historical materialism.[10] But *The Arcades Project* could not have been completed anyway because Benjamin conceived it as a work that could not be written. He must have realized early enough that the project is impossible to complete. In a letter to Scholem of 15 March 1929 he writes: "A perilous, breathtaking enterprise, repeatedly put off over the course of the winter, not without reason [...] thus sometimes paralyzing me, and as I have discovered, it was just as impossible to postpone as it is to complete at this time" (*The Correspondence of Walter Benjamin 1910–1940*, p. 348).

Following the idea of the library as a figure of the text, Benjamin perused and copied countless documents, to the extent that the excerpts began to predominate over the commentary. Apparently Benjamin failed even to produce a catalogue. Had he compiled one, we would certainly miss the commentaries but the clear ordering system would help us find our way through the amorphous mass of text. Instead, the existing work overflows with quotations whose sheer volume thwarts all attempts at systematization. Consequently, the reader has no access either to the works cited, which are only represented by their decontextualized fragments, or to the author's plan for putting the fragments in order. The author of *The Arcades Project* seems to hesitate between two possibilities: becoming a full-fledged copyist and devoting all his energies to copying books written by others, or relying on his own intuition and reducing the books to a system of index cards in which the original character of the books would be lost. In either case Benjamin's text could become the ideal library which either collects faithful copies of books or presents them cleverly, protecting them against dispersion. Neither of those utopian concepts was implemented, though. Or rather, both were implemented only partially. While the idea of being a library owner and writer-as-collector might seem a fascinating point of departure for writing an original book, the idea of the library as a figure of the text led the author astray. As a result the reader gets lost in *The Arcades Projects* as in the arcades of an unfamiliar city, and the text is not a copy or a signpost but a tangle of streets marked out by a mad urban planner. No wonder that as we move from the first stage of "editing," i.e., the idea of the text as a library, to the second stage, which is the implementation of the idea (the act of writing), the figure of the library gives way to the labyrinth.

---

10 Benjamin presents his utopian idea of combining metaphysics (which he persistently refers to as theology) with historical materialism in his famous "On the Concept of History" (see *Selected Writings*, vol. IV, pp. 389–400).

## The Labyrinth

Unlike the library, the labyrinth is a frequent metaphor in Benjamin's writings, so much so that he viewed it as the key to his imagination and work. In the autobiographical essay "Berlin Childhood around 1900" Benjamin notes:

> Not to find one's way around a city does not mean much. But to lose one's way in a city, as one loses one's way in a forest, requires some schooling. […] This art I acquired rather late in life; it fulfilled a dream, on which the first traces were labyrinths on the blotting papers in my school notebooks. ("Berlin Childhood around 1900," in: *Selected Writings*, vol. III, p. 352)

The same idea returns in "Central Park," which speaks of "the labyrinthine character of the city itself. The labyrinth, whose image has become part of the flâneur's flesh and blood" ("Central Park," in: *Selected Writings*, vol. IV, p. 189). Thus, both the traces of childhood dreams in Benjamin's school notebooks and his mature reflection on the phenomenon of the *flâneur*, which he observed in Baudelaire's work, involve the figure of the labyrinth. The labyrinth is the key to understanding many chapters of *The Arcades Project*, including "Arcades, *Magasins de Nouveautés*, Sales Clerks" (*The Arcades*, pp. 31–61), "Baudelaire" (*The Arcades*, pp. 228–387) or "The Flâneur" (*The Arcades*, pp. 416–455). However, in all those cases the labyrinth appears as a theme, or the basis for a comparison (the city as a labyrinth), while I am interested in the labyrinth as a particular kind of text or work on the text where the main writerly strategy is slowing down and losing one's way, and which manifests itself as obsessive quoting.

In "Central Park" Benjamin explicitly talks about slowness and delay as the essence of the labyrinth. "The labyrinth is the habitat of the dawdler. The path followed by someone reluctant to reach his goal easily becomes labyrinthine" ("Central Park," in: *Selected Writings*, vol. IV, p. 171). This statement reveals two essential aspects of the labyrinth: first, it is a structure; second, the person who decides to enter it has certain characteristics. As a structure, the labyrinth complicates and reverses the seemingly obvious relation between route and destination. Pragmatically, the destination is more important than the route, which should be short and free from obstacles or distractions. The route is only important in so far as it leads to the destination, even though one can stray off, stop, or even get lost on the way. The evaluation of literary works, especially in the positivistic vein, follows similar principles. The assessment is based on the completed work as intended by the author. The process of writing, documented by a labyrinth of notes, abandoned editions, and drafts, is inconsequential, perceived by as a mere scaffolding. In reality, however, the scaffolding is indispensable for constructing the text. As Benjamin states in *The Arcades Project*, "I shall purloin no valuables, appropriate no ingenious formulations. But the rags, the refuse – these I will not inventory but allow, in the only way possible, to come into their own: by making use of them" (*The Arcades*, p. 460). This statement discredits in advance any academic evaluations of his work, or rather, his "text" or "edition," given how discontinuous and fragmented *The Arcades Project* is, as if it resisted completion. The route becomes more important for Benjamin than the destination. Constant studies, accumulating quotations, filling numerous index cards in expectation of the ever receding work are fascinating in themselves, as Benjamin admits in his letters to friends (for example, in early 1934 he writes about it to Gretel Adorno and in December of that year to Siegfried Kracauer).

Another meaning of the labyrinth comes into play here: "The path followed by someone reluctant to reach his goal". Benjamin's correspondence shows that he was less often hindered by fear than by personal problems, especially financial difficulties. However, his personality was not without significance. He seemed to dread completion of the book and hence postpone the "editing" to collect more excerpts and quotations. He mentions "the Saturnian tempo of the thing" in a letter to Werner Kraft (25 May 1935 – *The Correspondence of Walter Benjamin 1910-1940*, p. 486). Scholem reminds us that the only book Benjamin managed to complete was *The Origin of German Tragic Drama*, his *Habilitation* thesis rejected by Frankfurt University.[11] Sontag regards Benjamin's tendency to procrastinate as one of the main features of his melancholy temperament.[12] Perhaps the author of *The Arcades Project* simply did not want to reach the end of his notes; maybe his love for "the rags, the refuse", of that which has been excluded from the mainstream of literary history, was so deep that he had to stray off the route and surrender to the charm of "monotonous wandering [which] is represented in the labyrinth" (*The Arcades*, p. 519). This is Benjamin's strategy as a writer. His main guide through the nineteenth century is Baudelaire, recognized as a symbol of his era by some contemporaries whose names, long since forgotten, can be found in the pages of *The Arcades Project*. For Benjamin to enter the labyrinth, the land of delay, was to linger over obscure books which even his brilliant friends had not heard about, such as Sigmund Engländer's *Geschichte der französischen Arbeiterassociationen*, which Benjamin mentions in a letter to Theodor Adorno (9 March 1934)[13]. This antiquarian attitude, hindered the "editing," which was

---

11 See Scholem, "Walter Benjamin," p. 184.
12 Sontag, "Under the Sign of Saturn," p. 115.
13 See Theodor Wiesengrund Adorno, Walter Benjamin, *The Complete correspondence 1928-1940*, ed. Henri Lonitz, trans. Nicholas Walker (Cambridge, Mass.: Harvard University Press, 1999), p. 29.

continually postponed. Benjamin clearly took more pleasure in studying, reading, and copying than in working on his own text, which disappeared under the mass of quotations and references. He lost his way and failed to reach the destination, if the destination was the completed work and published book. The melancholy *flâneur* prefers to roam around rather than head toward a specific point and never reaches the center of the labyrinth. Thus the labyrinth is not only a figure which retards the "editing" but also a space in which the melancholic, the *flâneur*, and the writer may lose their way.

Strikingly enough, not only *may* they lose their way but that want to do so. Benjamin often speaks of straying while doing research and taking notes, and describes his tendency to digress, which often interrupts his main argument. "What for the others are deviations are, for me, the data which determine my cours. – On the differentials of time (which, for others, distrub the main lines of the inquiry), I base my reckoning" (*The Arcades*, p. 456). In "One-Way Street" he marvels at the treatise, a genre he regards as the ideal of roaming: "The tractatus is an Arabic form. Its exterior is undifferentiated and unobtrusive, like the fasades of Arabian buildings, whose articulation begins only in the courtyard. [...] In the ornamental density of this presentation, the distinction between thematic and excursive expositions is abolished" ("One-Way Street," in: *Selected Writings*, vol. I, p. 462). What Benjamin finds particularly appealing is the blurred boundary between center and periphery. Again, he defends "the rags, the refuse" because they are just as important in the structure of the whole as the main argument. *The Arcades Project* provides an extreme example of this kind of structure. As the author's commentary virtually disappears, the reader joins the author in stumbling through a tangle of quotations, with a sense that s/he may never find a way out. But the wandering is pleasant; it does not annoy or cause anxiety. It is yet another manifestation of the melancholy of Benjamin's writing. Travel and wandering were perceived as typical activities of the melancholic at least from the early nineteenth century and the publication of François René Chateaubriand's novel *René*.[14] More importantly, since Robert Burton's *Anatomy of Melancholy* (1621) wandering among texts and objects had been seen as the key element of melancholy aesthetics. Burton, who

---

14 Benjamin comments on melancholy roving in "One-Way Street": "In a love affair, most people seek an eternal homeland. Others, but very few, eternal voyaging. The latter are melancholics, who believe that contact with Mother Earth is to be shunned. They seek the person who will keep the homeland's sadness far away from them. To that person they remain faithful. The medieval complexion-books understood the yearning of this human type for long journeys" ("One-Way Street," in: *Selected Writings*, vol. I, p. 466).

loved to linger on the backroads and constantly delayed explaining what melancholy was, writes:

> This roving humour... I have ever had, and like a ranging spaniel, that barks at every bird he sees, leaving his game, I have followed all.... I have read many books, but to little purpose, for want of good method; I have confusedly tumbled over divers authors in our libraries, with small profit, for want of art, order, memory, judgment. I never travelled but in map or card, in which mine unconfined thoughts have freely expatiated.[15]

In his correspondence from the *Arcades* period Benjamin describes a similar experience: "I actually spend the entire day in the library reading room" (letter to Adorno, 9 March 1934)[16], and "the most intensive writing" (letter to Scholem, 14 February 1929 – *The Correspondence of Walter Benjamin 1910–1940*, p. 346). Like Burton, Benjamin lacks a consistent method since he is always reformulating his principles and goals. The indecision is certainly associated with his search for a successful combination of theology and historical materialism. But Benjamin never manages to get beyond the preliminary stage, which consists in arranging the quotations and planning the sequence of chapters, described as a major success in a letter to Gretel Adorno of March 1934: "Although it is still far from a definite shape, it is still very far away from its initial form, and much closer to the final one. Much could be said about it, but there is no way to write. Enough to say that in recent days something has hatched, an initial arrangement of chapters; I have never gone that far before"[17]. Those words sound bizarre: Benjamin is boasting about something he ought to have done seven years earlier, when he first embarked on his project. It seems as if the actual book on the Paris arcades only existed in the author's mind, where it developed and acquired the qualities of a finished work: unity, coherence, completeness. What exists on paper is *The Arcades Project* as a tangled, thickening mass of text which overflows the boundaries of the intended work. The main reason for its amorphousness is Benjamin's obsession with quoting.

Quotations slow down the writing because they require commentary. Moreover, if the writer uses them immoderately, he is likely to become disoriented. The disorientation is often evident in *The Arcades Project*, which is made up of quotations followed by commentaries but lacks a clear line of argument which would

---

15 Robert Burton, "Democritus Junior to the Reader," in: *The Anatomy of Melancholy*, 22 June http://www.gutenberg.org/files/10800/10800-h/10800-h.htm.
16 Adorno, Benjamin, *The Complete correspondence 1928–1940*, p. 29.
17 Walter Benjamin, *Pasaże*, ed. Rolf Tiedemann, trans. Irenuesz Kania, postface Zygmunt Bauman (Kraków: Wydawnictwo Literackie, 2005), p. 1009.

contain the quotations within some kind of framework. Digressions often prevail over the author's conception of the work, just as in the Arab treatise described in "One-Way Street." Benjamin openly admitted his predilection for, or rather, obsession with quoting as he emphasized "necessity of paying heed over many years to every casual citation, every fleeting mention of a book" (*The Arcades*, p. 417). The quotation, which forcefully demands to be included in the book, often with no mention of its source, was to become the main structural principle of *The Arcades Project*: "This work has to develop to the highest degree the art of citing without quotation marks" (*The Arcades*, p. 458). The reader can never know who is talking since the narrator's identity is impossible to determine. This undermines the entire methodological and philosophical apparatus which Benjamin expounded with satisfaction in letters to Benjamin Adorno (e.g. on 6 November and 5 and 17 December 1934 or 20 May 1935) becomes questionable. I do not argue that Benjamin did not aspire to be a philosopher; conversely, he may have been a philosopher more than anything else. Scholem repeatedly stresses that his friend was a full-blooded metaphysician.[18] Nonetheless, it would be difficult to discern a central idea or unchanging method in Benjamin's philosophical thought. Interestingly, Scholem points out that the apparatus of *The Arcades Project* was "provisional," "determined by the method of commentary" and "dialectic,"[19] interpretative tools that reflect Benjamin's tendency to nonsystematic research and his literary passions rather than any philosophical aspirations.

However, the quotations which complicated Benjamin's text were more than just a game of hide-and-seek, and perhaps this is where we should look for a general philosophical method which invites the reader to pause and reflect. This function of the quotation is eloquently described in "One-Way Street": "Quotations in my work are like wayside robbers who leap out, armed, and relieve the idle stroller of his conviction" ("One-Way Street," in: *Selected Writings*, vol. I, p. 481). The role of the quotation is thus not so much to illustrate Benjamin's own argument as to disrupt the reader's complacency about understanding everything. In this context the modest authorial commentary, so sparing in *The Arcades Project*, no longer comes as a surprise. Commentary and interpretation prove insignificant, contrary to Adorno's opinion, expressed in a letter to Benjamin of 20 May 1935, that it is necessary to interpret the accumulated material.[20] In Benjamin's view the quotation can be compared to "the dialectical image" which *The Arcades*

---

18 See Scholem, "Walter Benjamin," p. 178.
19 Scholem, "Walter Benjamin," p. 181.
20 See Adorno, Benjamin, *The Complete correspondence 1928–1940*, p. 83.

*Project* refers to as "a flash" (*The Arcades*, p. 473). The quotation removes the object or thought from its context, preserving its "pastness," but only through the now of present cognition. In this sense the quotation perfectly fits the obsession with collecting, so characteristic of Benjamin's strategy as a writer. Unfortunately, since the quotation hovers between the absent original context and the new context of the artificially produced collection of excerpts, and because is very rarely provided with explanation, it destroys the coherence of the text. The reader gets lost in what s/he is reading. The text seems unstable, decentered; the author seems to pursue a variety of associations that come to his mind and obstinately hide the essence of his reflection. Or else, the writer does not proceed from observation to observation but from quotation to quotation. Benjamin was perfectly aware of the destructive power of quoting. He admired Jules Michelet, "an author who, wherever he is quoted, makes the reader forget the book in which the quotation appears" (*The Arcades*, p. 468). We might say that what seems a negative element (wandering, straying) was not negative for Benjamin, and the centrifugal force of the quotation determined his ideal of the text. But Benjamin's writing also displays a quality that is rather surprising in the light of the above statement.

This connoisseur of digression, a declared drifter and apologist for "rags and refuse," and an enemy of composition in its classic sense was also extraordinarily sensitive to matters of style. Scholem notes that Benjamin's style was always flawless and fascinating, and his speeches were often publishable without revision.[21] Indeed, *The Arcades Project* openly demands a precise, simple, and clear style and includes among its quotations a long passage from Joseph Joubert's essay "On Style" (*Du style*) (see *The Arcades*, p. 482). In his unexpected love of style Benjamin resembles Gustave Flaubert, with whom he actually has much more in common. Arguably, style was to be the remedy for Benjamin's shortcomings as writer. The reader and the author weave their way through a tangle of references, allusions, and quotations; they continually stumble on names of authors which cannot be found even in encyclopedias; the structure of the book threatens to collapse, and if it never does, it is solely because we are captivated by the scattered fragments. The vehicle of meaning is the style and not an idea or philosophical imperative, hardly ever mentioned in *The Arcades Project*. Benjamin again convinces his readers that his vocation is not only philosophy, but also, and perhaps primarily, writing. At the same time, Benjamin is a peculiar writer who converts the work into text and the idea of a huge library into ruins.

---

21  See Scholem, "Walter Benjamin," pp. 173, 182–183.

## The Ruin

We certainly cannot claim that Benjamin intended to create a flawed, unfinished, or fragmented work. On the contrary, in late March 1934 he writes to Gretel Adorno that he can now see the "definite shape"[22] of his book. He humbly agrees with Max Horkheimer's criticism, in a letter of 18 September 1935, that he is not paying enough attention to "forming the material."[23] However, Benjamin's efforts to organize the book cause a lot of anxiety, since the excess of material overshadows the commentary and thwarts all attempts at interpretation. Quotation marks and footnotes appear more frequently that authorial comments.

Benjamin seems to have fallen into the same trap as Bouvard and Pécuchet, the protagonists of Flaubert's last novel who tried to recreate the past and encountered the aporias involved in all attempts at objectivization and synthesis. They could not understand that writing about the past requires selecting the documents, arranging them in some order, and finally, interpretation, which can never be unbiased. Those limitations are inescapable and the only way to avoid them is to copy all the documents. This solution, however, is completely absurd because it does not lead to recreating history. Benjamin encountered a similar aporia, although he often commented on how absurd it was to try and write about the past from an ahistorical and uncritical perspective. "Central Park" and *The Arcades Project* abound in such remarks. Nonetheless, the countless hours he spent copying documents at the Bibliothèque Nationale in Paris and the new quotations and references he was always finding began to blur the underlying idea of his magnum opus. Benjamin had described a similar situation in "One-Way Street":

> The power of a text when it is read is different from the power it has when it is copied out. [...] Only the copied text thus commands the soul of him who is occupied with it, whereas the mere reader never discovers the new aspects of his inner self that are opened by the text, that road cut through the interior jungle forever closing behind it: because the reader follows the movement of his mind in the free flight of daydreaming, whereas the copier submits it to command. ("One-Way Street," in: *Selected Writings*, vol. I, p. 448)

This brilliant passage unwittingly describes the process of compiling *The Arcades Project*, or, more precisely, its final effect, which is the ruin. But against the optimism of the above statement, the literary consequences of copying are disastrous at two levels: the construction of the text and the identity of the writing subject.

The idea of the library, cataloguing, and copying dominated *The Arcades Project* to such an extent that what was intended to remain in the footnotes was converted

---

22 Benjamin, *Pasaże*, p. 1009.
23 Benjamin, *Pasaże*, p. 1065.

into the main text. It is not Benjamin's design that determines the selection and arrangement of the quotations; rather, it is the quotations that determine the direction his thought will take. Hence our increasing doubts as to whether we are still dealing with a coherent philosophical idea or with a disorderly literary technique. The scattered fragments of the unfinished work resemble the ruin as defined by Georg Simmel. According to the German sociologist, the ruin is produced by a clash between the human spirit and natural forces. Whenever a building is erected, the creating spirit gains a small advantage over nature. This advantage is lost, however, when the architectural form collapses. As Simmel argues, "the ruin of a building, however, means that where the work of art is dying, other forces and forms, those of nature, have grown; and that out of what of art still lives in the ruin and what of nature already lives in it, there has emerged a new whole, a characteristic unity".[24] In the new whole, inert matter and nature claim back their rights, violated by humans in the process of shaping the world according to their will. In the ruin "nature has transformed the work of art into material for her own expression, as she had previously served as material for art".[25] It is my sense that this statement captures the relation between the numerous quotations included in *The Arcades Project* and the "editing," that is, the unceasing search for the right "constructive moment" which Benjamin described in a letter to Gretel Adorno (16 August 1935 – *The Correspondence of Walter Benjamin 1910-1940*, p. 507). It was for the sake of "editing" that he appropriated hundreds of texts from the past to create his work, but this flood of texts eventually swallowed the "edition." The material, which Benjamin used rather crudely, removing the copied quotations from their original contexts and treating them as mere illustrations of his argument, overwhelmed the writer.

The faulty structure of the text affects the subject's identity. Benjamin's "I," responsible for the original idea of the work, has been incapacitated, drowned in the mass of quotations. The passage from "One-Way Street" cited above mentions the situation when "the reader follows the movement of his mind in the free flight of daydreaming, whereas the copier submits it to command." If this is the perfect strategy for a copyist, it may prove disastrous for a writer or philosopher, and it did destroy the structure of Benjamin's book. His work attempted in vain to become a sort of magnetic center, attracting slivers of quotations, allusions, and references. But as the mass of slivers exceeded the critical point, they began to slide down and

---

24 Georg Simmel, *Two Essays. The Handle, and the Ruin*, trans. David Kettler, *Hudson Review*, Autumn (1958), p. 380.
25 Simmel, *Two Essays*, p. 381.

detach from the center, producing a ruin of scattered quotes and pale commentaries. The energy of the work's center has been extinguished. Quoting has a similar impact on the subject who resorts to borrowing words. Benjamin developed the strategy of borrowing other people's words to such a degree that his own voice became inaudible. The work's ruined center corresponds to the subject's ruined "I," which disintegrates because it is exposed to ceaseless influence. The writing subject does not impose his perspective; rather, he is overwhelmed by the words of others and loses his identity. Not surprisingly, in a letter to Scholem of 26 July 1932 Benjamin described his book as "the real site of ruin or catastrophe, whose furthest boundary I am still unable to survey when I let my eyes wander over the next years of my life" (*The Correspondence of Walter Benjamin 1910–1940*, p. 396). The idea of the library has fallen to pieces, as has the idea of the sane librarian who can use his system of index cards to master the chaos of names and titles. Hence the embittered tone in Benjamin's correspondence: on 28 October 1931 Benjamin tells Scholem that he sees his work on *The Arcades Project* as endless "prolegomena and paralipomena" (*The Correspondence of Walter Benjamin 1910–1940*, p. 385), and in May 1935 he admits in a letter to Cohn, "Whether the book is going to be written at all, is still more doubtful than ever"[26]. Thus Benjamin's ambitious project became its own ruin.

The best description of this ruin can again be found in "One-Way Street," which states that "the work is the death mask of its conception" ("One-Way Street," in: *Selected Writings*, vol. I, p. 459). The work comes into being when its idea has died – but how can the work implement the idea if the idea is no longer there and cannot be referred to? Perhaps the work is not an accurate reflection of the idea but only a mask that covers the idea's failure. A mask: not a real face, not the incarnation of a thought but camouflage permeated by sadness and melancholy. The work does not reflect the beauty of the idea but testifies to its impossibility. The passage from "One-Way Street," which can also be applied to the relation between the metaphors of the ruin and the library, corresponds to Benjamin's observations in *The Origin of German Tragic Drama*, where he discusses the sense of "an empty world" produced by the Lutheran faith (*The Origin of German Tragic Drama*, p. 138). The secular world, which Lutheranism views as spiritually meaningless, is inhabited by sad people who believe in predestination and therefore see no meaning in their everyday actions. God has hidden in heaven and earthly existence has no impact on one's salvation or damnation. The burning question in such a world is, why live at all? Life itself is meaningless and is permeated by melancholy and mourning, which Benjamin defines as follows:

---

26  Benjamin, *Pasaże*, p. 1031.

> Mourning is the state of mind in which feeling revives the empty world in the form of a mask, and derives an enigmatic satisfaction in contemplating it.... Accordingly the theory of mourning, which emerged unmistakably as a *pendant* to the theory of tragedy, can only be developed in the description of that world which is revealed under the gaze of the melancholy man. For feelings, however vague they may seem when perceived by the self, respond like a motorial reaction to a concretely structured world. (*The Origin of German Tragic Drama*, p. 138)

The "empty world" is the world of objects which have been deprived both of their particular metaphysical value and of a unifying meaning. To preserve one's sanity in a world stripped bare, one has to cover the void with a mask, which is the product of human sorrow. Benjamin seems to be concealing a similar void in *The Arcades Project*. The ideal of the library, which was to provide the text with a metaphysical anchor, has proved impossible to implement. The conception of the work has fallen apart and all the writer is left with are countless index cards, notes, and footnotes. The "editing," a supposed remedy for the chaotic excess, turned into a deeply melancholy act. Firstly, it only disguises the absence of the work, thwarted by the author's unrealistic idea that, in his own words, "everything one is thinking at a specific moment in time must at all costs be incorporated into the project then at hand" (*The Arcades*, p. 546). Secondly, it leaves the writing subject among things (quotations, excerpts) which have lost their meaning, both as individual entities (because they have been removed from their original contexts) and as a whole (Benjamin failed to incorporate them effectively into his theologico-materialist vision of the nineteenth century). Thirdly, the "editing" is a sad and futile attempt to breathe life into the scattered fragments, and as such it only camouflages the melancholy of the lost subject who is drifting from word to word in search for certainty and order but cannot find them. According to Benjamin's concept of melancholy, "editing" is a melancholy act which shuts the individual in the world of allegory, a world of changing forms with no metaphysical grounding. There is nothing but words and the act of copying them, governed by the artificial and illusory principle of style.

"Sometimes I feel *crushed* by the mass of this work, which may fall flat after all." This could be another of Benjamin's laments as he sat in reading rooms and studied books and journals, endlessly copying excerpts and providing them with sparing commentary. In fact, the statement comes from Flaubert's letter to Ivan Turgenev of 8 December 1877 and refers to Flaubert's newly begun work on his last novel, *Bouvard and Pécuchet*.[27] Earlier, on 29 July 1874, a few days before he

---

27  Gustave Flaubert, *Correspondance*, ed. Bernard Masson, Jean Bruneau (Paris: Gallimard, 2002), p. 705.

started writing, Flaubert had shared his fears and doubts about the project with Turgenev: "But how I dread it! How anxious I am! It seems to me I am going on a long journey to unknown lands and will never come back."[28] Flaubert began to work on the actual text of the novel on 1 August 1874, after conducting a lot of library research, filling several thick notebooks with quotations, and taking a number of sightseeing trips which were to add credibility to his descriptions and enhance the scientific character of the novel. Claudine Gothot-Mersch draws our attention to a letter of January 1880, where Flaubert admits that he read over 1,500 books while preparing to write *Bouvard and Pécuchet*.[29] Like Benjamin, the French author often forgets himself in his work and spends countless hours over his manuscript, as he mentions in a letter to Edma Roger des Genettes of 15 February 1877: "This winter I have been working like crazy."[30] Given that Flaubert was constantly coming up with new plans and scenarios for the book, his anxiety seems only natural: "This damned book gives me shivers,"[31] he wrote to Zola on 5 October 1877. *Bouvard and Pécuchet* is indeed a impressive project, by virtue of both the extensive research that preceded the writing and the main idea. Flaubert intended to demonstrate the methodological shortcomings of the sciences, as stated in the book's original subtitle. To this purpose he designed a novel in two volumes, of which he only managed to complete volume one. The novel consists of ten chapters presenting a mad search for the Truth conducted by the two eponymous copyists. Volume two was to comprise excerpts and quotations from the books Bouvard and Pécuchet use in volume one.

Flaubert's undertaking seems to anticipate Benjamin's *Arcades*. Both projects embrace the metaphor of the library as they attempt to comprise and catalogue knowledge in its entirety. It is a mad desire to discover the absolute Truth, which, however, does not exist as such, separate from the method and instruments of cognition. Benjamin was perfectly aware of this aporia. As he states in his famous "On the Concept of History," "History is the subject of a construction whose site is not homogeneous, empty time, but time filled full by now-time" ("On the Concept of History," in: *Selected Writings*, vol. 4, p. 395). Nonetheless, he continued to amass quotations and compile inclusive lists of names. As a result he delayed the moment of "editing" and prolonged his roving among the excerpts. In this sense

---

28  Flaubert, *Correspondance*, p. 638.
29  Gustave Flaubert, *Bouvard et Pécuchet* avec un choix des scénarios, du *Sottisier*, *L'Album de la Marquise* et *Le Dictionnaire des idées reçues*, ed. Claudine Gothot-Mersch (Paris: Gallimard, 1999), p. 15.
30  Flaubert, *Correspondance*, p. 693.
31  Flaubert, *Correspondance*, p. 701.

*The Arcades Project* closely resembles Flaubert's notebooks. Both are chaotic and driven by the desire for totality. They are labyrinths made of names and titles, of words which do not illustrate any Truth but reflect the anxiety of the subject in quest. If Flaubert managed to arrange the fragments of other works in some order and incorporate them in a novel, it was because he created the characters of the two copyists who do in the fictional world exactly what Flaubert and later Benjamin did in the real world. Another quality shared by the literary labyrinths of *Bouvard and Pécuchet* and *The Arcades Project* is that neither of them has a center or a point of entrance and exit. The center does not exist, or rather, exists only as the fantasy of the subject who mistakes its own desires for reality. What is really important are the margins and footnotes, where all the "action" takes place. There is no entrance or exit because the quest does not allow leaving the boundaries of one's own self and one's own cognition to see things from another point of view, ahistorically and objectively. Flaubert and Benjamin are doomed to endless roving, which converts their ideal libraries into ruins. What kind of ruin is it? It is a fragment of an edifice erected upon positivist illusions, which turns out to be richer in meaning than the most orderly library. Sometimes it is better to wander the backroads than to read an encyclopedia. The three metaphors discussed above: the library, the labyrinth, and the ruin also define the transition from a writing strategy based upon faith in the objectifying power of "editing" to a strategy rooted in melancholia.

The melancholy strategy not only foregrounds the periphery or the margin at the expense of the center but also privileges delay, quoting, and enumeration over the seemingly coherent argument of a scholarly study. Scientific order is illusory because it will not admit its own metaphoric character and its status as a mask which tries to hide an emptiness. The sense of emptiness is perhaps Flaubert's and Benjamin's most poignant experience. The emptiness encapsulates the sadness of their writing and the melancholy of "editing." It cannot be controlled; each writer only strives to fill it with words. Finally, it is the emptiness Benjamin noticed in Albrecht Dürer's *Melancholia I* and so insightfully discussed in his book on the Trauerspiel, an emptiness reflecting meditation on the uselessness of the instruments of human cognition.

Translated by Magdalena Zapędowska

## Bibliography

1. Theodor Wiesengrund Adorno, Walter Benjamin, *The Complete correspondence 1928–1940*, ed. Henri Lonitz, trans. Nicholas Walker (Cambridge, Mass.: Harvard University Press, 1999).
2. Walter Benjamin, "Berlin Childhood around 1900," in: *Selected Writings*, ed. Michael W. Jennings and Marcus Bullock, Howard Eiland, Gary Smith, vol. III (Cambridge, MA: Belknap Press of Harvard University Press, 2002).
3. Walter Benjamin, "Central Park," in: *Selected Writings*, ed. Michael W. Jennings and Marcus Bullock, Howard Eiland, Gary Smith, vol. IV (Cambridge, MA: Belknap Press of Harvard University Press, 2003).
4. Walter Benjamin, "On the Concept of History," in: *Selected Writings*, ed. Michael W. Jennings and Marcus Bullock, Howard Eiland, Gary Smith, vol. IV (Cambridge, MA: Belknap Press of Harvard University Press, 2003).
5. Walter Benjamin, "One-Way Street," in: *Selected Writings*, ed. Michael W. Jennings and Marcus Bullock, Howard Eiland, Gary Smith, vol. I (Cambridge, MA: Belknap Press of Harvard University Press, 1996).
6. Walter Benjamin, *Pasaże*, ed. Rolf Tiedemann, trans. Ireneusz Kania, postface Zygmunt Bauman (Kraków: Wydawnictwo Literackie, 2005).
7. Walter Benjamin, *The Arcades Project*, trans. Howard Eiland and Kevin McLaughlin, prepared on the basis of the German volume edited by Rolf Tiedman (Cambridge Mass.: The Belknap Press of Harvard University Press, 1999).
8. Walter Benjamin, *The Origin of German Tragic Drama*, trans. John Osborne (London – New York: Verso, 1998).
9. Robert Burton, "Democritus Junior to the Reader," in: *The Anatomy of Melancholy*, 22 June http://www.gutenberg.org/files/10800/10800-h/10800-h.htm.
10. Gustave Flaubert, *Bouvard et Pécuchet avec un choix des scénarios, du Sottisier, L'Album de la Marquise et Le Dictionnaire des idées reçues*, ed. Claudine Gothot-Mersch (Paris: Gallimard, 1999).
11. Gustave Flaubert, *Correspondance*, ed. Bernard Masson, Jean Bruneau (Paris: Gallimard, 2002).
12. Willem van Reijen, "Labyrinth und Ruine. Die Wiederkehr des Barock in der Postmoderne," in: *Allegorie und Melancholie*, ed. Willem van Reijen (Frankfurt am Main: Suhrkamp, 1992).
13. Ryszard Różanowski, *Pasaże Waltera Benjamina. Studium myśli* (Wrocław: Wydawnictwo Uniwersytetu Wrocławskiego, 1997).

14. Gershom Scholem, "Walter Benjamin," in: *On Jews and Judaism in Crisis*, ed. Wrner J. Dannhauser (New York: Schocken Books, 1976).
15. Georg Simmel, *Two Essays. The Handle, and the Ruin*, trans. David Kettler, *Hudson Review*, Autumn (1958).
16. Susan Sontag, "Under the Sign of Saturn," in *Under the Sign of Saturn* (London: Vintage, 1996).
17. *The Correspondence of Walter Benjamin 1910-1940*, ed. Gershom Scholem and Theodor W. Adorno, trans. Manfred R. Jacobson and Evelyn M. Jacobson (Chicago and London: The University of Chicago Press, 1994).
18. Bryan S. Turner, "Ruine und Fragment. Anmerkungen zur Barockstil," in: *Allegorie und Melancholie*, ed. Willem van Reijen (Frankfurt am Main: Suhrkamp, 1992).

## Context-Based Approach

Krzysztof Trybuś

# Benjamin as a Commentator on Norwid

**Abstract:** The text focuses on shared elements in Benjamin's work and the work by Cyprian Norwid, the Polish Romantic poet who predated Benjamin's work. The discussion will revolve around the role of allegory in both authors' work, and around the aesthetic dimension of their contemporary Paris life. Norwid is positioned as a forerunner of Benjamin's critical historiography, which discovered those traces of the past, which have not permeated into collective memory.

**Keywords:** Paris; Rome; allegory; space; town

Benjamin as a commentator on Norwid's work? Obviously, it is impossible: they never met, never read each other's work or thought about it. Nonetheless, although they wrote during different time periods, they lived in the same era and the same city. And it is in the time and space of that city that they met. More precisely, they met in the labyrinth of its biography – the biography of Paris, the capital of the nineteenth century.

When I read *The Arcades Project* with its numerous variants, repetitions, and paralipomena, I cannot resist anticipating that in a moment, on the next page, in the next paragraph, alongside commentaries on the work of Victor Hugo, Teophile Gautier, or Eugene Sue I will see an excerpt from *Vade-mecum* juxtaposed with one from *The Flowers of Evil*. The nostalgia of the following lines by Baudelaire:

> Old Paris is no more (a town, alas,
> Changes more quickly than man's heart may change)[1]

could be followed by Norwid's observations about the close proximity of the old and the new, especially in architecture, the most important manifestation of the cityscape. This city has no marked boundaries, as in the lithographs of Gustave Doré, whom Norwid admired and about whom Benjamin writes as well. These lithographs commingle the contemporary and the old images of Paris, creating a vision outside of time, as in allegory.

For Norwid, as for Benjamin, the choice of allegory was related to the choice of place. The protagonist of *Quidam* asks:

---

1 Charles Baudelaire, *The Swan*, trans. Frank Pearce Sturm, in: *The Flowers of Evil*, ed. Marthiel and Jackson Mathews (New York: New Directions, 1955), p. 79.

> Man can be so closely associated with a place,
> Is thought so often connected with space
> That some frail thing or flimsy object
> Cast light or shade on it by comparison? (III, 103)[2]

As it assumes the form of an allegorical image, thought connected with space is only seemingly enclosed in space. In the city whose architecture had been based on repetition for almost two centuries, one could not avoid using allegory, dwelling in it, and remaining in its shade. Norwid, who saw Baudelaire's Paris from a closer distance than Benjamin did, anticipated Benjamin's discovery of allegory as a region with no boundaries. This is why Rome in the times of Hadrian in *Quidam* resembles Paris from before the modernization, when it was a city of unrelated districts, an intricate labyrinth of narrow streets. The project of rebuilding Rome, undertaken by Hadrian in Norwid's poem, reflects the events of the Haussmann period.[3]

The idea of encountering Norwid's era with its historical and social background in Benjamin's writings seems self-evident. Norwid has long been referred to as a poet of the merchant and industrial era which, however, has no distinct boundaries in his work, effacing the "here and now" of late nineteenth-century Paris. The context of Benjamin's *Arcades Project* makes it possible to discover the surface of things, blurred and unexpressed in Norwid's allegorical constructs. Almost from its beginnings the Paris of the Second Empire was an important element of the poet's reality. In December 1851, witnessing the fights in the streets of Paris during Louis-Napoleon Bonaparte's coup, Norwid wrote:

> Never in the memory of the living has the situation of France been so phenomenal as it is now – if it is not momentary bewilderment, it must be a fall on a grand scale. It seems that for three years the struggle with no plan or banners has been arrested by great effort.
>
> Fifty steps from those who fall under gunfire stand people in smocks and non-smocks, virtually yawning.... I have never imagined the indifference of a crowd of spectators in such proximity.
>
> Looking closely, looking into the pale faces of those fighting, it becomes clear – it is not happening but half-happening... The aura of falling Rome can be sensed – leagues are a purpose to themselves – the emperor is trying his fortune – the rhetors have been

---

[2] All quotations from Norwid come from: Cyprian Norwid, *Pisma wszystkie*, ed. Juliusz Wiktor Gomulicki, vol. I–XI (Warszawa: PIW, 1971–1976). Henceforth they are marked parenthetically in the text as *PWsz* followed by volume number (in Roman numerals) and page number (in Arabic numerals).

[3] See Krzysztof Trybuś, *Epopeja w twórczości Cypriana Norwida* (Wrocław: Ossolineum, 1993), pp. 74–83.

banished as the dailies are closed. We – the pale emigrant faces, like those of the Nazarenes who know what will happen in a thousand years but what they have at their hands is obscure and inaccessible – camps – fires surrounded by cuirassiers. Barbarians from the Neva, from afar... from afar. (*PWsz*, VIII, 145–146)

Characteristically, Norwid transforms the present, captured as the "here and now," into the universal "always and everywhere." A similar process can be observed in his literary writings from that period: the ancient costume superimposed on Paris reality transforms the immediate present into a sort of illusion of timelessness. The concepts of eternal, circular, mythical, still time deployed by Norwid are characteristic of neoclassical writers.

The above depiction of the coup d'état which preceded the proclamation of the empire in France conveys an unreservedly negative recognition of "a fall on a grand scale." Norwid captures the atrophy of the elements that create the emergent reality but does not offer any concretization of the events on the streets of Paris. His view of the birth of the Second Empire seems to find complementation, and a sort of prefiguration, in the excerpt from *Les Miserables* quoted by Benjamin in *The Arcades Project*:

> At the time of the insurrection of May 12, 1839, on the Rue Saint Martin, a little infirm old man, drawing a handcart surmounted by a tricolored rag, in which there were decanters filled with some liquid, went back and forth from the barricade to the troops and from the troops to the barricade, impartially offering glasses of cocoa". (*The Arcades*, p. 719)

Norwid's recognition of the critical dimension of reality (which is not happening but half-happening) is complemented by Benjamin's historiography of detail, which makes it possible to reconstruct the emergence of Norwid's parable at the surface level of phenomena and things, things which, mediated in the poet's everyday experience, describe the accident of his Paris existence. It would be futile to seek biographical detail in Norwid's representation of Paris, either in his letters or literary writings. I argued elsewhere that the colorful air of Paris which has inspired so many poets and painters becomes transparent under Norwid's pen.[4] Now, forced into Benjamin's *Arcades Project*, Paris air regains its colors.

Benjamin asks:

> What would the nineteenth century be to us if we were bound to it by tradition? How would it look as religion or mythology? We have no tactile <*tektisch*> relation to it. That is, we are trained to view things, in the historical sphere, from a romantic distance. To account for the directly transmitted inheritance is important. But it is still too early, for

---

4   See Krzysztof Trybuś, *Stary poeta: Studia o Norwidzie* (Poznań: Wydawnictwo Naukowe UAM, 2000), p. 88 ff.

example, to form a collection. Concrete, materialistic deliberation on what is nearest is now required. "Mythology," as Aragon says, drives things back into the distance. Only the presentation of what relates to us, what conditions us, is important. The nineteenth century – to borrow the Surrealists' terms – is the set of noises that invades our dream, and which we interpret on awakening. (*The Arcades*, p. 831)

A similar idea of reading the nineteenth century was proposed in Poland in Benjamin's times. Interestingly, it was developed with reference to Norwid. In 1933, at the beginnings of his career as a literary critic, Kazimierz Wyka published a now classic essay on "Norwid in Old Age" in the journal *Droga* [The Pathway]. It appeared alongside his teacher Stefan Kołaczkowski's article on Norwid's irony. Both essays radically departed from the earlier eulogistic approach to the poetry of Polish romanticism. Scholars usually ascribe this change to Wyka and his intellectual circle's rejection of the tradition of Polish modernism, noting that it was inspired by the modernist Stanisław Brzozowski's *Legend of Young Poland*.[5]

In his investigation of Norwid in old age, Wyka did much more than examine the reality of St. Casimir's Institution, where the poet spent the last years of his life. He extended the notion of old age to Norwid's entire artistic stance, relating all of the poet's life and work after 1848 to the historical and cultural change taking place in France during his immigrant period. Viewing Norwid's biography retrospectively, from the windows of St. Casimir's Institution, Wyka observed: "Gone were the worldly years, the years of great love for a great lady. Gone was the time of frantic national hopes; memorable and important years had passed – in France, for example, to which he remained the most faithful, so many changes occurred between 1848 to 1877, the year when he had to seek refuge in a shelter."[6] In Wyka's own phrase, his essay on the poet's old age reverberates with a sort of "catastrophic echo." The catastrophic tone results from the critic's deep compassion for Norwid's tragic fate as well as from his strategy of relating the poet's life to a broader panorama of contemporary culture, as in his discussion of the "capitalization" of art in the short story "Ad Leones."

Wyka, who in 1933 received a Fund for National Culture fellowship to do research in Paris, had an opportunity to establish what Benjamin would call "a tactile relationship" with the nineteenth century as embodied by the city that was the capital of the world. Indeed, the Paris of those years was still the capital of the

---

[5] See Maria Janion, "Badania nad romantyzmem polskim," in: *Rozwój wiedzy o literaturze polskiej po 1918 roku*, ed. Janusz Maciejewski (Warszawa: Czytelnik, 1986), p. 131.

[6] Kazimierz Wyka, "Starość Norwida," in: *Cyprian Norwid. Studia, artykuły, recenzje*, ed. Henryk Markiewicz and Marta Wyka (Kraków: Wydawnictwo Literackie, 1989), p. 182.

world. Among the many documents that confirm it, suffice it to quote Czesław Miłosz's description of those times in his "Rue Descartes":

> Passing Descartes Street
> I walked down toward the Seine, a young barbarian on his journey
> Intimidated by his arrival in the capital of the world.[7]

As the author of "Norwid in Old Age" and other essays from that period, Wyka is first and foremost a cultural critic, an attitude that finds perhaps the most forceful expression in his "Norwid as a Poet of Culture," where Wyka underscores "the constantly recurring concept of culture as a dual phenomenon"[8] in Norwid's work and talks about "the realism of culture, its close connection with material conditions and collective life, so clearly distinguishing Norwid's thought from that of others."[9] It is in this essay that Wyka illustrates his reflections on Norwid's "cultural collecting" with an excerpt from Cezary Jellenta, who compares the poet to "a greedy museum which wishes to possess all the treasures of ruins and excavations."[10]

Wyka's later study "A Poet and Conjurer" seems to continue his earlier tendencies, first started in the 1930s, to read Norwid in the context of related European authors and literary movements, and to seek in his writings "architectural components of an independent poetic vision."[11] Applied to Norwid's text, Benjamin's remarks about the domestic interior appear to elaborate on Wyka's observations. Quoting them will not only help us identify the many columns and arches of Norwid's poetry as references to Paris architecture, but will also encompass in our reading of Paris the world of things, which is beyond the scope of Norwid's attention:

> The interior is the asylum of art. The collector is the true resident of the interior. He makes his concern the transfiguration of things. To him falls the Sisyphean task of divesting things of their commodity character by taking possession of them. (*The Arcades*, p. 9)

> The interior is not just the universe but also the étui of the private individual. To dwell means to leave traces. In the interior, these are accentuated. Coverlets and antimacassars, cases and containers are devised in abundance; in these, the traces of the most ordinary subjects are imprinted." (*The Arcades*, p. 9)

---

7   Czesław Miłosz, *Wiersze* (Kraków: Wydawnictwo Literackie, 1985), vol. II, p. 363.
8   Wyka, "Starość Norwida," p. 176.
9   Wyka, "Starość Norwida," pp. 176–177.
10  Quoted after: Wyka, "Starość Norwida," p. 174.
11  Wyka, "Starość Norwida," p. 100.

Such remarks make it possible to discover in everyday domestic life of nineteenth-century Paris those times what Norwid will perceive as his era's *raison d'être*. *Quidam*'s Emperor Hadrian, who "thought of something new: / To express each century with different buildings," (*PWsz*, III, 98) is, just like Napoleon III, a great collector who transforms the capital of the world into a vast collection of architectural forms – "a form of practical memory," (*The Arcades*, 883) to use Benjamin's phrase. The German writer's comments about the relationship between collecting and memory seem to pertain, in Norwid's words, to "Trajan's Column, bronze-coated, / In Napoleon's grand name," (*PWsz*, I, 108) that is, the famous column from Vendôme Square.

Benjamin writes:

> Everything remembered, everything thought, everything conscious becomes socle, frame, pedestal, seal of his possession. It must not be assumed that the collector, in particular would find anything strange in the *topos hyperouránios* – that place beyond heavens which, for Plato, shelters the unchangeable archetypes of things. (*The Arcades*, p. 205)

These unchanging patterns, the patterns of wielding power, are what the monumental protagonists of the poem "Vendôme" converse about.

Benjamin writes:

> Perhaps the most deeply hidden motive of the person who collects can be described this way: he takes up the struggle against dispersion. Right from the start, the great collector is struck by the confusion, by the scatter, in which the things of the world are found. (*The Arcades*, p. 211)

Read as a commentary on Quidam's vicissitudes as a "speck," "a tiny plant," "a lost grain," this fragment foregrounds the spatial aspect of the unfolding tragedy. Even when it takes the form of a body politic, the vast collection remains an infinite entity founded upon the principle of exclusion.

Benjamin writes: "Empire is the style of revolutionary terrorism, for which the state is an end in itself" (*The Arcades*, p. 4).

In one of his later commentaries on *Quidam* Norwid states that "Hadrian's era was the renaissance of Augustus's era and modeled itself on it as today does on Napoleon I" (*PWsz*, IX, 263). He found that era on the streets and squares of the Second Empire; he may also have found it in his apartment in Count Choiseul's summer palace, where his studio resembled an old Roman domicile with a fastigium and a garden.

On the basis of Benjamin's topography of detail concerning "Empire's austere world of forms" (*The Arcades*, p. 5) we can read Quidam's petrified world, separating it into individual pieces of marble. But we may also discover the real structure of this world in the Pompeian column "cast in zinc" if we descend into the unconscious (see *The Arcades*, p. 4). The dreamlike structure of this world is the structure of a narrative.

Reversing the relation between *Quidam* and *The Arcades Project*, we can ramble with Quidam through Benjamin's book of quotations and mark a route, find a path. We can distinguish between a boundary and a threshold, and see how "Out of the field of experience proper to the threshold evolved the gateway that transforms whoever passes under its arch" (*The Arcades*, p. 856). Following Norwid into the depth of allegory, Benjamin could have arrived at Hadrian's Pantheon and recognize it as a *topos hyperouránios*. He might see "the protomodel of things" in the designs of Etienne-Louis Boullée, the "mad architect" of the Revolution whose designs of monuments were based on a spherical dome with openings and revolutionized space since they refused to give people any sense of orientation. The "mad architect" believed that, just like his monuments, streets should have no beginning or end either.[12] Is the cult of perspective during the Second Empire a response to Boullée proposal? This is an unwritten part of *The Arcades Project*.

Following Quidam into Norwid's allegory, Benjamin could have admired the Numidian marble of the Pantheon, brought in by Hadrian from what is today's north-western Tunisia. He could have marveled at the colorful stones: the porphyry from Mons Claudianus in Egypt, the *africano* from Ionia, the *pavonazetto* from Phrygia, the *serpentino* (green porphyry) from the Peloponnese, the *verde antico* from Thessaly. After all, seeing is believing – in the Rome of the Caesars this rule, referred to stone symbolism, served to legitimize power.[13] However, in Hadrian's Rome Benjamin could have found yet another idea defining the relationship between the human being and place, or more precisely, between the human body and place. The first Christians believed that the stronger the faith in God, the lesser the attachment to the place where one lives. In his *Flesh and Stone: The Body and the City in Western Civilization* Richard Sennett reminds us that Roman Christians adopted this belief from the long tradition of Judaism.[14]

Thus, rambling with Quidam, Benjamin could perhaps have discovered the beginning of his dream, found yet another chance of awakening, and recognized his own fate in the life of Norwid's protagonist.

---

12 See Richard Sennett, *Flesh and Stone: The Body and the City in Western Civilization* (New York: Norton, 1994).
13 Janusz Skoczylas, Marek Żyromski, *Symbolika kamienia jako element procesu legitymizowania władzy w cywilizacji europejskiej* (Poznań: Wydawnictwo Naukowe UAM, 2007), p. 56.
14 Sennett, *Flesh and Stone*, p. 76.

Although we may agree that Benjamin's *Arcades Project* tells about a world with no axis, it certainly is not a story without an axis or structural principle. *The Arcades Project* can be read in an indefinite number of ways. We can read it as the author designed it to be read, with no assumption of a whole, or however we want, backwards, as fragments. We can read it in passing, browsing through the book from time to time. Or we can read and reread it, almost infinitely, in the way Benjamin read the nineteenth century. But regardless of the kind and pattern of reading, the choice of quotation and commentary, Benjamin's negative perspective will always unravel the text like Penelope's shroud. After all, the subject of *The Arcades Project* is the twilight of the arcades and a diminishing world without any idea of passage, a world in decline from the times of Louis-Phillippe to the fall of the Second Empire and further.

*Ubi defuit orbis – When the world was no more.* This epigraph to Norwid's poem "Spartacus" could be applied to Benjamin's *Arcades Project*.

The invasion of perspective in urban space and the destruction of the arcades, which entailed the end of the myth of passage, is the story told by both Norwid and Benjamin. It is the theme of all of Norwid's writings and the main topic of Benjamin's work. It is also the story of the lives of these two newcomers, passers-by, and wanderers who only seemingly, owing to an incident of chronology, did not know each other.

Thus, Benjamin can be seen as not only a commentator on Norwid but also a writer from the same family, the family of great solitaries. It is astonishing how their oeuvres complement and illuminate each other. In essence, Norwid's and Benjamin's writings relate a similar adventure, an adventure in a world which is a city. They describe that world according to the same principle, found in observation of the world during a stroll through the streets of their era. The negative perspective which invades that world destroys the material, breaks the composition into fragments, opens up the text. And it reveals passages.

Translated by Magdalena Zapędowska

## Bibliography

1. Charles Baudelaire, *The Swan*, trans. Frank Pearce Sturm, in: *The Flowers of Evil*, ed. Marthiel and Jackson Mathews (New York: New Directions, 1955).
2. Walter Benjamin, *The Arcades Project*, trans. Howard Eiland and Kevin McLaughlin, prepared on the basis of the German volume edited by Rolf Tiedman (Cambridge Mass.: The Belknap Press of Harvard University Press, 1999).

3. Maria Janion, "Badania nad romantyzmem polskim," in: *Rozwój wiedzy o literaturze polskiej po 1918 roku*, ed. Janusz Maciejewski (Warszawa: Czytelnik, 1986).
4. Czesław Miłosz, *Wiersze*, vol. II (Kraków: Wydawnictwo Literackie, 1985).
5. Cyprian Norwid, *Pisma wszystkie*, ed. Juliusz Wiktor Gomulicki, vol. I–XI (Warszawa: PIW, 1971–1976).
6. Richard Sennett, *Flesh and Stone: The Body and the City in Western Civilization* (New York: Norton, 1994).
7. Janusz Skoczylas, Marek Żyromski, *Symbolika kamienia jako element procesu legitymizowania władzy w cywilizacji europejskiej* (Poznań: Wydawnictwo Naukowe UAM, 2007).
8. Krzysztof Trybuś, *Epopeja w twórczości Cypriana Norwida* (Wrocław: Ossolineum, 1993).
9. Krzysztof Trybuś, *Stary poeta: Studia o Norwidzie* (Poznań: Wydawnictwo Naukowe UAM, 2000).
10. Kazimierz Wyka, "Starość Norwida," in: *Cyprian Norwid. Studia, artykuły, recenzje*, ed. Henryk Markiewicz and Marta Wyka (Kraków: Wydawnictwo Literackie, 1989).

Michał Mrugalski
# Myths in the Polish People's Republic. Iwaszkiewicz *avec* Benjamin

**Abstract:** In this article, the poet and high-ranking official Iwaszkiewicz is presented as a symptomatic figure for Communist Poland's relation to nature and the history of Western culture, which in both cases, closely entwined, met features of the mythical worship as Benjamin conceived of it. My contention is that although Iwaszkiewicz worshipped myth diligently and fervently, he did it like the Hop o'My Thumb, the youngest child who triumphed at the end of the fable, because the more diligently he served, the more damage he did in the sorcerer's house.

**Keywords:** Iwaszkiewicz; myth; symbol; nature; fable

Kierkegaard said that paganism is a "sensuousness, but it is a sensuousness that has a relation to spirit, although spirit is not in the deepest sense posited as spirit."[1] Jarosław Iwaszkiewicz, on the other hand, often said that the spirit in its deepest sense is realized a nature and beauty.[2] Fear, and the nothing that corresponds to it, are loathed both by Christians and by pagans like Iwaszkiewicz. The nothingness of fear is, according to Kierkegaard, a destiny, a fate. "Fate is a relation to spirit as external. It is a relation between spirit and something else that is not spirit and to which fate nevertheless stands in a spiritual relation. Fate may also signify exactly the opposite, because it is the unity of necessity and the accidental."[3] Iwaszkiewicz can be called a victim of fate: he entangled himself in a worship of nature. The aesthete considered art to be the ultimate fulfilment of the spirit, ready and stored in works of art, ignoring the infinite striving which is the essence of the spirit which absorbs, according to Solger,[4] a truly modern, Christian, allegoric art.

---

1   Søren Kierkegaard, *The Concept of Anxiety: A Simple Psychologically Orienting Deliberation on the Dogmatic Issue of Hereditary Sin*, trans. Reidar Thomte and Albert B. Anderson (Princeton: Princeton University Press, 1980), p. 96.
2   According to Artur Sandauer (and other critics) for Iwaszkiewicz art is a "substitute for religion" (*Poeci trzech pokoleń* [Warszawa: Czytelnik, 1996], p. 75).
3   Kierkegaard, *The Concept of Anxiety*, p. 96.
4   Karl Wilhelm Ferdinand Solger, "Erwin, or Four Dialogues on Beauty and Art," trans. Joyce Crick, in: *German Aesthetic and Literary Criticism: The Romantic Ironists and Goethe,* ed. Kathleen M. Wheeler (Cambridge: Cambridge University Press, 1984), pp. 129–150.

Iwaszkiewicz usually did not go beyond contemplation of symbols possible only in the world of mythology and the eternal return of the fullness of the world. He worshipped myth diligently and fervently, but he did it like the Hop o'My Thumb, the youngest child who, unlike the proud sorcerer's apprentice, triumphed at the end of the story, because the more diligently he served, the more damage he did in the mythic sorcerer's house. Walter Benjamin called the fable "the earliest arrangements that mankind made to shake off the nightmare which myth had placed upon its chest" ("The Storyteller. Observations on the Works of Nikolai Leskov," in: *Selected Writings*, vol. III, p. 157). This inadvertent sabotage of fate can lead to a new association of chance and necessity, an association different from fate – that association is art. But it must be the kind of art that does not demand worship, an art that is fun enough by itself.

## Deathly Beauty and Animal Religion

Recent times brought a revival of interest in Iwaszkiewicz and his poetry. The leading author of the People's Democratic Republic is still an important "poet of culture." But of what culture? And how? It is certainly not enough to say that he weaved his works on a warp of "intertextual references," and stuffed them with "topoi." That would mean admitting defeat in the face of culture's stupendous legacy, which, instead of reverberating in Iwaszkiewicz's works, muffled and paralysed the author's voice. Iwaszkiewicz's masochism, or the bliss he derived from culture as the source of suffering, has been identified by several interpreters, especially by those fascinated with queer studies. For example, the motto of one of his works can be interpreted accordingly: "Wer die Schönheit angeschaut mit Augen/Ist dem Tode schon anheimgegeben…" [Who watched the beauty with his eyes / is given out to death already]. It is possible to read the heading of *Metop z Selinuntu II*, an epigraph quoted from August von Platen's *Tristan*, as "a tragic formula of an impossible homoerotic desire."[5] German Ritz hesitates, but finally makes this concession in his critical essay. The conclusion is possible, since anything goes, but the reading nullifies the already reduced interpretative capacity of Iwaszkiewicz's work: it either becomes a collection of homoerotic topoi (de-historicization) or a coded, implicit documentary of privations of not-yet-emancipated homosexuals in those times (which is the reverse, a historicization). Iwaszkiewicz's relevance

---

5   German Ritz, *Jarosław Iwaszkiewicz: pogranicza nowoczesności*, trans. Andrzej Kopacki (Kraków: Universitas, 1999), p. 84. (Professor Ritz's study was translated from German into Polish by Andrzej Kopacki. The translator of this paper rendered the quotation in English).

is not a timeless one, common to all humanity. Neither is it imposed as a duty to remember the history which is closed today. It is more fair to read him verbatim: beauty as beauty, and death as death. Only in this way it is possible to avoid dabbing into the private life of a dead hero. What strikes in Iwaszkiewicz's work today, is the relation between a human being and beauty in the given historical situation. The situation made it necessary to refer, anachronistically, to Platen, and to feel the fascinating, destructive force of art. This situation is occurring now, too, regardless of our (in)ability to realize it.

As a part of the great interdependence of culture, Iwaszkiewicz becomes a seismograph (the metaphor is by Hofmannsthal)[6] which records changing intensity of the mythic violence directed against the poet, any poet, in the People's Republic. The poems, above all, are the record of the seismic disturbances, and they demand a close scrutiny. In this way, close reading will reveal the meaning of the poet's great story, whereas biographical evidence will extract details which can become sensual images of an allegory, emblems of the poet. The mythic quality of culture in the People's Republic is confirmed by the poet's powerlessness when, confronted with the living presence of the past, he cannot decide what is still living, what needs to be revived, and what is returning, time and again, as a living corpse which sucks life out of life. That is why the living person fears beauty, which attracts and leads to death, demands worship, and a sacrifice of life. Arcadian moments are rare in Iwaszkiewicz's poetry, for example in *Stary ogród* (The Old Garden) is a place where "pamięć i niepamięć [...] to dwa wieńce splecione w sam raz na mą głowę" [remeberance and forgetting [...] are two entangled wreaths, made just right for my head] (*Wiersze*, p. 472).[7] The tangle of memory and forgetting encourages people and moments to return, however unwillingly. Time is regained, as it were, without effort of will. Usually, however, Iwaszkiewicz describes a terrible

---

6   Hugo von Hofmannsthal, "The Poet and Our Time," in: *Hugo von Hoffmanstahl and the Austrian Idea: Selected Essays and Speeches, 1906–1927*, trans. and ed. David S. Luft (West Lafayette: Purdue University Press, 2011), p. 44. Hofmannsthal compares a poet to a "seismograph that starts to oscillate form every quake, even if it is thousands of miles away. It is not that he thinks constantly about all the things in the world. But they think of him. Even his dullest hours, his depressions, his confusions are impersonal states; they are like the tremors of the seismograph."

7   The following editions of Iwaszkiewicz's works have been used: Jarosław Iwaszkiewicz, *Wiersze* (Warszawa: Czytelnik, 1977), vol. II; Jarosław Iwaszkiewicz, *Muzyka wieczorem* (Warszawa: Czytelnik, 1980); Jarosław Iwaszkiewicz, *Opowiadania*, vol. I–III (Warszawa: Czytelnik, 1980). When quoting from these texts, page numbers are included in the text. (Philological translations are by the translator of this paper).

compulsion to remember everything. The wreath changes into a tool of torture, forcing a prisoner to speak.

Walter Benjamin wanted to break the spell of tradition, magically turned into myth. The "scientific communism" which ruled Poland and other Soviet satellites, did not break with the *bourgeoisie*-capitalist practice of production of prehistory in history. On the contrary, prehistory was unexpectedly reinforced when the socialist propaganda tried to present socialism as the end of prehistory and the beginning of a truly human history, the outcome of emancipating effort of the entire humanity. The capitalist societies left behind, as Marx said, would be the closing stages of the "prehistory of human society."[8] The end of capitalism would mean the emergence from the state of nature into a truly general history,[9] and the consequent rejection of totemism and fetishism, signs of the capitalistic entanglement in the "natural religion"[10], described by Marx as an analogy to Hegel's

---

8   Karl Marx, "A Contribution to the Critique of Political Economy," tansl. Salomea Wolfovna Ryazanskaya, in: *Marx/Engels Collected Works*, vol. XXXI (Moscow: Progress Publishers, 1970), www.marxists.org/archive/marx (for the purposes of this translation, date of access to all Marx's works at www.marxist.org is 21 Nov. 2007).

9   See Karl Marx, Friedrich Engels, "The German Ideology," in: *Marx/Engels Collected Works*, vol. V (Moscow: Progress Publishers, 1968), (especially section 1) http://www.marxists.org/archive/marx/works/1845/german-ideology/ch01a.htm

10  Marx, Engels, *The German Ideology*. On the entanglement of the human species in nature, and the "natural history of humanity" that Marx plans to conduct to the moment of emergence from the state of nature, see (for example) "Economic and Philosophical Manuscripts," trans. Martin Mulligan, in *Marx/Engels Collected Works*, vol. III (Moscow: Progress Publishers, 1975), especially section XXVI: "only naturalism is capable of comprehending the action of world history," and a dialectical reversal in the next section: "History is the true natural history of man." In footnote 4 to the 13th chapter of 1st volume of *Capital*, Marx insists that development of technology, or society's productive organs, should be investigated in the same manner as Darwin applied to investigation of productive organs of plants and animals. Marx refers to Vico's principle of real facts (*verum factum*), or direct accessibility of history to humanity that was formed by it. It seems that Marx does only because he wants to question Vico's fundamental distinction between human history and natural one (which is distant and estranged from people), because he would always study processes of production of life, biological or social. Also: the end of the first article of the "Debates on the Law of Thefts of Wood" (*Marx/Engels Collected Works*, vol. I [Moscow: Progress Publishers, 1975]); the chapters on primitive accumulation in *Capital*, and in *Outline of the Critique of Political Economy*. Marxist critique of human nature and nature in general, the natural history of man, should be the foundation of all political and gender-oriented interest in literature. In very early "Debates on Freedom of Press," conducted in the *Rheinishe Zeitung* in 1842, he claims that licensing

"animal religion." (In the epoch of animalistic religion, fighting groups of people were formed by shared interests and identified with an animal, while trying to hunt and devour other groups[11]. Relics can be still seen in today's language: the big fish eat small fish, Asian tigers hunt fat cats. The most abstract processes can be described by means of botanical or aquatic metaphors, hence Hegel's "plant religion": process of growth and rising levels of this and that.) It is small wonder, then, that communist countries, seeing how they fail the hopes of young Marx, lied about their cultural affluence: the entirety of culture was supposedly available to every individual. The meaning of history was clear and self evident to every member of the saved portion of humanity. Robert Weimann, a leading literary critic of the German Democratic Republic, attacked Adorno for his views of tradition, views supposedly derived from folktale imagination. Adorno, apparently, wanted to cheat the false and oppressive tradition, so that it would give its most precious treasured to those, who seem to care the least:

> Poetry rescues its real content where, in closest contact with tradition, it rejects tradition. Who does not want to betray the blissful happiness that tradition still promises in some images, the potentiality covered and hidden by its ruins, must turn away from tradition

---

of the right to participate in public debate leads to the situation where "press, instead of being a bond uniting the nation, would be a sure means of dividing it, that the difference between the estates would thus be fixed intellectually, and the history of literature would sink to the level of the natural history of the particular intelligent breeds of animals" – http://www.marxists.org/archive/marx/works/1842/free-press/ch06.htm In German, the wording is even more radical: *und die Literaturgeschichte zur Naturgeschichte der besonderen geistigen Tierrassen herabsänke* – 20 July 2007 http://www.mlwerke.de/me/me01/me01_066.htm). This topic is discussed in, most importantly, in Theodor Wiesengrund Adorno's *Negative Dialectic: Philosophy and the Possibility of Critical Rationality*. The idea, developed in *Dialectic of the Enlightenment*, was Adorno's concern from the beginning of his work, e.g. in "The Idea of Natural History," *Gesammelte Schriften*, vol. 1 (Frankfurt am Main: Suhrkamp, 1973). Further comments in Karl Löwith's *Meaning of History: The Theological Implications of the Philosophy of History* (Chicago: University of Chicago Press, 1949), and *From Hegel to Nietsche: The Revolution in Nineteenth Century Thought*, trans. David E. Green (New York: Columbia UP, 1964). Additionally, Alfred Schmidt's "Die in Naturgeschichte verstrickte Menschheit," in: *Krise und Kritik. Zur Aktualität der Marxschen Theorie*, ed. Gerhard Schweppenhäser (Springe: Dietrich zu Klampen, 1987). On the role of animals in Marx's thought (animals will be very important in this reading of Iwaszkiewicz's work), see Heinz Schandl, *Der Naturbegriff nach Karl Marx. Über den Mehrwert und die Rolle des Tieres in der Marx'schen Theorie*, 18 June 2006 http://www.iff.ac.at/socec/backdoor/ws0405-se-usoz/BarlaJosef.pdf

11   Georg Wilhelm Friedrich Hegel, *The Phenomenology of Spirit*, trans. Arnold V. Miller (Oxford: Clarendon Press, 1977), p. 387 and ff.

that transforms meaning and potentiality into a lie. Tradition can only return in what relentlessly resists it.[12]

Weimann knows, like Adorno and Benjamin did, that the present constantly redetermines its relation to the past, but this very knowledge does not allow him to see that something wrong is happening to tradition. Tradition is sacred: this is the dogma of modernity, consecrated by blood spilled in class struggles, completed and won long before 1953, when communist authorities lost their trust in society. The socialist critic of culture, by rejecting criticism of the present, starts to worship tradition:

> acceleration of the march to future can, and must, be accompanied by deeper assimilation of the legacy of the past. [...] Material efficiency, which has greatly increased today, must be based upon, and support spiritual self-consciousness, which a working personality derives from becoming conscious of the quality of its trained relation to society. [...] Members of a socialist community, as they expand their understanding of 'the whole movement of history' as an 'absorbed and conscious movement of their own coming to existence' (Marx), increasingly relate their present life to the unity of those material and spiritual achievements, in which important human powers objectified themselves in the course of human history. The deeper they understand their transformative process as a social one, the more conscious they become that history of literature is the history of their own spiritual and aesthetic powers.[13]

In an eulogy of socialist culture, the incongruity of images (since the scientific terminology is yoked into a fantastic poem), is an indication that the train of reasoning is kept together by the force of desire, not by facts: old-time feats and privations "objectified themselves" into artefacts of culture, which we decode today, to find out what we know (i.e. to know our trained, acquired relation with society). Reversely, the more we learn about ourselves, the better we see the past. The ultimate objectification of tradition, the inevitable goal of construction of socialist societies, was determination of the correct shape of tradition. Preservation and consolidation of history would be completed thanks to developing productive forces that served all members of society. Collective consciousness of history would catch up with the present. However, objectification also means reification. In Weimann's vision, no new technique is employed to explore the past. The present (modernity) has been omitted in his exploration of the past. The best

---

12 Theodor Wiesengrund Adorno, "O tradycji," in: *Sztuka i sztuki*, trans. Krystyna Krzemienowa, Karol Saureland, (Warszawa: PIW, 1990), p. 57.
13 Robert Weimann, "Współczesność a przeszłość w historii literatury," in: *Literatura: produkcja i recepcja. Studia z metodologii historii literatury*, ed. Hubert Orłowski (Warszawa: PIW, 1978), p. 18.

# Myths in the Polish People's Republic. Iwaszkiewicz *avec* Benjamin

indication of this fact is the inscription of the past into the 19th century vision of culture (e.g. Hegel's "objective spirit"). Benjamin called this procedure a "reifying" representation of culture: "The riches [...] amassed in the aerarium of civilization henceforth appear as though identified for all time" (*The Arcades*, p. 14). Absorbing this kind of culture is like swallowing the stones of Venice after work. The dissonance between technical possibilities and real production relations (in this case, production and consumption of culture) is the cycle which determines beginnings of new epochs according to Marx, or which is a factor responsible for the permanent disaster according to Benjamin. The effect of this dissonance is that "the new forms of behavior and the new economically and technologically based creations [...] enter tne univers of a phantasmagoria," (*The Arcades*, p. 14) or myth. Members of a socialist society receives a mythicized past, a colourful screen that cuts them off from their very own capabilities, determined by none other than history. Whereas the dialectic image, the basic technique of the *Arcade Project* heals not only history, but also the present. One of the reasons why the "now" must collide with the "then" is because we must learn to *predict the present*, according to words of a politician lost in the *Arcades*.

Reification of legacy had its inevitable consequences: fetishization reinstates animism. In things of the past there live malignant powers that the seemingly tame lives a secret life, ready to strike at careless manipulators. The feeling was that forty and a half centuries are looking down at curators of culture, which brought about a paranoid suspiciousness (against culture), a characteristic of people afflicted by guilt complex. At a meeting of the Polish Literary Association, when Communist authorities forced the controversial production of *Dziady* off the stage, Leszek Kołakowski said, with Iwaszkiewicz listening as the chair:

> It is a classic, textbook example of positive feedback: the means designed to suppress resistance (nobody is thinking about its real sources), lead to the situation in which more means of oppression are needed, and thus the process continues infinitely. Naturally, the resistance will find it way, when pressed out of the natural ways, into accidental, arbitrary areas. In this way, the most innocent circumstances will lose their neutrality, and become dangerous trouble spots. [...] We have arrived at the embarrassing situation, where all the world's dramatic works, from Aeschylus, through Shakespeare, to Ionesco, became a set of dangerous innuendos related to the People's Republic of Poland.[14]

Benjamin, in his monumental essay on Goethe's *Elective Affinities*, read the novel as history of unsuccessful emancipation. Thus, he established the correlation between

---

14 Marta Fik, *Kultura marcowa. Wokół Dziadów – Literaci i władza – Kampania marcowa* (Warszawa: Wydawnictwo Wodnika, 1995), p. 138.

*myth, guilt, and fate*, which is essential for his historiography. This correlation assumes the same shape as Freud's Oedipal patricide.[15] Like in Freud, repression of mythic forces, present in the fictional world but ignored by characters, leads to a "return of the repressed content" which becomes increasingly destructive, in accordance with the logic of positive feedback. The nightmare can be averted by the sacrifice of Ottilie, Goethe's beloved character, whose beauty augurs her fate (i.e. redemptive death). Ten years after the essay on *Elective Affinities,* Benjamin wrote that the aura of hopelessness surrounding Kafka's defendants makes them his only beautiful characters (see "Franz Kafka. On the Tenth Anniversary of His Death," in: *Selected Writings*, vol. II, part 2, pp. 797–798). Sadly, all sacrifices are made too late, and this is not just because the lives of other characters have been destroyed, never to be so cheerful as before the opening of action (and before the reaction of the demonic). Myth closes in around the victim, and turns around, like it always did, *in the circle of eternal return*: "The essence of the mythical event is return. Inscribed as a hidden figure in such events is the futility that furrows the brow of some of the heroic personages of the underworld (Tantalus, Sisyphus, the Danaides)" (*The Arcades*, p. 119). It is not possible to break free from myth, such is its centripetal force. Sometimes, however, it can be stopped and held back, like in the dialectical image of Kafka-Sysyphus, a flash photograph of hell. Kafka "moves the mass of historical happenings the way Sisyphus rolled the stone. As he does so, its nether side comes to light; it is not a pleasant sight, but Kafka is capable of bearing it" ("Franz Kafka. On the Tenth Anniversary of His Death," in: *Selected Writings*, vol. II, part 2, p. 808). He stares, motionless.

Among the sins committed by the heroes of *Elective Affinities*, removal of the old cemetery, and replacing it with the landscape garden, seems to be especially grave for Benjamin. Destruction of graves is a sin against memory, because, according to Benjamin, the dead support the ground under the feet of the living; and this, not only according to myth, but also according to religion, the spiritual order (see "Goethe's *Elective Affinities*," in: *Selected Writings*, vol. I, pp. 302–303). We are not going to emancipate ourselves by forgetting old superstitions or by ignoring death. Coming of age would be possible only through a new, better remembrance; it would establish a new, different relation between the living and the dead, which would radically transform the meaning of "history" and "nature." An authentic taming of myth can happen through healing of memory, which is synonymous

---

15 The similarity has been pointed out by Winfried Menninghaus in *Schwellenkunde. Walter Benjamins Passage des Mythos* (Frankfurt am Main: Suhrkamp, 1986), p. 21. See also Rolf-Peter Janz, "Mythos und Moderne bei Walter Benjamin," in: *Mythos und Moderne*, ed. Karl Heinz Bohrer (Frankfurt am Main: Suhrkamp, 1983).

with a truly rational organization of society, because relations between the living are determined by their relations with the dead.

The notion of *nature* must be added to the constellation of myth, guilt, and fate. Fate is an inclusion of every living thing into the union based on guilt and retribution, Benjamin's "guilt among the living," ("Goethe's *Elective Affinities*," in: *Selected Writings*, vol. I, p. 307) and this union is destructive not only for the living, but above all for life itself. Granted, Benjamin shares Gundolf's view that notions of law, fate, and character in *Elective Affinities* are constructed analogously to bud, flower, and fruit, in accordance with Goethe's natural science. However, at the same time Benjamin fervently protests against the thought that fate and misfortune could be ascribed to workings of innocent plants. Comparing a human being to a fruit is only an allegory, and only human faults can deform nature, a force which imprisons the characters in prehistory. People relate to nature, by considering themselves as something external, but in fact something intimately linked, or perhaps as something which is more of themselves than they (themselves) are. Caught in the magnetic force field of the earth, the characters do not shape nature, but become its tragic actors and stage engineers (see "Goethe's *Elective Affinities*," in: *Selected Writings*, vol. I, p. 303). "The mythic is the real material content of this book; its content appears as a mythic shadowplay staged in the costumes of the Age of Goethe" ("Goethe's *Elective Affinities*," in: *Selected Writings*, vol. I, p. 309). The heroes of the novel do not fulfil the ideal of *Bildung*; instead, they settle for typicality, which turns into a sign of eternal return of the same, of fate. This is probably because the characters constantly make elective choices (*Wahl*), instead of saving themselves by making a decision (*Entscheidung*). Their modernity is but a re-enactment of old acts. In *The Arcades Project*, the saving decision is made through dialectic image.

The heroes of *Elective Affinities* establish a spiritual relation with something that is not a spirit, thus, in accordance with Kierkegaard's diagnosis, falling into the trap of fate. This fate can be concretized in the language of Marx: "The newly emancipated powers of wealth become, through a strange play of destiny, sources of privation. […] The result of all our inventions and progress seems to be that material powers become invested with spiritual life, while human life deteriorates into a material force."[16] Human life is dominated by forces which it cannot comprehend. Comparing the fetishist world of goods to the mythic fate, and the promise that communism would overcome the fate: these are the tenets of

---

16 Karl Marx, *Die Revolution von 1848 und das Proletariat* (1849) (quoted after: Löwith, *Meaning in History*, p. 36).

Marxist criticism, e.g. "how does it happen that trade, which after all is nothing more than the exchange of products of various individuals and countries, rules the whole world through the relation of supply and demand – a relation which, as an English economist says, hovers over the earth like the fate of the ancients, and with invisible hand allots fortune and misfortune to men, sets up empires and overthrows empires, causes nations to rise and to disappear – while with the abolition of the basis of private property, with the communistic regulation of production (and, implicit in this, the destruction of the alien relation between men and what they themselves produce), the power of the relation of supply and demand is dissolved into nothing, and men get exchange, production, the mode of their mutual relation, under their own control again?"[17] Fight against myth is the theological secret, an element of pure Judaism[18] in Marx's philosophy (in spite of his anti-Semitic association of capital with Jews). It is a permissible conclusion, then, that the young Benjamin, an openly religious thinker, was ready for his conversion to Marxism, a conversion of great importance for someone who wanted to preserve rudiments of theology in a secularized world. Through this conversion, Benjamin's theology could be adjusted to the state of creation, keeping alive and in contact with reality, instead of turning to dust in empty libraries. If we treat Iwaszkiewicz as an instrument that records the mythic state of affairs in Communist Poland, our reading will confirm the observation that the People's Republic did not abolish myth and its fetishism. Instead, his works contain flash images of myth, images which destroy myth from within. Returning to *Elective Affinities*: life of nature, into which the characters slide, runs the circular path of eternal return, thus: beauty, death, myth, guilt, forgetting, fate, union, nature.

---

17  Marx, Engels, *The German Ideology*, 20 Novembre 2007 http://www.marxists.org/archive/marx/works/1845/german-ideology/ch01a.htm

18  The opposition between Judaism and myth is discussed, for example, in Julius Gutman's fundamental work, *Philosophies of Judaism: The History of Jewish Philosophy from Biblical Times to Franz Rosenzweig*, trans. Dawid W. Silverman (New York: Shocken Books, 1973), p. 9 and ff. Of course, rabbi Gutman, with his wary attitude to mystical strains of Judaism (they were a lasting and formative influence on Benjamin), creates a rather static, undialectic opposition between myth and Judaist ethical, voluntaristic personalism. This makes his work unsuitable for a reading of Iwaszkiewicz through Benjamin. However, the desire to distance oneself from myth is the defining quality of every Judaism, and of "the Christian heresy." Myth threatens these religions both from outside and from inside.

## Dogs and people

> *Für das Tier ist die menschliche Gestalt das Höchste,*
> *wie der Geist demselben erscheint.*
> *Aber für den Geist ist sie nur die erste Erscheinung desselben*
> *und die Sprache sogleich sein vollkommenerer Ausdruck.*
> Hegel, *Enzyklopädie* § 411

Iwaszkiewicz, reconsidered, is not a poet of culture, but one of nature: not only because his work equivocally expresses two seemingly contradictory urges, the desire to become one with both culture and nature. The combination is typical for literature of the turn of the 20th century, which is why Tadeusz Konwicki called Iwaszkiewicz an "eminent 19th century writer." From this temporal position, Iwaszkiewicz raids the borders of modernity. Iwaszkiewicz could repeat the motto of young Rilke: the poet, who becomes a new kind of landscape painter, should unite with great currents of nature, *sich selbst irgendwo an ihre [Natur – M.M.] großen Zusammenhänge einzufügen* (emphasis mine)[19]. Universalistic demands of the hermeneutic, represented by Gadamer's thought, is based precisely on the same process: every poet is considered to be a poet of culture, even natural scientists become inadvertent poets of culture, because tradition, synonymous with truth, makes poets and scientists perceive things as things, perceive in a particular way, so that perception (*wahrnehmen*) turns out to be reception-in-truth (wahr-*nehmen*). This is accompanied by a countermovement of naturalization of language, this *Zwischenwelt der Sprache*, which, as long as we can listen to it wisely, becomes the source of all truth, immune to falsities of ideology.[20] Deculturalization of nature and naturalization of culture are two examples of numerous circular, inverting structures that organize both Gadamer's thought and Iwaszkiewicz's literary art. The universal structures, however, are too general to explain the specific quality of Iwaszkiewicz's writing and his peculiar complex of culture and nature, which organizes his poetical universe. Unlike the German philosopher, Iwaszkiewicz looks at culture, as it were, from the inside of nature. He compares himself, a poet, to a stork in Ryczywół:[21] the animal is looking at a church and clattering nonsensically,

---

19   Rainer Maria Rilke, "Worpswede. Monographien einer Landschaft und ihrer Maler," in: *Sämliche Werke*, ed. Ernst Zinn (Frankfurt am Main: Suhrkamp Verlag, 1965), vol. 5, p. 14.
20   See Hans-Georg Gadamer, "Text and Interpretation," in: *The Gadamer Reader. A Bouquet of the Later Writings*, ed. and trans. Richard E. Palmer (Evanston, Illinois: Northwestern University Press, 2007), p. 166.
21   In Polish, the name is (or used to be) a synonym of stagnation and decline. (It is a village to the south of Warsaw.)

but it is keeping a rhythm (*Muzyka wieczorem*). Contemplation of beauty pushes the poet into animal existence, making him aware of his inferiority, frailty, vulnerability, and unsurpassable obtuseness. Natural and artificial beauty combine in a strange entanglement: the series of poems *Psy i ptaki* from *Śpiewnik włoski* gives human voice (in first or third person) only to animals painted and carved by human craft. Still, the animals are beautiful, and thus able to evoke animal delight: "Bo ja czasami śpię i widzę w nocy / zarysy boskie gór, z radości szczekam / i jestem chyba jak ty, biało-czarny / pies horacjański" [Because I am sometimes asleep and see at night / divine outlines of mountains, I bark of joy / and I seem to be like you, the black-and-white / Horatian dog] (p. 445); it is a dog painted on the wall of Horace's villa. The euphoric barking disturbs any thought, but the thought (sometimes) can take advantage of the fact that the crowd is gathering around the source of noise, and takes a totally different path in an act of evasion.

In *The Old Poet* animalism combines with humanity into a hierarchy of incomprehensibility. The result if a proportional relation: hieroglyphs of cosmos are as incomprehensible to people as human words are to animals. In general, Iwaszkiewicz seems to build a cosmology that includes analogical steps of the levels of Hegelian pantheism[22]: from religion of elements (geological), e.g. The cult of water, through religion of plants, to religion of animals. The stratification of creation is reflected, in the temporal aspect of Iwaszkiewicz's work, by the shift of interest from plants to animals in the 1960s. The same shift is described in the VIII b chapter of the *Phenomenology of Spirit*, as the step from calm contemplation of different atoms of spirit to an adverse agitation. The innocence of religion of flowers, the impersonal image of the self, transforms into the solemn, fighting spirit of life, into the guilt (*Schuld*) of religion of animals: quiet and powerless contemplating individual, into the destructive *Für-sich-sein*. But Iwaszkiewicz's "animal religion" does not identify the self with a fighting predator; instead the self is a domesticated, tame animal, a victim rather than aggressor.

Nevertheless, those tame pets can give a lesson of resoluteness to historical materialists, e.g. the white poodle of St. Augustine in Benozzo Gozzola's fresco (*Benozzo Gozzoli*, p. 453):

> Święty Augustyn bardzo się zamyślił przed podróżą z Rzymu do Mediolanu. Wie że tyle spraw od tego zależy. Jest jakby niezdecydowany. I ludzie którzy go wyprawiają są

---

[22] I know about two monographic discussions of Iwaszkiewicz's religiousness: Zbigniew Chojnowski, *Poetycka wiara Jarosława Iwaszkiewicza* (Olsztyn: WSP, 1999); Piotr Mitzner, *Na progu: doświadczenia religijne w tekstach Jarosława Iwaszkiewicza* (Warszawa: UKSW, 2003).

niepewni. Ale biały pudel pod brzuchem jego konia kroczy pełen decyzji i odwagi. Wie o co chodzi. On idzie pewnie i wie że dojdzie choć jest trochę za tłusty. Może rzeczywiście zwierzęta lepiej wiedzą jak trzeba żyć?
[St. Augustine sank deep in thought before his journey from Rome to Milan. He knows that so many matters depend on the outcome. He seems to be irresolute. And the people who prepare him for the travel are in doubt, too. But the white poodle under the belly of his horse strides on, full of resolution and courage. He knows what it is about. He walks confidently, and he knows he will get there, even though he is a bit too fat.
So perhaps animals indeed know better how to live?]

The poodle resolutely strides among people afflicted by doubt, but does not go beyond the frames, not wishing to be seen in the corner of the painting. Perhaps, thanks to its easy stride, the contrast between the margin and the "ideological content" will become the main theme of the painting. The poodle, which does not go beyond the painting, while introducing the right kind of dissonance, becomes an allegorical emblem of the fact, that happiness can be anticipated only within the frames of myth, because happiness does not like breaking thresholds. Manninghaus provides numerous quotations supporting the statement that in Benjamin "levelling thresholds, or ripping the apart, is not an act of liberation, but a disaster, intrusion of chaos into a mythically formed world."[23] Chaos means unleashing mythic powers uninhibited by any thresholds. Similarly, in Iwaszkiewicz's *Powrót Prozerpiny*, one of the *Italian Novelettes*, Mme Cannet's intervention leads to a disaster, when she wants to interrupt the cyclical misfortune of Dick Wames, who loses his Persephone for the larger portion of each year. The Persephone (Kora), persuaded by Mme Cannet to abandon her husband and children, so that she can enjoy her affair with Wames, becomes so emancipated that she marries a chance encounter, a theatrical agent, whereas Dick Wames drinks himself to death. The theatrical agent has Dionisian attributes, just like Dick,[24] who destroys himself among Corybants. Besides, Dionysius is Hades, as Heraclitus tells us (fragment 33). Mme Cannet, in spite of her best intentions, has to carry the burden of a terrible guilt. Myth has not been destroyed; Cannet's unthinking action only intensified its ruthless operation. Cannet's wisdom, revealed in the moral of the story, has been won too late: "Persephone must return to the land of the dead." The wisdom, however, is ambiguous, since Persephone will end up in hell anyway. Only when myth is made open, is it possible to conduct Kierkegaard's "opening forward," into a

---

23 Menninghaus, *Schwellenkunde*, p. 40.
24 See Małgorzata Łukasiewicz, "Szanse happy endu – *Powinowactwa z wyboru, Śmierć w Wenecji, Powrót Prozerpiny*", in: *Recepcja literacka i proces literacki*, ed. German Ritz, Gabriela Matuszek (Kraków: Universitas, 1999), p. 294.

real novelty whose relation with the past is not an eternal repetition of the same in the new, but a preservation of the archaic and the incredible in the jubilant tension. Thus Benjamin: "Eternal recurrence is an attempt to combine the two antinomic principles of happiness: that of eternity and that of the 'yet again.' – The idea of eternal recurrence conjures the speculative idea (or phantasmagoria) of happiness from the misery of the times" ("Central Park," in: *Selected Writings*, vol. IV, p. 184). "Dialectic of happiness: dual willing: the incredible, the astonishing, the summit of bliss. And: the eternal again of the same situation, an eternal restoring of the original, first happiness" (VI, p. 202). This, among other things, is the dialectic of conservative and revolutionary tendencies in messianic thought.[25]

According to Adorno, the language of Goethe's *Iphigenia in Tauris* reconciliates myth with itself.[26] Language contains what Orestes is silent about, too, both in Goethe's and in Aeschylus' tragedy. Benjamin used Orestes' silence as the base for his demonstration of escape from myth and law in the world of Greek tragedy. The tragic hero is silent, terrified by his/her moral superiority over gods, with their inhuman fondness for strict natural law that pushes heroes, in a circular movement, from the top to the bottom, making triumph synonymous with fall. Orestes is silent in *Eumenides* (see *The Origin of German Tragic Drama*, p. 109), where only his divine defender, Apollo, speaks in human voice. In the words of Florien Chrystian Rang, who taught Benjamin a lot about tragedy: "Only through the shape of verbal expression, tragedy makes it possible to break with astrology, to escape from the message of stars, escape from fate (Rang, *Briefe* I, 336)."[27] Only through the voice confronted with absurd of fate, adds Benjamin, can tragedy become an introduction to prophecy. The word and the silence of pre-time, in which the voice tries to be heard, are tragic. Suffering and death, which release the voice, are also tragic. Tragedy, however, can never be reduced to the pragmatic content of the plot (see *The Origin of German Tragic Drama*, p. 118). Iwaszkiewicz, having shown us Persephone freed from hell into free hell, shifts his attention to Orestes, who escaped from myth, running straight into modernity:

---

25  See Gershom Scholem, *The Messianic Idea in Judaism and other Essays on Jewish Spirituality* (New York: Schocken Books, 1971).
26  Theodor Wisengrund Adorno, "On the Classicism of Goethe's Iphigenia," in: *Notes on Literature*, trans. Shierry Weber Nicholsen (New York: Columbia University Press, 1992), p. 13 and ff.
27  Quoted after Carrie S. Asman, "Theater and Agon/Agon and Theater: Walter Benjamin and Florens Christian Rang," *MLN*, vol. 107, No. 3 (1992).

Orestes biegnie mostem
Zabił matkę
Zgwałcił siostrę
Porzucił Pyladesa

Dokąd prowadzi ten most?

Most łączy brzegi
tam i tam
Co jest tam?

Dokąd biegnie Orestes?

Zawieszony nad światem
Co widzi Orestes?

Widzi krew
Widzi brzeg
Widzi brzask

A może widzi zieloną łąkę
usianą tarczami
i kwiaty

Czy to anemony?

[Orestes is running across a bridge / He killed his mother / He raped his sister / Abandoned Pylades / Where does this bridge lead? / The bridge connects shores / here and there / What is there? / Where is Orester running? / Hung above the world / What does Orestes see? / He sees blood / He sees the shore / He sees dawn / Or perhaps he sees a green meadow / spotted with shields / and flowers / Are these anemones?]

The flowers are perceived, received-in-truth and as beautiful as anemones. *Ecce homo*, Orestes is nothing like Iwaszkiewicz's happy animals. Fortunately, we still do not understand what he sees quite clearly.

Hope dwells only in conscious blabbering. To anticipate resurrection, by reaching back to the moment of birth, is to know that one still cannot talk, and play with words and things with the stubbornness of a child or an animal. Iwaszkiewicz plays thus, eschatologically, in *Podróż do Patagonii*, when he attempts to purify the word, so that it becomes the word of Judgement:

Obrazy z barw się oczyszczają,
  Kwiaty ulatują jak ptaki,
    Zostaje, jak szkielet,
      Słowo
        I prawda (s. 201).

[Images purge themselves of colours, / Flowers fly away like birds, / What remains, like a skeleton / Is word / And truth]

But what truth remains? That the Word is hidden in blabbering:

> Sonaty i sonety, yachty i jogurty,
>         Rozmiecione jak karty igry
> Na pachnących deltach wyspy Tigre,
> Strzaskane tablice starych praw,
>         Fanfary kirem zamroczone,
> Zamglone cyprysy słów,
>         I prawda jasna jak dzień (p. 203).

[Sonatas and sonnets, yachts and yoghurts, / Scattered like playing cards / Over perfumed deltas of Tigre river, / Broken tablets of old laws, / Flourishes stunned by pall, / Hazy cypresses of words, / And the truth that is clear as day]

Indeed, Iwaszkiewicz, as a prophet of the truth clear as day, is like a dog barking at the sun:

> Kwiaty, owoce, liście, książki, szafy, graty,
> Złamane klawikordy, czarne futerały,
> Rozdartych nut kaskady, wazon popielaty,
> Pulpit pod ewangelię i dwa pastorały,
>
> Potargane paprocie, drewniane buławy,
> Lalka, koń z włosiennicy, stoliczek kulawy,
> Okręt bez żagli, i ja na tym leżę
> Jak wielkie, pobrudzone, zachwycone zwierzę. (*Rzeczy*, *Muzyka wieczorem*, p. 14)

[Flowers, fruit, leaves, books, wardrobes, odds and ends, / Broken clavichords, black instrument cases, / Cascades of torn music scores, a grey vase, / A Gospel pulpit and two crosiers, / Shattered ferns, wooden maces, / A doll, a horse made of sackcloth, a crooked stool, / A ship without sails, and me too on the pile / Like a big, soiled, delighted animal.]

For an animal, an accidental object, found by chance, broken and thrown away, can become a treasure, for reasons (cause) that the animal does not understand (because it does not understand the notion of cause), though the reasons must be very important. Hence, several species of animals collect objects. Benjamin interprets Goethe's collecting passion as an expression of superstition: fear that is an effect of entanglement in myth (see "Goethe's *Elective Affinities*," in: *Selected Writings*, vol. I, pp. 319–320). For the Polish poet the awakening of a collecting instinct is not an example of the "reifying vision of culture," but brings a totally different relation to artefacts of the past, which are cherished and treasured because they are ambiguous, historically undetermined. This attitude is particularly well seen in the language that blabbers about them, turning every collected object, piled up in a lair or nest, into a hieroglyph of mysterious wisdom. This, also, is a way of cheating myth that imprisons us: by serving it as best as we can, but without understanding. The service was criticized by Hegel as cheap pantheism, in the opening of the chapter of *Aesthetics* devoted to pantheism of art: the pantheism that worships everything, i.e. cans and tins, houses, lichens, maces, stools, instead of cherishing the all-encompassing Everything, or substantiality, the immanent quality of every thing, abstracted from every thing's particular details, their empirical reality. Iwaszkiewicz surrenders to things, while ignoring the general soul of the world; the Everything loses its totality, when it slides into the aggregate of objects, whose pile is growing with new and new acquisitions. This is a totally different kind of desire for everything. By attempting to preserve every bit of tradition, the delighted animal inadvertently contributes to the revelation that tradition is but a huge pile of trash. The passéist unintentionally informs us about the nature of progress and integration of the past by humanity, on its way to the fullness of humanity. Iwaszkiewicz, who was never a resolute person (and who turned this into an advantage as an author), does not learn much resoluteness from the dogs and cats in *Śpiewnik włoski*, but he shares their fondness of peace and quiet, disregard of the human peace and human moralizing. He does not care about human matters. An example: at a long sitting of a committee Zygmunt Mycielski is passing a card to Iwaszkiewicz with a complaint about boredom and purposelessness of it. Iwaszkiewicz, who has been enduring the same hours, answers: "Je m'en Fiche. J.Iw."[28] He did not care about the great myths of the mythicized culture, and treated them in a cavalieric manner, although he could not escape from them. He would combine Odysseus' circular route with Moses's exodus from Egypt; he did not find them mutually exclusive. Thus, travelling to Patagonia, where he never arrived, he presents himself as Moses, standing on Mount Nebo, and watching Odysseus' conversations with the dead. From there, from Iwaszkiewicz's way, we can see that Benjamin was not afraid of ridicule either. Precisely at the moments of greatest pathos, he can be most ironic. Benjamin's writings are a transcendental masquerade, their author, like a clown, changed acts and costumes incessantly. His cheerful irresponsibility, an authentic sense of adventure, cannot be contained in the boring, ashamed morality play of post-war Germany, whose minimalist moralizing found its apogee in Jurgen Habermas's theory of communicative action. Benjamin does not fit into the boring pop-foolishness either. He is freed by his own misfortune, his death, when he contradicts it, opens it with laughter. It could be a redundant, needless gesture. Iwaszkiewicz, likewise, softened death not

---

28 Zygmunt Mycielski, *Dziennik 1960–1969* (Warszawa: Iskry, 2001) p. 325.

only in his poems, where he derided death, but also in his own funeral, which he organized as masquerade. Dressed up in a miner's uniform, incensed by a priest, he juxtaposed the two deepest-nagging Polish myths: the "incredibly rowdy"[29] Catholicism clashed with the chthonic, pagan power based on exploration of powers hidden underground by magic.

## Bibliography

1. Theodor Wisengrund Adorno, *Negative Dialectics*, trans. E.B. Ashton (New York & London: Continuum, 2007).
2. Theodor Wisengrund Adorno, "On the Classicism of Goethe's Iphigenia," in: *Notes on Literature*, trans. Shierry Weber Nicholsen (New York: Columbia University Press, 1992).
3. Theodor Wiesengrund Adorno, "O tradycji," in: *Sztuka i sztuki*, trans. Krystyna Krzemienowa, Karol Saureland, (Warszawa: PIW, 1990).
4. Theodor Wiesengrund Adorno, "The Idea of Natural History," *Gesammelte Schriften*, vol. 1 (Frankfurt am Main: Suhrkamp, 1973).
5. Carrie S. Asman, "Theater and Agon/Agon and Theater: Walter Benjamin and Florens Christian Rang," *MLN*, vol. 107, No. 3 (1992).
6. Zbigniew Chojnowski, *Poetycka wiara Jarosława Iwaszkiewicza* (Olsztyn: WSP, 1999).
7. Friedrich Engels, *Outline of the Critique of Political Economy*, trans. Martin Milligan, 20 July 2007 https://www.marxists.org/archive/marx/works/1844/df-jahrbucher/outlines.htm.
8. Marta Fik, *Kultura marcowa. Wokół Dziadów – Literaci i władza – Kampania marcowa* (Warszawa: Wydawnictwo Wodnika, 1995).
9. Hans-Georg Gadamer, "Text and Interpretation," in: *The Gadamer Reader. A Bouquet of the Later Writings*, ed. and trans. Richard E. Palmer (Evanston, Illinois: Northwestern University Press, 2007).

---

29 From Iwaszkiewicz's letter to Mycielski, with a comment on the celebrations of the 1000th anniversary of Poland's conversion to Christianity: "In times when we desperately need some national movement of common sense, in reaction to the shameful behaviour of both sides, the incredibly rowdy Church and the incredible foolishness of the other side ("Polish government and Mr. Gomułka's clique") – at least a few individuals in Poland must maintain some standards of decency and seriousness" (quoted in Mycielski, *Dziennik 1960–1969*, p. 447).

Myths in the Polish People's Republic. Iwaszkiewicz *avec* Benjamin    179

10. Julius Gutman, *Philosophies of Judaism: The History of Jewish Philosophy from Biblical Times to Franz Rosenzweig*, trans. Dawid W. Silverman (New York: Shocken Books, 1973).
11. Georg Wilhelm Friedrich Hegel, *The Phenomenology of Spirit*, trans. Arnold V. Miller (Oxford: Clarendon Press, 1977).
12. Hugo von Hofmannsthal, "The Poet and Our Time," in: *Hugo von Hoffmanstahl and the Austrian Idea: Selected Essays and Speeches, 1906–1927*, trans. and ed. David S. Luft (West Lafayette: Purdue University Press, 2011).
13. Jarosław Iwaszkiewicz, *Muzyka wieczorem* (Warszawa: Czytelnik, 1980).
14. Jarosław Iwaszkiewicz, *Opowiadania*, vol. I–III (Warszawa: Czytelnik, 1980).
15. Jarosław Iwaszkiewicz, *Wiersze* (Warszawa: Czytelnik, 1977).
16. Rolf-Peter Janz, "Mythos und Moderne bei Walter Benjamin," in: *Mythos und Moderne*, ed. Karl Heinz Bohrer (Frankfurt am Main: Suhrkamp, 1983).
17. Søren Kierkegaard, *The Concept of Anxiety: A Simple Psychologically Orienting Deliberation on the Dogmatic Issue of Hereditary Sin*, trans. Reidar Thomte and Albert B. Anderson (Princeton: Princeton University Press, 1980).
18. Karl Löwith, *From Hegel to Nietsche: The Revolution in Nineteenth Century Thought*, trans. David E. Green (New York: Columbia UP, 1964).
19. Karl Löwith, *Meaning of History: The Theological Implications of the Philosophy of History* (Chicago: University of Chicago Press, 1949).
20. Małgorzata Łukasiewicz, "Szanse happy endu – *Powinowactwa z wyboru, Śmierć w Wenecji, Powrót Prozerpiny*", in: *Recepcja literacka i proces literacki*, ed. German Ritz, Gabriela Matuszek (Kraków: Universitas, 1999).
21. Karl Marx, "A Contribution to the Critique of Political Economy," tansl. Salomea Wolfovna Ryazanskaya, in: *Marx/Engels Collected Works*, vol. XXXI (Moscow: Progress Publishers, 1970), 21 Nov. 2007 www.marxists.org/archive/marx.
22. Karl Marx, *Capital*, vol. I–III, 21 Nov. 2007 www.marxists.org/archive/marx
23. Karl Marx, "Debatten über Preßfreiheit und Publikation der Landständischen Verhandlungen," 20 July 2007 http://www.mlwerke.de/me/me01/me01_066.htm.
24. Karl Marx, "Debates on the Law of Thefts of Wood," in: *Marx/Engels Collected Works*, vol. I (Moscow: Progress Publishers, 1975).
25. Karl Marx, "Economic and Philosophical Manuscripts," trans. Martin Mulligan, in *Marx/Engels Collected Works*, vol. III (Moscow: Progress Publishers, 1975).
26. Karl Marx, Friedrich Engels, "The German Ideology," in: *Marx/Engels Collected Works*, vol. V (Moscow: Progress Publishers, 1968), 21 Nov. 2007 http://www.marxists.org/archive/marx/works/1845/german-ideology/ch01a.htm

27. Winfried Menninghaus, *Schwellenkunde. Walter Benjamins Passage des Mythos* (Frankfurt am Main: Suhrkamp, 1986).
28. Piotr Mitzner, *Na progu: doświadczenia religijne w tekstach Jarosława Iwaszkiewicza* (Warszawa: UKSW, 2003).
29. Zygmunt Mycielski, *Dziennik 1960–1969* (Warszawa: Iskry, 2001).
30. Rainer Maria Rilke, "Worpswede. Monographien einer Landschaft und ihrer Maler," in: *Sämliche Werke*, vol. 5, ed. Ernst Zinn (Frankfurt am Main: Suhrkamp Verlag, 1965).
31. German Ritz, *Jarosław Iwaszkiewicz: pogranicza nowoczesności*, trans. Andrzej Kopacki (Kraków: Universitas, 1999).
32. Artur Sandauer, *Poeci trzech pokoleń* (Warszawa: Czytelnik, 1996).
33. Heinz Schandl, *Der Naturbegriff nach Karl Marx. Über den Mehrwert und die Rolle des Tieres in der Marx'schen Theorie*, 18 June 2006 http://www.iff.ac.at/socec/backdoor/ws0405-se-usoz/BarlaJosef.pdf.
34. Alfred Schmidt, "Die in Naturgeschichte verstrickte Menschheit," in: *Krise und Kritik. Zur Aktualität der Marxschen Theorie*, ed. Gerhard Schweppenhäser (Springe: Dietrich zu Klampen, 1987).
35. Gershom Scholem, *The Messianic Idea in Judaism and other Essays on Jewish Spirituality* (New York: Schocken Books, 1971).
36. Karl Wilhelm Ferdinand Solger, "Erwin, or Four Dialogues on Beauty and Art," trans. Joyce Crick, in: *German Aesthetic and Literary Criticism: The Romantic Ironists and Goethe,* ed. Kathleen M. Wheeler (Cambridge: Cambridge University Press, 1984).
37. Robert Weimann, "Współczesność a przeszłość w historii literatury," in: *Literatura: produkcja i recepcja. Studia z metodologii historii literatury*, ed. Hubert Orłowski (Warszawa: PIW, 1978).

**Literary and Cultural Theory**
General editor: Wojciech H. Kalaga

Vol. 1 Wojciech H. Kalaga: Nebulae of Discourse. Interpretation, Textuality, and the Subject. 1997.

Vol. 2 Wojciech H. Kalaga / Tadeusz Rachwał (eds.): Memory – Remembering – Forgetting. 1999.

Vol. 3 Piotr Fast: Ideology, Aesthetics, Literary History. Socialist Realism and its Others. 1999.

Vol. 4 Ewa Rewers: Language and Space: The Poststructuralist Turn in the Philosophy of Culture. 1999.

Vol. 5 Floyd Merrell: Tasking Textuality. 2000.

Vol. 6 Tadeusz Rachwał / Tadeusz Slawek (eds.): Organs, Organisms, Organisations. Organic Form in 19th-Century Discourse. 2000.

Vol. 7 Wojciech H. Kalaga / Tadeusz Rachwał: Signs of Culture: Simulacra and the Real. 2000.

Vol. 8 Tadeusz Rachwal: Labours of the Mind. Labour in the Culture of Production. 2001.

Vol. 9 Rita Wilson / Carlotta von Maltzan (eds.): Spaces and Crossings. Essays on Literature and Culture in Africa and Beyond. 2001.

Vol. 10 Leszek Drong: Masks and Icons. Subjectivity in Post-Nietzschean Autobiography. 2001.

Vol. 11 Wojciech H. Kalaga / Tadeusz Rachwał (eds.): Exile. Displacements and Misplacements. 2001.

Vol. 12 Marta Zajac: The Feminine of Difference. Gilles Deleuze, Hélène Cixous and Contempora-ry Critique of the Marquis de Sade. 2002.

Vol. 13 Zbigniew Bialas / Krzysztof Kowalczyk-Twarowski (eds.): Alchemization of the Mind. Literature and Dissociation. 2003.

Vol. 14 Tadeusz Slawek: Revelations of Gloucester. Charles Olsen, Fitz Hugh Lane, and Writing of the Place. 2003.

Vol. 15 Carlotta von Maltzan (ed.): Africa and Europe: En/Countering Myths. Essays on Literature and Cultural Politics. 2003.

Vol. 16 Marzena Kubisz: Strategies of Resistance. Body, Identity and Representation in Western Culture. 2003.

Vol. 17 Ewa Rychter: (Un)Saying the Other. Allegory and Irony in Emmanuel Levinas's Ethical Language. 2004.

Vol. 18 Ewa Borkowska: At the Threshold of Mystery: Poetic Encounters with Other(ness). 2005.

Vol. 19 Wojciech H. Kalaga / Tadeusz Rachwał (eds.): Feeding Culture: The Pleasures and Perils of Appetite. 2005.

Vol. 20 Wojciech H. Kalaga / Tadeusz Rachwał (eds.): Spoiling the Cannibals' Fun? Cannibalism and Cannibalisation in Culture and Elsewhere. 2005.

| | | |
|---|---|---|
| Vol. | 21 | Katarzyna Ancuta: Where Angels Fear to Hover. Between the Gothic Disease and the *Meat*aphysics of Horror. 2005. |
| Vol. | 22 | Piotr Wilczek: (Mis)translation and (Mis)interpretation: Polish Literature in the Context of Cross-Cultural Communication. 2005. |
| Vol. | 23 | Krzysztof Kowalczyk-Twarowski: *Glebae Adscripti*. Troping Place, Region and Nature in America. 2005. |
| Vol. | 24 | Zbigniew Białas: The Body Wall. Somatics of Travelling and Discursive Practices. 2006. |
| Vol. | 25 | Katarzyna Nowak: Melancholic Travelers. Autonomy, Hybridity and the Maternal. 2007. |
| Vol. | 26 | Leszek Drong: Disciplining the New Pragmatism. Theory, Rhetoric, and the Ends of Literary Study. 2007. |
| Vol. | 27 | Katarzyna Smyczyńska: The World According to Bridget Jones. Discourses of Identity in Chicklit Fictions. 2007. |
| Vol. | 28 | Wojciech H. Kalaga / Marzena Kubisz (eds.): Multicultural Dilemmas. Identity, Difference, Otherness. 2008. |
| Vol. | 29 | Maria Plochocki: Body, Letter, and Voice. Construction Knowledge in Detective Fiction. 2010. |
| Vol. | 30 | Rossitsa Terzieva-Artemis: Stories of the Unconscious: Sub-Versions in Freud, Lacan and Kristeva. 2009. |
| Vol. | 31 | Sonia Front: Transgressing Boundaries in Jeanette Winterson's Fiction. 2009. |
| Vol. | 32 | Wojciech Kalaga / Jacek Mydla / Katarzyna Ancuta (eds.): Political Correctness. Mouth Wide Shut? 2009. |
| Vol. | 33 | Paweł Marcinkiewicz: The Rhetoric of the City: Robinson Jeffers and A. R. Ammons. 2009. |
| Vol. | 34 | Wojciech Małecki: Embodying Pragmatism. Richard Shusterman's Philosophy and Literary Theory. 2010. |
| Vol. | 35 | Wojciech Kalaga / Marzena Kubisz (eds.): Cartographies of Culture. Memory, Space, Representation. 2010. |
| Vol. | 36 | Bożena Shallcross / Ryszard Nycz (eds.): The Effect of Pamplisest. Culture, Literature, History. 2011. |
| Vol. | 37 | Wojciech Kalaga / Marzena Kubisz / Jacek Mydla (eds.): A Culture of Recycling / Recycling Culture? 2011. |
| Vol. | 38 | Anna Chromik: Disruptive Fluidity. The Poetics of the Pop *Cogito*. 2012. |
| Vol. | 39 | Paweł Wojtas: Translating Gombrowicz's Liminal Aesthetics. 2014. |
| Vol. | 40 | Marcin Mazurek: A Sense of Apocalypse. Technology, Textuality, Identity. 2014. |
| Vol. | 41 | Charles Russell / Arne Melberg / Jarosław Płuciennik / Michał Wróblewski (eds.): Critical Theory and Critical Genres. Contemporary Perspectives from Poland. 2014. |
| Vol. | 42 | Marzena Kubisz: Resistance in the Deceleration Lane. Velocentrism, Slow Culture and Everyday Practice. 2014. |
| Vol. | 43 | Bohumil Fořt: An Introduction to Fictional Worlds Theory. 2016. |

Vol. 44  Agata Wilczek: Beyond the Limits of Language. Apophasis and Transgression in Contemporary Theoretical Discourse. 2016.

Vol. 45  Witold Sadowski / Magdalena Kowalska / Magdalena Maria Kubas (eds.): Litanic Verse I. *Origines, Iberia, Slavia et Europa Media*. 2016.

Vol. 46  Witold Sadowski / Magdalena Kowalska / Magdalena Maria Kubas (eds.): Litanic Verse II. *Britannia, Germania et Scandinavia*. 2016.

Vol. 47  Julia Szołtysek: A Mosaic of Misunderstanding: Occident, Orient, and Facets of Mutual Misconstrual. 2016.

Vol. 48  Manyaka Toko Djockoua: Cross-Cultural Affinities. Emersonian Transcendentalism and Senghorian Negritude. 2016.

Vol. 49  Ryszard Nycz: The Language of Polish Modernism. Translated by Tul'si Bhambry. 2017.

Vol. 50  Alina Silvana Felea: Aspects of Reference in Literary Theory. Poetics, Rhetoric and Literary History. 2017.

Vol. 51  Jerry Xie: Mo Yan Thought. Six Critiques of Hallucinatory Realism. 2017.

Vol. 52  Paweł Stachura / Piotr Śniedziewski / Krzysztof Trybuś (eds.): Approaches to Walter Benjamin's *The Arcades Project*. 2017.

www.peterlang.com